DEMOSTHENES, SPEECHES 50–59

THE ORATORY OF CLASSICAL GREECE

Translated with Notes • *Michael Gagarin, Series Editor*

VOLUME 6

DEMOSTHENES, SPEECHES 50–59

Translated by Victor Bers

 UNIVERSITY OF TEXAS PRESS, AUSTIN

First edition, 2003

Requests for permission to reproduce material from
this work should be sent to Permissions, University
of Texas Press, Box 7819, Austin, TX 78713-7819.

♾ The paper used in this book meets the mini-
mum requirements of ANSI/NISO Z39.48-1992
(R1997) (Permanence of Paper).

Library of Congress Cataloging-in-Publication Data

Demosthenes.
    [Selections. English. 2003]
    Speeches 50–59 / translated by Victor Bers.
        p.   cm. — (The oratory of classical Greece ;
    v. 6)
    Includes bibliographical references and index.
    ISBN 978-0-292-70922-5

    1. Demosthenes—Translations into English.
2. Speeches, addresses, etc., Greek—Translations
into English.   I. Bers, Victor.   II. Title.
III. Series.
    PA3951 .E5   2003
    885'.01—dc21   2002012299

For Diane

CONTENTS

❖❖

SERIES EDITOR'S PREFACE

This is the sixth volume in a series of translations of *The Oratory of Classical Greece*. The aim of the series is to make available primarily for those who do not read Greek up-to-date, accurate, and readable translations with introductions and explanatory notes of all the surviving works and major fragments of the Attic orators of the classical period (ca. 420–320 BC): Aeschines, Andocides, Antiphon, Demosthenes, Dinarchus, Hyperides, Isaeus, Isocrates, Lycurgus, and Lysias. This volume is the first to appear with speeches of Demosthenes, under whose name are preserved more than a third of all the surviving works of Attic oratory.

On behalf of all the translators, I would like again to thank Alan Boegehold, who read the volume for the Press and made many helpful comments and suggestions, and also once again my colleagues at the University of Texas Press, especially Director Joanna Hitchcock, Humanities Editor Jim Burr, Managing Editor Carolyn Wylie, Copyeditor Nancy Moore, and the production staff.

—M. G.

TRANSLATOR'S PREFACE

I record here my gratitude to five scholars who worked assiduously to improve successive drafts of my manuscript: Alan Boegehold (reader for the University of Texas Press), Debra Hamel, Adriaan Lanni, Barbara Tsakirgis, and especially Michael Gagarin, ever-vigilant and helpful shepherd of his flock of translators. Warm thanks also to Nancy Moore, who prepared this book for the University of Texas Press, for her good ear and sharp eye, and to Jared Hudson, who prepared the index. The mistakes, however, are my very own—which will not surprise my daughter Diane, to whom this book is dedicated.

—V. B.

SERIES INTRODUCTION
Greek Oratory

❧❧❧

By Michael Gagarin

ORATORY IN CLASSICAL ATHENS

From as early as Homer (and undoubtedly much earlier) the Greeks placed a high value on effective speaking. Even Achilles, whose greatness was primarily established on the battlefield, was brought up to be "a speaker of words and a doer of deeds" (*Iliad* 9.443); and Athenian leaders of the sixth and fifth centuries,[1] such as Solon, Themistocles, and Pericles, were all accomplished orators. Most Greek literary genres —notably epic, tragedy, and history—underscore the importance of oratory by their inclusion of set speeches. The formal pleadings of the envoys to Achilles in the *Iliad,* the messenger speeches in tragedy reporting events like the battle of Salamis in Aeschylus' *Persians* or the gruesome death of Pentheus in Euripides' *Bacchae,* and the powerful political oratory of Pericles' funeral oration in Thucydides are but a few of the most notable examples of the Greeks' never-ending fascination with formal public speaking, which was to reach its height in the public oratory of the fourth century.

In early times, oratory was not a specialized subject of study but was learned by practice and example. The formal study of rhetoric as an "art" (*technē*) began, we are told, in the middle of the fifth century in Sicily with the work of Corax and his pupil Tisias.[2] These two are

---

[1] All dates in this volume are BC unless the contrary is either indicated or obvious.

[2] See Kennedy 1963: 26–51. Cole 1991 has challenged this traditional picture, arguing that the term "rhetoric" was coined by Plato to designate and denigrate an activity he strongly opposed. Cole's own reconstruction is not without problems,

scarcely more than names to us, but another famous Sicilian, Gorgias of Leontini (ca. 490–390), developed a new style of argument and is reported to have dazzled the Athenians with a speech delivered when he visited Athens in 427. Gorgias initiated the practice, which continued into the early fourth century, of composing speeches for mythical or imaginary occasions. The surviving examples reveal a lively intellectual climate in the late fifth and early fourth centuries, in which oratory served to display new ideas, new forms of expression, and new methods of argument.[3] This tradition of "intellectual" oratory was continued by the fourth-century educator Isocrates and played a large role in later Greek and Roman education.

In addition to this intellectual oratory, at about the same time the practice also began of writing speeches for real occasions in public life, which we may designate "practical" oratory. For centuries Athenians had been delivering speeches in public settings (primarily the courts and the Assembly), but these had always been composed and delivered impromptu, without being written down and thus without being preserved. The practice of writing speeches began in the courts and then expanded to include the Assembly and other settings. Athens was one of the leading cities of Greece in the fifth and fourth centuries, and its political and legal systems depended on direct participation by a large number of citizens; all important decisions were made by these large bodies, and the primary means of influencing these decisions was oratory.[4] Thus, it is not surprising that oratory flourished in Athens,[5] but it may not be immediately obvious why it should be written down.

The pivotal figure in this development was Antiphon, one of the fifth-century intellectuals who are often grouped together under the

---

but he does well to remind us how thoroughly the traditional view of rhetoric depends on one of its most ardent opponents.

[3] Of these only Antiphon's Tetralogies are included in this series. Gorgias' *Helen* and *Palamedes,* Alcidamas' *Odysseus,* and Antisthenes' *Ajax* and *Odysseus* are translated in Gagarin and Woodruff 1995.

[4] Yunis 1996 has a good treatment of political oratory from Pericles to Demosthenes.

[5] All our evidence for practical oratory comes from Athens, with the exception of Isocrates 19, written for a trial in Aegina. Many speeches were undoubtedly delivered in courts and political forums in other Greek cities, but it may be that such speeches were written down only in Athens.

name "Sophists."[6] Like some of the other sophists he contributed to the intellectual oratory of the period, but he also had a strong practical interest in law. At the same time, Antiphon had an aversion to public speaking and did not directly involve himself in legal or political affairs (Thucydides 8.68). However, he began giving general advice to other citizens who were engaged in litigation and were thus expected to address the court themselves. As this practice grew, Antiphon went further, and around 430 he began writing out whole speeches for others to memorize and deliver. Thus began the practice of "logography," which continued through the next century and beyond.[7] Logography particularly appealed to men like Lysias, who were metics, or noncitizen residents of Athens. Since they were not Athenian citizens, they were barred from direct participation in public life, but they could contribute by writing speeches for others.

Antiphon was also the first (to our knowledge) to write down a speech he would himself deliver, writing the speech for his own defense at his trial for treason in 411. His motive was probably to publicize and preserve his views, and others continued this practice of writing down speeches they would themselves deliver in the courts and (more rarely) the Assembly.[8] Finally, one other type of practical oratory was the special tribute delivered on certain important public occasions, the best known of which is the funeral oration. It is convenient to designate these three types of oratory by the terms Aristotle later uses: forensic (for the courts), deliberative (for the Assembly), and epideictic (for display).[9]

---

[6] The term "sophist" was loosely used through the fifth and fourth centuries to designate various intellectuals and orators, but under the influence of Plato, who attacked certain figures under this name, the term is now used of a specific group of thinkers; see Kerferd 1981.

[7] For Antiphon as the first to write speeches, see Photius, *Bibliotheca* 486a7–11 and [Plut.], *Moralia* 832c–d. The latest extant speech can be dated to 320, but we know that at least one orator, Dinarchus, continued the practice after that date.

[8] Unlike forensic speeches, speeches for delivery in the Assembly were usually not composed beforehand in writing, since the speaker could not know exactly when or in what context he would be speaking; see further Trevett 1996.

[9] *Rhetoric* 1.3. Intellectual orations, like Gorgias' *Helen,* do not easily fit into Aristotle's classification. For a fuller (but still brief) introduction to Attic oratory and the orators, see Edwards 1994.

THE ORATORS

In the century from about 420 to 320, dozens—perhaps even hundreds—of now unknown orators and logographers must have composed speeches that are now lost, but only ten of these men were selected for preservation and study by ancient scholars, and only works collected under the names of these ten have been preserved. Some of these works are undoubtedly spurious, though in most cases they are fourth-century works by a different author rather than later "forgeries." Indeed, modern scholars suspect that as many as seven of the speeches attributed to Demosthenes may have been written by Apollodorus, son of Pasion, who is sometimes called "the eleventh orator." [10] Including these speeches among the works of Demosthenes may have been an honest mistake, or perhaps a bookseller felt he could sell more copies of these speeches if they were attributed to a more famous orator.

In alphabetical order the Ten Orators are as follows: [11]

* AESCHINES (ca. 395–ca. 322) rose from obscure origins to become an important Athenian political figure, first an ally, then a bitter enemy of Demosthenes. His three speeches all concern major public issues. The best known of these (Aes. 3) was delivered at the trial in 330, when Demosthenes responded with *On the Crown* (Dem. 18). Aeschines lost the case and was forced to leave Athens and live the rest of his life in exile.

* ANDOCIDES (ca. 440–ca. 390) is best known for his role in the scandal of 415, when just before the departure of the fateful Athenian expedition to Sicily during the Peloponnesian War (431–404), a band of young men mutilated statues of Hermes, and at the same time information was revealed about the secret rites of Demeter. Andocides was exiled but later returned. Two of the four speeches

---

[10] See Trevett 1992.

[11] The Loeb volumes of *Minor Attic Orators* also include the prominent Athenian political figure Demades (ca. 385–319), who was not one of the Ten; but the only speech that has come down to us under his name is a later forgery. It is possible that Demades and other fourth-century politicians who had a high reputation for public speaking did not put any speeches in writing, especially if they rarely spoke in the courts (see above n. 8).

in his name give us a contemporary view of the scandal: one pleads for his return, the other argues against a second period of exile.

- ANTIPHON (ca. 480–411), as already noted, wrote forensic speeches for others and only once spoke himself. In 411 he participated in an oligarchic coup by a group of 400, and when the democrats regained power he was tried for treason and executed. His six surviving speeches include three for delivery in court and the three Tetralogies—imaginary intellectual exercises for display or teaching that consist of four speeches each, two on each side. All six of Antiphon's speeches concern homicide, probably because these stood at the beginning of the collection of his works. Fragments of some thirty other speeches cover many different topics.

- DEMOSTHENES (384–322) is generally considered the best of the Attic orators. Although his nationalistic message is less highly regarded today, his powerful mastery of and ability to combine many different rhetorical styles continues to impress readers. Demosthenes was still a child when his wealthy father died. The trustees of the estate apparently misappropriated much of it, and when he came of age, he sued them in a series of cases (27–31), regaining some of his fortune and making a name as a powerful speaker. He then wrote speeches for others in a variety of cases, public and private, and for his own use in court (where many cases involved major public issues), and in the Assembly, where he opposed the growing power of Philip of Macedon. The triumph of Philip and his son Alexander the Great eventually put an end to Demosthenes' career. Some sixty speeches have come down under his name, about a third of them of questionable authenticity.

- DINARCHUS (ca. 360–ca. 290) was born in Corinth but spent much of his life in Athens as a metic (a noncitizen resident). His public fame came primarily from writing speeches for the prosecutions surrounding the Harpalus affair in 324, when several prominent figures (including Demosthenes) were accused of bribery. After 322 he had a profitable career as a logographer.

- HYPERIDES (390–322) was a political leader and logographer of so many different talents that he was called the pentathlete of orators. He was a leader of the Athenian resistance to Philip and Alexander and (like Demosthenes) was condemned to death after Athens' final surrender. One speech and substantial fragments of five others have been recovered from papyrus remains; otherwise, only fragments survive.

- ISAEUS (ca. 415–ca. 340) wrote speeches on a wide range of topics, but the eleven complete speeches that survive, dating from ca. 390 to ca. 344, all concern inheritance. As with Antiphon, the survival of these particular speeches may have been the result of the later ordering of his speeches by subject; we have part of a twelfth speech and fragments and titles of some forty other works. Isaeus is said to have been a pupil of Isocrates and the teacher of Demosthenes.

- ISOCRATES (436–338) considered himself a philosopher and educator, not an orator or rhetorician. He came from a wealthy Athenian family but lost most of his property in the Peloponnesian War, and in 403 he took up logography. About 390 he abandoned this practice and turned to writing and teaching, setting forth his educational, philosophical, and political views in essays that took the form of speeches but were not meant for oral delivery. He favored accommodation with the growing power of Philip of Macedon and panhellenic unity. His school was based on a broad concept of rhetoric and applied philosophy; it attracted pupils from the entire Greek world (including Isaeus, Lycurgus, and Hyperides) and became the main rival of Plato's Academy. Isocrates greatly influenced education and rhetoric in the Hellenistic, Roman, and modern periods until the eighteenth century.

- LYCURGUS (ca. 390–ca. 324) was a leading public official who restored the financial condition of Athens after 338 and played a large role in the city for the next dozen years. He brought charges of corruption or treason against many other officials, usually with success. Only one speech survives.

- LYSIAS (ca. 445–ca. 380) was a metic—an official resident of Athens but not a citizen. Much of his property was seized by the Thirty during their short-lived oligarchic coup in 404–403. Perhaps as a result he turned to logography. More than thirty speeches survive in whole or in part, though the authenticity of some is doubted. We also have fragments or know the titles of more than a hundred others. The speeches cover a wide range of cases, and he may have delivered one himself (Lys. 12), on the death of his brother at the hands of the Thirty. Lysias is particularly known for his vivid narratives, his *ēthopoiïa,* or "creation of character," and his prose style, which became a model of clarity and vividness.

THE WORKS OF THE ORATORS

As soon as speeches began to be written down, they could be preserved. We know little about the conditions of book "publication" (i.e., making copies for distribution) in the fourth century, but there was an active market for books in Athens, and some of the speeches may have achieved wide circulation.[12] An orator (or his family) may have preserved his own speeches, perhaps to advertise his ability or demonstrate his success, or booksellers may have collected and copied them in order to make money.

We do not know how closely the preserved text of these speeches corresponded to the version actually delivered in court or in the Assembly. Speakers undoubtedly extemporized or varied from their text on occasion, but there is no good evidence that deliberative speeches were substantially revised for publication.[13] In forensic oratory a logographer's reputation would derive first and foremost from his success with jurors. If a forensic speech was victorious, there would be no reason to alter it for publication, and if it lost, alteration would probably not deceive potential clients. Thus, the published texts of forensic speeches were probably quite faithful to the texts that were provided to clients, and we have little reason to suspect substantial alteration in the century or so before they were collected by scholars in Alexandria (see below).

In addition to the speaker's text, most forensic speeches have breaks for the inclusion of documents. The logographer inserted a notation in his text—such as *nomos* ("law") or *martyria* ("testimony")—and the

---

[12] Dover's discussion (1968) of the preservation and transmission of the works of Lysias (and perhaps others under his name) is useful not just for Lysias but for the other orators too. His theory of shared authorship between logographer and litigant, however, is unconvincing (see Usher 1976).

[13] See further Trevett 1996: 437–439.

speaker would pause while the clerk read out the text of a law or the testimony of witnesses. Many speeches survive with only a notation that a *nomos* or *martyria* was read at that point, but in some cases the text of the document is included. It used to be thought that these documents were all creations of later scholars, but many (though not all) are now accepted as genuine.[14]

With the foundation of the famous library in Alexandria early in the third century, scholars began to collect and catalogue texts of the orators, along with many other classical authors. Only the best orators were preserved in the library, many of them represented by over 100 speeches each (some undoubtedly spurious). Only some of these works survived in manuscript form to the modern era; more recently a few others have been discovered on ancient sheets of papyrus, so that today the corpus of Attic Oratory consists of about 150 speeches, together with a few letters and other works. The subject matter ranges from important public issues and serious crimes to business affairs, lovers' quarrels, inheritance disputes, and other personal or family matters.

In the centuries after these works were collected, ancient scholars gathered biographical facts about their authors, produced grammatical and lexicographic notes, and used some of the speeches as evidence for Athenian political history. But the ancient scholars who were most interested in the orators were those who studied prose style, the most notable of these being Dionysius of Halicarnassus (first century BC), who wrote treatises on several of the orators,[15] and Hermogenes of Tarsus (second century AD), who wrote several literary studies, including *On Types of Style*.[16] But relative to epic or tragedy, oratory was little studied; and even scholars of rhetoric whose interests were broader than style, like Cicero and Quintilian, paid little attention to the orators, except for the acknowledged master, Demosthenes.

Most modern scholars until the second half of the twentieth century continued to treat the orators primarily as prose stylists.[17] The re-

---

[14] See MacDowell 1990: 43–47; Todd 1993: 44–45.

[15] Dionysius' literary studies are collected and translated in Usher 1974–1985.

[16] Wooten 1987. Stylistic considerations probably also influenced the selection of the "canon" of ten orators; see Worthington 1994.

[17] For example, the most popular and influential book ever written on the orators, Jebb's *The Attic Orators* (1875) was presented as an "attempt to aid in giving Attic Oratory its due place in the history of Attic Prose" (I.xiii). This modern focus

evaluation of Athenian democracy by George Grote and others in the nineteenth century stimulated renewed interest in Greek oratory among historians; and increasing interest in Athenian law during that century led a few legal scholars to read the orators. But in comparison with the interest shown in the other literary genres—epic, lyric, tragedy, comedy, and even history—Attic oratory has been relatively neglected until the last third of the twentieth century. More recently, however, scholars have discovered the value of the orators for the broader study of Athenian culture and society. Since Dover's groundbreaking works on popular morality and homosexuality,[18] interest in the orators has been increasing rapidly, and they are now seen as primary representatives of Athenian moral and social values, and as evidence for social and economic conditions, political and social ideology, and in general those aspects of Athenian culture that in the past were commonly ignored by historians of ancient Greece but are of increasing interest and importance today, including women and the family, slavery, and the economy.

GOVERNMENT AND LAW IN CLASSICAL ATHENS

The hallmark of the Athenian political and legal systems was its amateurism. Most public officials, including those who supervised the courts, were selected by lot and held office for a limited period, typically a year. Thus a great many citizens held public office at some point in their lives, but almost none served for an extended period of time or developed the experience or expertise that would make them professionals. All significant policy decisions were debated and voted on in the Assembly, where the quorum was 6,000 citizens, and all significant legal cases were judged by bodies of 200 to 500 jurors or more. Public prominence was not achieved by election (or selection) to public office but depended rather on a man's ability to sway the majority of citizens in the Assembly or jurors in court to vote in favor of a pro-

---

on prose style can plausibly be connected to the large role played by prose composition (the translation of English prose into Greek, usually in imitation of specific authors or styles) in the Classics curriculum, especially in Britain.

[18] Dover (1974, 1978). Dover recently commented (1994: 157), "When I began to mine the riches of Attic forensic oratory I was astonished to discover that the mine had never been exploited."

posed course of action or for one of the litigants in a trial. Success was never permanent, and a victory on one policy issue or a verdict in one case could be quickly reversed in another.[19] In such a system the value of public oratory is obvious, and in the fourth century, oratory became the most important cultural institution in Athens, replacing drama as the forum where major ideological concerns were displayed and debated.

Several recent books give good detailed accounts of Athenian government and law,[20] and so a brief sketch can suffice here. The main policy-making body was the Assembly, open to all adult male citizens; a small payment for attendance enabled at least some of the poor to attend along with the leisured rich. In addition, a Council of 500 citizens, selected each year by lot with no one allowed to serve more than two years, prepared material for and made recommendations to the Assembly; a rotating subgroup of this Council served as an executive committee, the Prytaneis. Finally, numerous officials, most of them selected by lot for one-year terms, supervised different areas of administration and finance. The most important of these were the nine Archons (lit. "rulers"): the eponymous Archon after whom the year was named, the Basileus ("king"),[21] the Polemarch, and the six Thesmothetae. Councilors and almost all these officials underwent a preliminary examination (*dokimasia*) before taking office, and officials submitted to a final accounting (*euthynai*) upon leaving; at these times any citizen who wished could challenge a person's fitness for his new position or his performance in his recent position.

---

[19] In the Assembly this could be accomplished by a reconsideration of the question, as in the famous Mytilenean debate (Thuc. 3.36–50); in court a verdict was final, but its practical effects could be thwarted or reversed by later litigation on a related issue.

[20] For government, see Sinclair 1988, Hansen 1991; for law, MacDowell 1978, Todd 1993, and Boegehold 1995 (Bonner 1927 is still helpful). Much of our information about the legal and political systems comes from a work attributed to Aristotle but perhaps written by a pupil of his, *The Athenian Constitution* (*Ath. Pol.*—conveniently translated with notes by Rhodes 1984). The discovery of this work on a papyrus in Egypt in 1890 caused a major resurgence of interest in Athenian government.

[21] Modern scholars often use the term *archōn basileus* or "king archon," but Athenian sources (e.g., *Ath. Pol.* 57) simply call him the *basileus*.

There was no general taxation of Athenian citizens. Sources of public funding included the annual tax levied on metics, various fees and import duties, and (in the fifth century) tribute from allied cities; but the source that figures most prominently in the orators is the Athenian system of liturgies (*leitourgiai*), by which in a regular rotation the rich provided funding for certain special public needs. The main liturgies were the *chorēgia,* in which a sponsor (*chorēgos*) supervised and paid for the training and performance of a chorus which sang and danced at a public festival,[22] and the trierarchy, in which a sponsor (trierarch) paid to equip and usually commanded a trireme, or warship, for a year. Some of these liturgies required substantial expenditures, but even so, some men spent far more than required in order to promote themselves and their public careers, and litigants often try to impress the jurors by referring to liturgies they have undertaken (see, e.g., Lys. 21.1–n5). A further twist on this system was that if a man thought he had been assigned a liturgy that should have gone to someone else who was richer than he, he could propose an exchange of property (*antidosis*), giving the other man a choice of either taking over the liturgy or exchanging property with him. Finally, the rich were also subject to special taxes (*eisphorai*) levied as a percentage of their property in times of need.

The Athenian legal system remained similarly resistant to professionalization. Trials and the procedures leading up to them were supervised by officials, primarily the nine Archons, but their role was purely administrative, and they were in no way equivalent to modern judges. All significant questions about what we would call points of law were presented to the jurors, who considered them together with all other issues when they delivered their verdict at the end of the trial.[23] Trials were "contests" (*agōnes*) between two litigants, each of whom presented his own case to the jurors in a speech, plaintiff first, then de-

---

[22] These included the productions of tragedy and comedy, for which the main expense was for the chorus.

[23] Certain religious "interpreters" (*exēgētai*) were occasionally asked to give their opinion on a legal matter that had a religious dimension (such as the prosecution of a homicide), but although these opinions could be reported in court (e.g., Dem. 47.68–73), they had no official legal standing. The most significant administrative decision we hear of is the refusal of the Basileus to accept the case in Antiphon 6 (see 6.37–46).

fendant; in some cases each party then spoke again, probably in rebuttal. Since a litigant had only one or two speeches in which to present his entire case, and no issue was decided separately by a judge, all the necessary factual information and every important argument on substance or procedure, fact or law, had to be presented together. A single speech might thus combine narrative, argument, emotional appeal, and various digressions, all with the goal of obtaining a favorable verdict. Even more than today, a litigant's primary task was to control the issue—to determine which issues the jurors would consider most important and which questions they would have in their minds as they cast their votes. We only rarely have both speeches from a trial,[24] and we usually have little or no external evidence for the facts of a case or the verdict. We must thus infer both the facts and the opponent's strategy from the speech we have, and any assessment of the overall effectiveness of a speech and of the logographer's strategy is to some extent speculative.

Before a trial there were usually several preliminary hearings for presenting evidence; arbitration, public and private, was available and sometimes required. These hearings and arbitration sessions allowed each side to become familiar with the other side's case, so that discussions of "what my opponent will say" could be included in one's speech. Normally a litigant presented his own case, but he was often assisted by family or friends. If he wished (and could afford it), he could enlist the services of a logographer, who presumably gave strategic advice in addition to writing a speech. The speeches were timed to ensure an equal hearing for both sides,[25] and all trials were completed within a day. Two hundred or more jurors decided each case in the popular courts, which met in the Agora.[26] Homicide cases and certain other religious trials (e.g., Lys. 7) were heard by the Council of the Areopagus or an associated group of fifty-one Ephetae. The Areopagus was composed of all former Archons—perhaps 150–200 members at most

---

[24] The exceptions are Demosthenes 19 and Aeschines 2, Aeschines 3 and Demosthenes 18, and Lysias 6 (one of several prosecution speeches) and Andocides 1; all were written for major public cases.

[25] Timing was done by means of a water-clock, which in most cases was stopped during the reading of documents.

[26] See Boegehold 1995.

times. It met on a hill called the Areopagus ("rock of Ares") near the Acropolis.

Jurors for the regular courts were selected by lot from those citizens who registered each year and who appeared for duty that day; as with the Assembly, a small payment allowed the poor to serve. After the speakers had finished, the jurors voted immediately without any formal discussion. The side with the majority won; a tie vote decided the case for the defendant. In some cases where the penalty was not fixed, after a conviction the jurors voted again on the penalty, choosing between penalties proposed by each side. Even when we know the verdict, we cannot know which of the speaker's arguments contributed most to his success or failure. However, a logographer could probably learn from jurors which points had or had not been successful, so that arguments that are found repeatedly in speeches probably were known to be effective in most cases.

The first written laws in Athens were enacted by Draco (ca. 620) and Solon (ca. 590), and new laws were regularly added. At the end of the fifth century the existing laws were reorganized, and a new procedure for enacting laws was instituted; thereafter a group of Law-Givers (*nomothetai*) had to certify that a proposed law did not conflict with any existing laws. There was no attempt, however, to organize legislation systematically, and although Plato, Aristotle, and other philosophers wrote various works on law and law-giving, these were either theoretical or descriptive and had no apparent influence on legislation. Written statutes generally used ordinary language rather than precise legal definitions in designating offenses, and questions concerning precisely what constituted a specific offense or what was the correct interpretation of a written statute were decided (together with other issues) by the jurors in each case. A litigant might, of course, assert a certain definition or interpretation as "something you all know" or "what the lawgiver intended," but such remarks are evidently tendentious and cannot be taken as authoritative.

The result of these procedural and substantive features was that the verdict depended largely on each litigant's speech (or speeches). As one speaker puts it (Ant. 6.18), "When there are no witnesses, you (jurors) are forced to reach a verdict about the case on the basis of the prosecutor's and defendant's words alone; you must be suspicious and examine their accounts in detail, and your vote will necessarily be cast on the basis of likelihood rather than clear knowledge." Even the testimony of witnesses (usually on both sides) is rarely decisive. On the other hand, most speakers make a considerable effort to establish facts and provide legitimate arguments in conformity with established law. Plato's view of rhetoric as a clever technique for persuading an ignorant crowd that the false is true is not borne out by the speeches, and the legal system does not appear to have produced many arbitrary or clearly unjust results.

The main form of legal procedure was a *dikē* ("suit") in which the injured party (or his relatives in a case of homicide) brought suit against the offender. Suits for injuries to slaves would be brought by the slave's master, and injuries to women would be prosecuted by a male relative. Strictly speaking, a *dikē* was a private matter between individuals, though like all cases, *dikai* often had public dimensions. The other major form of procedure was a *graphē* ("writing" or "indictment") in which "anyone who wished" (i.e., any citizen) could bring a prosecution for wrongdoing. *Graphai* were instituted by Solon, probably in order to allow prosecution of offenses where the victim was unable or unlikely to bring suit himself, such as selling a dependent into slavery; but the number of areas covered by *graphai* increased to cover many types of public offenses as well as some apparently private crimes, such as *hybris*.

The system of prosecution by "anyone who wished" also extended to several other more specialized forms of prosecution, like *eisangelia* ("impeachment"), used in cases of treason. Another specialized prosecution was *apagōgē* ("summary arrest"), in which someone could arrest a common criminal (*kakourgos,* lit. "evil-doer"), or have him arrested, on the spot. The reliance on private initiative meant that Athenians never developed a system of public prosecution; rather, they presumed that everyone would keep an eye on the behavior of his political enemies and bring suit as soon as he suspected a crime, both to harm his opponents and to advance his own career. In this way all public officials would be watched by someone. There was no disgrace in admitting that a prosecution was motivated by private enmity.

By the end of the fifth century the system of prosecution by "any one who wished" was apparently being abused by so-called sykophants (*sykophantai*), who allegedly brought or threatened to bring false suits against rich men, either to gain part of the fine that would be levied or to induce an out-of-court settlement in which the accused would pay to have the matter dropped. We cannot gauge the true extent of this problem, since speakers usually provide little evidence to support their claims that their opponents are sykophants, but the Athenians did make sykophancy a crime. They also specified that in many public procedures a plaintiff who either dropped the case or failed to obtain one-fifth of the votes would have to pay a heavy fine of 1,000 drachmas. Despite this, it appears that litigation was common in Athens and was seen by some as excessive.

Over the course of time, the Athenian legal and political systems have more often been judged negatively than positively. Philosophers and political theorists have generally followed the lead of Plato (427–347), who lived and worked in Athens his entire life while severely criticizing its system of government as well as many other aspects of its culture. For Plato, democracy amounted to the tyranny of the masses over the educated elite and was destined to collapse from its own instability. The legal system was capricious and depended entirely on the rhetorical ability of litigants with no regard for truth or justice. These criticisms have often been echoed by modern scholars, who particularly complain that law was much too closely interwoven with politics and did not have the autonomous status it achieved in Roman law and continues to have, at least in theory, in modern legal systems.

Plato's judgments are valid if one accepts the underlying presuppositions, that the aim of law is absolute truth and abstract justice and that achieving the highest good of the state requires thorough and systematic organization. Most Athenians do not seem to have subscribed to either the criticisms or the presuppositions, and most scholars now accept the long-ignored fact that despite major external disruptions in the form of wars and two short-lived coups brought about by one of these wars, the Athenian legal and political systems remained remarkably stable for almost two hundred years (508–320). Moreover, like all other Greek cities at the time, whatever their form of government, Athenian democracy was brought to an end not by internal forces but by the external power of Philip of Macedon and his son Alexander. The legal system never became autonomous, and the rich sometimes complained that they were victims of unscrupulous litigants, but there is no indication that the people wanted to yield control of the legal process to a professional class, as Plato recommended. For most Athe-

nians—Plato being an exception in this and many other matters—
one purpose of the legal system was to give everyone the opportunity
to have his case heard by other citizens and have it heard quickly and
cheaply; and in this it clearly succeeded.

Indeed, the Athenian legal system also served the interests of the
rich, even the very rich, as well as the common people, in that it provided a forum for the competition that since Homer had been an important part of aristocratic life. In this competition, the rich used the
courts as battlegrounds, though their main weapon was the rhetoric of
popular ideology, which hailed the rule of law and promoted the ideal
of moderation and restraint.[27] But those who aspired to political lead-
ership and the honor and status that accompanied it repeatedly entered
the legal arena, bringing suit against their political enemies whenever
possible and defending themselves against suits brought by others
whenever necessary. The ultimate judges of these public competitions
were the common people, who seem to have relished the dramatic
clash of individuals and ideologies. In this respect fourth-century oratory was the cultural heir of fifth-century drama and was similarly ap-
preciated by the citizens. Despite the disapproval of intellectuals like
Plato, most Athenians legitimately considered their legal system a hallmark of their democracy and a vital presence in their culture.

THE TRANSLATION OF GREEK ORATORY

The purpose of this series is to provide students and scholars in all
fields with accurate, readable translations of all surviving classical Attic oratory, including speeches whose authenticity is disputed, as well
as the substantial surviving fragments. In keeping with the originals,
the language is for the most part nontechnical. Names of persons and
places are given in the (generally more familiar) Latinized forms, and
names of officials or legal procedures have been translated into English
equivalents, where possible. Notes are intended to provide the necessary historical and cultural background; scholarly controversies are
generally not discussed. The notes and introductions refer to scholarly
treatments in addition to those listed below, which the reader may
consult for further information.

---

[27] Ober 1989 is fundamental; see also Cohen 1995.

Cross-references to other speeches follow the standard numbering system, which is now well established except in the case of Hyperides (for whom the numbering of the Oxford Classical Text is used).[28] References are by work and section (e.g., Dem. 24.73); spurious works are not specially marked; when no author is named (e.g., 24.73), the reference is to the same author as the annotated passage.

ABBREVIATIONS:

Aes.   = Aeschines
And.   = Andocides
Ant.   = Antiphon
Arist.   = Aristotle
Aristoph. = Aristophanes
Ath. Pol. = *The Athenian Constitution*
Dem.   = Demosthenes
Din.   = Dinarchus
Herod.   = Herodotus
Hyp.   = Hyperides
Is.   = Isaeus
Isoc.   = Isocrates
Lyc.   = Lycurgus
Lys.   = Lysias
Plut.   = Plutarch
Thuc.   = Thucydides
Xen.   = Xenophon

NOTE: The main unit of Athenian currency was the drachma; this was divided into obols and larger amounts were designated minas and talents.

1 drachma = 6 obols
1 mina   = 100 drachmas
1 talent = 60 minas (6,000 drachmas)

It is impossible to give an accurate equivalence in terms of modern currency, but it may be helpful to remember that the daily wage of

---

[28] For a listing of all the orators and their works, with classifications (forensic, deliberative, epideictic) and rough dates, see Edwards 1994: 74–79.

some skilled workers was a drachma in the mid-fifth century and 2–2½ drachmas in the later fourth century. Thus it may not be too misleading to think of a drachma as worth about $50 or £33 and a talent as about $300,000 or £200,000 in 1997 currency.

BIBLIOGRAPHY OF WORKS CITED

Boegehold, Alan L., 1995: *The Lawcourts at Athens: Sites, Buildings, Equipment, Procedure, and Testimonia.* Princeton.

Bonner, Robert J., 1927: *Lawyers and Litigants in Ancient Athens.* Chicago.

Cohen, David, 1995: *Law, Violence and Community in Classical Athens.* Cambridge.

Cole, Thomas, 1991: *The Origins of Rhetoric in Ancient Greece.* Baltimore.

Dover, Kenneth J., 1968: *Lysias and the Corpus Lysiacum.* Berkeley.

———, 1974: *Greek Popular Morality in the Time of Plato and Aristotle.* Oxford.

———, 1978: *Greek Homosexuality.* London.

———, 1994: *Marginal Comment.* London.

Edwards, Michael, 1994: *The Attic Orators.* London.

Gagarin, Michael, and Paul Woodruff, 1995: *Early Greek Political Thought from Homer to the Sophists.* Cambridge.

Hansen, Mogens Herman, 1991: *The Athenian Democracy in the Age of Demosthenes.* Oxford.

Jebb, Richard, 1875: *The Attic Orators,* 2 vols. London.

Kennedy, George A., 1963: *The Art of Persuasion in Greece.* Princeton.

Kerferd, G. B., 1981: *The Sophistic Movement.* Cambridge.

MacDowell, Douglas M., 1978: *The Law in Classical Athens.* London.

———, ed. 1990: *Demosthenes, Against Meidias.* Oxford.

Ober, Josiah, 1989: *Mass and Elite in Democratic Athens.* Princeton.

Rhodes, P. J., trans., 1984: *Aristotle, The Athenian Constitution.* Penguin Books.

Sinclair, R. K., 1988: *Democracy and Participation in Athens.* Cambridge.

Todd, Stephen, 1993: *The Shape of Athenian Law.* Oxford.

Trevett, Jeremy, 1992: *Apollodoros the Son of Pasion.* Oxford.

————, 1996: "Did Demosthenes Publish His Deliberative Speeches?" *Hermes* 124: 425–441.

Usher, Stephen, 1976: "Lysias and His Clients," *Greek, Roman and Byzantine Studies* 17: 31–40.

————, trans., 1974–1985: *Dionysius of Halicarnassus, Critical Essays.* 2 vols. Loeb Classical Library. Cambridge, MA.

Wooten, Cecil W., trans., 1987: *Hermogenes' On Types of Style.* Chapel Hill, NC.

Worthington, Ian, 1994: "The Canon of the Ten Attic Orators," in *Persuasion: Greek Rhetoric in Action,* ed. Ian Worthington. London: 244–263.

Yunis, Harvey, 1996: *Taming Democracy: Models of Political Rhetoric in Classical Athens.* Ithaca, NY.

ADDENDA

Carey, Christopher, 1997: *Trials from Classical Athens.* London.

Usher, Stephen, 1999: *Greek Oratory: Tradition and Originality.* Oxford.

DEMOSTHENES, SPEECHES 50–59

INTRODUCTION TO DEMOSTHENES

By Michael Gagarin

Since antiquity Demosthenes (384–322 BC) has usually been judged the greatest of the Attic orators. Although the patriotic and national-istic tenor of his message has been more highly regarded in some pe-riods of history than in others, he is unique in his mastery of so many different rhetorical styles and his ability to blend them into a powerful ensemble.

LIFE

Demosthenes was born into an old wealthy Athenian family. His father Demosthenes owned workshops that made swords and furni-ture. His maternal grandfather, Gylon, had been exiled from Athens and lived in the Crimea, where his mother Cleobule was born (per-haps to a Scythian mother). When Demosthenes was seven, his father died leaving his estate in the trust of several guardians. According to Demosthenes' own account, the guardians mismanaged and defrauded the estate to the point that when he turned eighteen, the age of ma-jority, he received almost nothing. He devoted the next several years to recovering his property, first studying forensic pleading and then bringing a series of suits against the guardians to recover his patrimony (speeches 27–31). He won the first case (27, *Against Aphobus I*), but then had to bring several more suits in order to collect the amount awarded him by the court. In the course of these trials he gained a reputation as a successful speaker, became sought after by others, and began to write speeches for a wide range of private suits, including inheritance, shipping loans, assault and trespass. His clients included one of the richest men in Athens, the banker Phormio; the speech *For Phormio* (36) involves a dispute over twenty talents (equivalent to several million dollars today). Demosthenes' vivid characterization of the honest, hard-working Phormio and his malicious and extravagant opponent proved so convincing that the jurors reportedly refused to listen to the other side and took the highly unusual step of voting immediately for Phormio.

In 355 Demosthenes became involved in his first major public case (22, *Against Androtion*). By this time it was common for ambitious or influential citizens to bring legal charges against their political opponents on matters of public interest. Charges of proposing an illegal decree (the *graphē paranomōn*) were particularly common; these involved the indictment of the proposer of a decree on the ground that it conflicted with existing law.[1] Although these speeches addressed the specific issue of a conflict between laws, it was generally accepted that the merits of the decree, and of its proposer, were also relevant factors, and these cases formed a major arena for the ongoing political struggles between leading figures in the city.

About the same time Demosthenes also began to publish speeches on public issues which he delivered in the assembly, and after 350, although he continued from time to time to write speeches for private disputes, he turned his attention primarily to public policy, especially relations between Athens and the growing power of Macedon under King Philip. Demosthenes' strategy throughout was to increase Athens' military readiness, to oppose Philip's expansion and to support other Greek cities in their resistance to it. Most notable in support of these objectives were the three *Olynthiacs* (1–3) in 349 unsuccessfully urging support for the city of Olynthus (which soon afterwards fell to Philip) and the four *Philippics* (4, 6, 9, 10) in 351–341 urging greater opposition to Philip. But Philip continued to extend his power into Greece, and in 338 he defeated a combined Greek force (including Athens) at the battle of Chaeronea in Boeotia, north of Attica. This battle

---

[1] One might compare the U.S. procedure of challenging the constitutionality of a law in court. Differences include the fact that today no charge is brought against the proposer of the law and that the case is heard by a small panel of professional judges, not the hundreds of untrained jurors who would have heard the case in Athens.

is usually taken to mark the end of the Greek cities' struggle to remain independent.

After Chaeronea Demosthenes continued to urge resistance to Philip, but his efforts were largely ineffectual and his successes and failures are more a matter of internal Athenian politics. His most prominent opponent during this period was Aeschines, who had been acquitted earlier (343) when Demosthenes brought a suit against him in connection with a delegation to Philip on which both men had served (19, cf. Aeschines 2). After Chaeronea, when a minor ally of Demosthenes named Ctesiphon proposed a decree awarding a crown to Demosthenes in recognition of his service to the city, Aeschines brought a *graphē paranomōn* against Ctesiphon (Aeschines 3). The suit, which was not tried until 330, raised legal objections to the proposed decree but also attacked the person and career of Demosthenes at considerable length. Demosthenes responded with his most famous speech *On the Crown* (18), often known by its Latin name *De Corona*. The verdict was so one-sided that Aeschines was fined for not receiving one-fifth of the votes and went into exile. This was Demosthenes' greatest triumph. The last years of his life, however, resulted in notable defeats, first in the rather shadowy Harpalus affair (324–323), from which no speech of his survives (but see Dinarchus 1). Shortly afterwards he was condemned to death at the instigation of pro-Macedonian forces and committed suicide.

WORKS

Sixty-one speeches and some miscellaneous works, including a collection of letters, have come down to us under Demosthenes' name. The authenticity of many of these has been challenged, often because of the allegedly poor quality of the work; but this reason is less often accepted today, and most of the public speeches and many of the private speeches are now thought to be authentic. Among the main exceptions are a group of private speeches (45, 46, 49, 50, 52, 53, 59 and possibly 47 and 51) that were delivered by Apollodorus and are now commonly thought to have been composed by him (Trevett 1992).

Apart from a funeral oration (60) and collections of proems and letters, Demosthenes' works fall into two groups, the assembly speeches (1–17) and the court speeches (18–59); the latter can be further divided into public and private speeches, though these are not formal legal categories. Notable among the public forensic speeches are *Against Meidias* (21), which has recently drawn attention for its pronouncements on Athenian public values, and his last surviving speech, *On the Crown* (18), generally recognized as his masterpiece. In this speech he uses his entire repertory of rhetorical strategies to defend his life and political career. He treats the legal issues of the case briefly, as being of minor concern, and then defends his conduct during the past three decades of Athenian history, arguing that even when his policy did not succeed, on each occasion it was the best policy for the city, in contrast to Aeschines' policies, which, when he ventured to propose any, were disastrous. Demosthenes' extensive personal attack on Aeschines' life and family may be too harsh for modern taste, but the blending of facts, innuendoes, sarcasm, rhetorical questions and other devices is undeniably effective.

Demosthenes' private speeches have recently begun to attract more interest from scholars, who draw from them insight into Athenian social, political, and economic life. Only the speeches concerned with recovering his inheritance (27–31) were delivered by Demosthenes himself; the rest were written for delivery by other litigants. We have already noted *For Phormio,* which is one of several having to do with banking. *Against Conon* (54) alleges an assault by several young rowdies spurred on by their father, and *Against Neaera* (59), delivered and probably written by Apollodorus, recounts the life of a former slave woman and her affairs with different Athenian men.

STYLE

Demosthenes is a master of Greek prose style; he paid careful attention to style, and to the oral delivery of his speeches. His Roman counterpart, Cicero, modeled his oratorical style (and some other features of his work) in part on Demosthenes' Greek. Although Demosthenes' style varied considerably over the course of time and among the different types of speeches, later assessments of his style are based primarily on the public forensic speeches, and especially the last of these, *On the Crown.* Long and sometimes elaborate sentences are one feature of his style, but Demosthenes' true greatness is his ability to write in many styles and to vary his style, mixing different features together both to suit the topic and to give variety and vigor to his speeches. The final product required great skill and practice to deliver effectively, and the stories about Demosthenes' rigorous training in delivery (see in general Plutarch, *Life of Demosthenes* 6–7), even if not literally true, accurately reflect his priorities. Indeed, only by reading aloud sections of *On the Crown* in Greek can one truly appreciate the power and authority of his prose.

SIGNIFICANCE

Demosthenes played a vital role in Athenian public affairs for some thirty years. His advocacy of the vigilant defense of Greece against foreign invaders, though ultimately unsuccessful in preserving Greek freedom, inspired his fellow Athenians with patriotic loyalty, and has similarly inspired many others in later times. In recent times political rhetoric has not been so widely admired as in the past, and Demosthenes is less read today than he used to be. But he still represents the greatest achievement of Greek oratory and stands as one of the greatest orators of any age.

SUPPLEMENTARY BIBLIOGRAPHY

Carey, Christopher, 1992: *Greek Orators VI: Apollodorus Against Neaira: [Demosthenes] 59*. Warminster.

Carey, Christopher, 1997: *Trials from Classical Athens*. London.

Carey, C., and R. A. Reid, 1985: *Demosthenes: Selected Private Speeches*. Cambridge.

Christ, Matthew, 1998: *The Litigious Athenian*. Baltimore.

Cohen, Edward E., 1992: *Athenian Economy and Society*. Princeton.

Davies, J. K., 1971: *Athenian Propertied Families*. Oxford.

Gabrielsen, V., 1994: *Financing the Athenian Fleet: Public Taxation and Social Relations*. Baltimore and London.

Hamel, Debra, 1998: *Athenian Generals: Military Authority in the Classical Period*. Leiden.

Hansen, M. H., 1976: *Apagoge, Endeixis* and *Ephegesis against Kakourgoi, Atimoi and Pheugontes*. Odense.

Hansen, M. H., 1999: *The Athenian Democracy in the Age of Demosthenes.* Norman, OK.

Harrison, A. R. W., 1968–1971 (2 volumes): *The Law of Athens.* Oxford (republished with a new foreword and additional bibliography provided by D. M. MacDowell). London, 1998.

Johnstone, Steven, 1999: *Disputes and Democracy.* Austin.

Kapparis, Konstantinos, 1999: *Apollodoros 'Against Neaira' [D.] 59.* Berlin.

Pearson, Lionel, 1976: *The Art of Demosthenes.* Meisenheim am Glan.

Sandys, J. E., 1886–1896 (2 volumes): *Select Private Orations of Demosthenes with Supplementary Notes by F. A. Paley.* Cambridge.

Thompson, Homer, and R. E. Wycherly, 1972: *The Athenian Agora Volume XIV: The Agora of Athens.* Princeton.

Usher, Stephen, 1999: *Greek Oratory: Tradition and Originality.* Oxford.

Wallace, Robert W., 1989: *The Areopagus Council.* Baltimore and London.

Wycherly, R. E., 1957: *The Athenian Agora Volume III: Literary and Epigraphical Testimonia.* Princeton.

Note: A comprehensive list of all known Athenians, with precise references to the literary and epigraphical sources relevant to each one, is given in M. J. Osborne and S. G. Byrne, *A Lexicon of Greek Personal Names* (Oxford, 1994). For noncitizens living in the city, one may consult the same authors' *The Foreign Residents of Athens* (Leuven, 1996).

INTRODUCTION TO THIS VOLUME

❖❖

By Victor Bers

Although this volume of *The Oratory of Classical Greece* bears the title *Demosthenes, Speeches 50–59,* only one speech in the group, *Against Conon* (54), has been unanimously regarded by antiquity and modern scholars as the work of Demosthenes. Some scholars have doubted whether Demosthenes wrote *On the Trierarchic Crown* (51). Most accept *Against Callicles* (55) and *Against Eubulides* (57) as authentic Demosthenic compositions, though conceding that the former has technical characteristics different from Demosthenes' mature prose and that the latter is unpolished. *Against Dionysodorus* (56) remains controversial: the authors of one book (Carey and Reid 1985) express doubt that Demosthenes could have written the speech, but even more recently Usher 1999: 257 writes: "His participation in the case, in some capacity, [is] highly likely." [1] Doubt over the authorship of *Against Theocrines* (58), a speech that condemns Demosthenes for abandoning a just cause (§42), goes back to at least the first century AD.

The speeches *Against Polycles* (50), *Against Callippus* (52), *Against Nicostratus* (53), and *Against Neaera* (59), as well as *Against Stephanus II* (46) and *Against Timotheus* (49), are in all probability by the well-known politician Apollodorus, the son of Pasion. Apollodorus is important enough in the history of Greek oratory to have been called (in

---

[1] "In some capacity" is an important qualification, since it is unclear what portion of a speech was contributed by the speechwriter (*logographos*), what portion by the man who commissioned and delivered the speech. See the Series Introduction, p. xix, for a more optimistic statement.

modern times) "The Eleventh Attic Orator." See below for a short account of Apollodorus' career and the matter of authorship.

Aside from *On the Trierarchic Crown* (51), which is addressed to the
Council of Five Hundred (*boulē*), all the speeches in this volume were
written for delivery before large, often boisterous, popular courts, the
dikastēria. Even though we have only the written form in which they
have been transmitted to us, all the speeches presented here, indeed all
Greek oratory meant to be delivered and not just read, hold many
signs that the orator needed to be something of a performer. For many
hours at a time, speakers had to hold the interest of their audiences—
spectators as well as members of the legislative or judicial bodies
they were addressing. They strove to do this by a variety of strategies.
On the level of content, speakers often claim that the verdict given in
their case will have enduring consequences for good or evil well beyond the matter at hand and their own interests: excellent examples
include 56.48 and 59.114. On the level of style, speakers exploit the
linguistic resources of the Greek language, including its rich store of
particles,[2] facility with clauses of great complexity, flexibility of word
order, wide repertory of rhetorical figures, and overall sense of shape.
Even the speeches in this volume that are regarded as unworthy of Demosthenes himself seem vigorous in style and capable of maintaining
the audience's sustained interest.

These ten speeches fall into a variety of procedural types (see the
Introductions to the individual speeches); a modern reader will probably see other classifications as more pertinent. Although they involve
individual citizens and do not directly involve policy decisions ema-
nating from the Council of Five Hundred and the Assembly, the ma-

---

[2] Greek prose writers normally connected every sentence to the one just before
using these short "nonlexical" words. A particular favorite was *gar*, a word usually
translated "for," but which I have generally rendered as "you see." The word is
generally used in aid of an argument to introduce some fact or consideration and
thereby insist on the logic of the sequence; but sometimes it is not much more than
a filler linking assertions and holding the listener's attention. In *Against Conon*, a
work of about sixteen pages in the Oxford Classical Text, Demosthenes uses *gar*
thirty-four times. In English, this type of repetition is associated with naïve speech
style.

jority involve relations of individual Athenians with state institutions
and life in the public sphere. The first two (50 and 51) have to do with
the conduct of one branch of the Athenian military, the outfitting and
management of warships. The speeches *Against Eubulides* (57) and
Against Neaera (59) arose from challenges to citizenship. *Against Theocrines* (58) argues that the defendant is in debt to the state and therefore barred from acting as prosecutor. The speech *Against Dionysodorus* (56) was written for a commercial case in which the principals were
not Athenian citizens or even resident aliens (*metoikoi*); nevertheless,
the jury is reminded that the supply and price of grain were very important to the city. The speech *Against Conon* (54) describes brawling
in both the streets of Athens and a military camp, an extension of
Athenian "civic space." A soured friendship forms the background of
Against Nicostratus (53), but here too the city was in some sense an interested party, since it stood to gain from the sale of private slaves to
the public treasury. We find explicit charges of abuse of the city's judicial system (*sykophantia*) in most of the speeches, including *Against
Callicles* (55), which describes a dispute between two neighboring families over trivial flood damage, if the speaker can be trusted about the
extent of the damage. Finally, whenever a speaker, co-speaker (*synēgoros*),[3] opponent, or witness was a man of prominence, the particular
issue to be judged might have been less important than the protracted
struggle of aristocrats for status and power in public competition
judged by common citizens.[4] This was certainly the case whenever
Demosthenes, Apollodorus, or their associates were involved.

These "private speeches," then, are hardly divorced from the larger
community, in both its organized and informal aspects. That said, it
is also true that some speeches derive from the world of private, even
intimate, associations. Although one must never make the mistake of
assuming any speaker's account to be entirely credible, we do find stories of rural neighbors (53 and 55), bands of young men joined in raucous, intentionally shocking behavior (54), families in severe economic
distress (57), and the intricate involvement of prostitutes with the lives

---

[3] See Lene Rubinstein, *Litigation and Cooperation* (Stuttgart, 2000), for a wide-
ranging treatment of *synēgoroi.*
[4] See the Series Introduction, p. xxviii.

of citizens (59). Similarly, though forensic speeches were stylized speech events that to a greater or lesser extent conformed to an etiquette specific to the lawcourts, we can at least get an occasional snatch of colloquial Attic speech, especially in speeches thought to have been written by Apollodorus.

APOLLODORUS [5]

From several points of view, there is considerable irony in the incorporation of speeches by Apollodorus, son of Pasion, into the corpus of Demosthenic speeches.[6] The two orators descended from families about as different from each other as possible in the Athens of the fifth and fourth centuries BC. At least during one period, moreover, their personal relations are likely to have been unfriendly in the extreme (see *For Phormio* [36]). If scholars have correctly identified those speeches that were attributed to Demosthenes by the manuscripts but were in fact composed by Apollodorus, there are very large stylistic differences between the two.[7]

Demosthenes descended from a family of undoubted Athenian citizenship whose wealth can, with some probability, be traced back to his paternal grandfather. By contrast, Apollodorus' father Pasion was a slave; worse, he was not even of Greek origin but probably came from Phoenicia. But Pasion was extraordinarily lucky in his owners,

---

[5] For a detailed treatment, see Trevett 1992.

[6] Many manuscripts bearing the name of an ancient Greek author contain works probably or certainly not by that person. Unscrupulous booksellers, unhampered by enforceable copyright, are likely to have enhanced the commercial value of some manuscripts by putting a prestigious name on a text by an obscure author; honest error might sometimes have been to blame, and indeed it may be that an uncritical collector simply lumped together speeches written by Demosthenes himself with others found in his library after his death.

[7] By contrast, Demosthenes' style is sometimes very close to that of Lysias, as the literary critic Dionysius of Halicarnassus observed. He quotes narrative taken from Lys. Fr. 2 *Against Teisis* and Dem. *Against Conon* (54) to show that the style of one passage so closely resembles the style of the other that few could easily tell who wrote which (*Demosthenes* 11–13).

his character, and his commercial acumen. He was the chattel of two bankers doing business in Athens and served his masters so well that they freed him from slavery. At some point, he acquired ownership of their successful bank and also came to own a factory that made shields. Pasion lavished part of his growing wealth on the city. In gratitude, the Athenians granted him citizenship, elevating him from the status of *metoikos*.[8]

Apollodorus, Pasion's first son, was born about 394, some ten years earlier than Demosthenes. As a man with a foreign accent, Apollodorus' father would probably not have been able to make more than a token effort at speaking in an Athenian court.[9] The son, however, spoke perfect Attic Greek and presumably received some rhetorical training. He was therefore prepared in his early twenties to argue in court over a matter that arose from his father's bank (see *Against Callippus* [52]). About seven years later, Apollodorus undertook a similar case when he prosecuted the general Timotheus to recover money borrowed from his father (*Against Timotheus* [Dem. 49]). Apollodorus later became embroiled in a protracted legal battle with Phormio, the ex-slave to whom Pasion entrusted first his bank and eventually his wife (Apollodorus' mother): he had provided in his will that Phormio marry her after his own death (see Dem. 36 and 45). As a rich Athenian citizen, Apollodorus was required to perform liturgies (Series Introduction, p. xxiii), starting with a trierarchy in 368. But even as liturgies confirmed high status, they could also provoke litigation (see *Against Polycles* [50]).

Apollodorus was also in court with his neighbor in a dispute connected, at least in part, with the conflict with Phormio (see *Against Nicostratus* [53]). Apollodorus' views on foreign and domestic politics are controversial,[10] but in 348 he was clearly close to Demosthenes' position on the need to resist Philip of Macedon (see *Against Neaera* [59.3]). Apollodorus' actions brought him into conflict with the politician Stephanus, and that conflict forms the real background to *Against*

---

[8] See Dem. 59.2 with note.

[9] Cf. what is said about Phormio in Demosthenes (36.1 and 45.30).

[10] For a largely agnostic review of various theories, see the fifth chapter, "The Political Career of Apollodoros," in Trevett 1992.

Neaera, a speech written for a trial that ostensibly deals with a Corinthian prostitute's usurpation of Athenian citizenship. That trial took place not later than 340, after which Apollodorus disappears from our evidence.

As already suggested (pp. xxix, 9, 12), the authorship of forensic speeches is never a simple matter. In the case of Demosthenes and Apollodorus there are some special complications arising from the legal combat between Apollodorus and Phormio. A speech in defense of Phormio attributed to Demosthenes (36) was so stunningly effective that it stymied Apollodorus' prosecution. Despite that setback, Apollodorus persisted in his legal pursuit, delivering two speeches, *Against Stephanus I* and *Against Stephanus II* (45 and 46), attacking a man who had appeared as a witness favorable to Phormio. Thus we have three speeches concerned with Phormio that the manuscripts attribute to Demosthenes, the first favoring Apollodorus' opponent, the second and third favoring Apollodorus, indeed written for him to deliver. The attributions might be flatly wrong, or perhaps Demosthenes switched sides. If the latter is true, the switch can be regarded as proof that a speechwriter of that period resembled a modern lawyer who, in principle at least, works for clients without regard to his personal beliefs. Making no such allowance for professional impartiality, Demosthenes' enemy Aeschines condemned him for disloyalty and avarice (see Aes. 2.165 with note in *The Oratory of Classical Greece,* Vol. 3). Even if Demosthenes did switch sides, there is the further possibility that 45 and 46 are the collaborative work of Demosthenes and Apollodorus.

The relations of the two men aside, there are good grounds for believing that Apollodorus was the author of a number of works that found their way into the collected speeches of Demosthenes. With the exception of *Against Stephanus I* (45), all the speeches written for trials in which Apollodorus was a principal player show a looser and more repetitious style than speeches certainly written by Demosthenes. Several technical characteristics, especially the frequency of runs of three short syllables and hiatus,[11] confirm this general impression. It is there-

---

[11] I.e., the "gap" or (as the ancients conceived it) "clash" of vowel sounds at the close of one word and the start of the next.

fore extremely probable that speeches 50, 52, 53, and 59 in this volume are all the work of Apollodorus.[12]

TEXT

This translation normally follows the Oxford Classical Text of W. Rennie (Oxford, 1931).

---

[12] As already mentioned, speeches 46 and 49 are also securely attributed to Apollodorus. Trevett 1992: 73 regards 47 as possibly his work too.

DEMOSTHENES, SPEECHES 50–59

Translated by Victor Bers

50. AGAINST POLYCLES IN THE MATTER OF A PERIOD OF SUPPLEMENTARY SERVICE AS TRIERARCH

〰〰〰〰〰〰〰〰〰〰〰〰〰〰〰〰〰〰〰〰〰〰〰〰〰〰〰〰〰〰〰〰〰〰〰〰〰〰〰

INTRODUCTION

This speech, delivered by Apollodorus, son of Pasion, is almost certainly his own composition, not Demosthenes' (see the Introduction to this volume). Regardless of the authorship, the text is one of the most revealing sources of information on the trierarchy, a liturgy (see the Series Introduction, p. xxiii) that involved not only paying for much of the cost of the maintenance and operation of a warship (*triērēs*) for one year, both its equipment and manpower, but also commanding the vessel. Since the trierarchy was notable for its expense and military importance, it provided an important arena for political and social competition.

Apollodorus has come to court to complain, in essence, that Polycles,[1] the man appointed to succeed him as trierarch for the following year, had refused to do so. In consequence, Apollodorus tells us, he was forced to remain in office well beyond his own term (the additional service is called *epitriērarkhēma*) at great financial and personal cost. The text does not specifically identify the form of legal action Apollodorus is pursuing, and there is no consensus as to which category it fell into. Some assign it to the *dikai triērarchikai*, "suits dealing with trierarchies"; others think it was a *dikē blabēs*, a "suit for damages." If the former, Apollodorus would be attempting simply to recover the costs

---

[1] This is apparently Polycles son of Polycrates of the deme Anagyros. From this speech and several inscriptions he is known to have been assigned a number of liturgies.

Polycles should have borne; if the latter, Apollodorus could hope for double damages.[2]

Apollodorus' trierarchy began in September, 362 (see §4). The trial for which the speech was written took place sometime between 360 and 358.[3]

For a detailed analysis of the speech, see Theodore Ballin, "A Commentary on [Demosthenes] 50, *Against Polykles*" (unpublished Ph.D. dissertation, University of Washington, 1978). Many aspects of the trierarchy are discussed by Gabrielsen 1994. Also useful are Trevett 1992 and Hamel 1998.

50. AGAINST POLYCLES IN THE MATTER OF A PERIOD OF SUPPLEMENTARY SERVICE AS TRIERARCH

[1] Gentlemen of the jury, it is right that those who are going to decide a case of this sort pay especially close attention. You see, this trial is not just a private matter between Polycles and myself but something that involves the whole city. When the complaints are private, but the damages public, it is surely to be expected (*eikos*) that you hear the matter and then make the correct judgment. Now *if* I had come before you over a quarrel with Polycles about some private arrangement, then the trial would be my business and his; but in fact, my case concerns the transfer of command over a ship and the trierarch's expenses over a period of five months and six days, and it concerns the laws— whether they are to be valid or not. [2] I think I must tell you everything from the start. And by the gods, gentlemen, don't suppose that I'm chattering away if I recount my expenses and actions at length, explaining how they were all opportune and in the city's interest. If someone can show that I am lying, let him stand up and use my allotted time[4] to refute me on any point where he claims I am not telling you the truth. But if it is true and no one other than Polycles would disagree with me, I put to all of you a just request: [3] those of you who

---

[2]Cf. Harrison 1968–1971, Vol. 2: 21-22, Edward E. Cohen, *Ancient Athenian Maritime Courts* (Princeton, 1973), 14 n. 31, and Ballin 1978 (see below): 43–44.

[3]Trevett 1992: 43 favors the first part of this period.

[4]Lit. "in my water," a reference to the waterclock used to time speeches. See the Series Introduction, p. xxiv.

were on military service and were present at the events, please recall what happened and tell the men sitting beside you of my eagerness, and of the difficult circumstances that faced the city at that juncture, so you will know what sort of a person I am when it comes to your commands.[5] You, on the other hand, who stayed here, I ask that you listen to me in silence as I tell you everything,[6] at each point presenting the laws and decrees of both the Council and the Assembly and the depositions of witnesses.

[4] On the twenty-fourth day of the month Metageitnion, during the archonship of Molon,[7] there was a meeting of the Assembly, and many grave situations were reported to you. You voted that the trierarchs, of whom I was one, were to launch our ships. I don't need to describe the emergency that faced the city then, but you yourselves should recall it. Tenos had been captured by Alexander and its inhabitants enslaved.[8] [5] Miltocythes had revolted from Cotys[9] and had sent ambassadors to you to discuss an alliance: he requested that you help him, and he said he would return the Chersonesus. At the meeting of the Assembly, delegates from Proconessus, your ally, implored you to

---

[5] It was customary to speak to members of a particular jury panel as representative both of jurors and voters at the Assembly, even if the event under discussion happened before most or all of the jurors being addressed were eligible for jury service, or even born. For instance, Aes. 1.173, delivered about fifty-three years after the event, states: "You executed Socrates the sophist." This would not be literally true of any juror younger than eighty-three.

[6] Jurymen were often boisterous, to judge from frequent requests for silence and criticisms of their deportment by Plato, a severe critic of the Athenian democracy. Cf. 57.1n.

[7] Some time in late summer, 362.

[8] Tenos is one of the Cycladic islands of the southern Aegean. Alexander, tyrant of Pherae in Thessaly from 369 to 358 (not to be confused with Alexander the Great of Macedon), had been an Athenian ally.

[9] Cotys, a Thracian king, was on friendly terms with Athens until his activities in the cities on the coast of Thrace (northwest Aegean); Miltocythes had been one of his subjects. The Chersonesus is the peninsular landmass forming the north shore of the Hellespont. From Dem. 23.104, 169–170 we know that Miltocythes was in Hieron Oros (Sacred Hill), a place of uncertain location, but perhaps of great strategic value to Athens, which would justify the phrase "return the Chersonesus" (see Ballin's commentary).

help them, saying that they were pressed by Cyzicus in warfare by land and sea and asking you not to allow them to be ruined.[10] [6] At that meeting you heard what these men said for themselves and also from those who spoke in their behalf. You also heard that the merchants and ship owners were sailing away from the Black Sea and that men from Byzantium, Chalcedon,[11] and Cyzicus were forcing those ships to put in to shore because they needed grain. You saw that grain was getting a high price in Piraeus[12] and the supply for sale was limited. You voted that the trierarchs launch their ships and bring them around to the jetty, that the Council members and demarchs[13] make lists of the deme members and supply sailors,[14] and that an expedition be sent out quickly to bring help to each of the areas. This is the decree of Aristophon[15] that the Assembly passed:

[DECREE]

[7] You have heard the decree, gentlemen of the jury. Now, since the sailors conscripted by the deme members[16] did not appear, except for a few incompetents whom I dismissed, I pledged my own property, and borrowed money, and I was the first of the trierarchs to man his boat.[17] I hired the best sailors possible, giving each man gifts and a large advance payment. Besides, I equipped the ship with all my own equip-

---

[10] Proconessus is an island in the western part of the Propontis (Sea of Marmara); Cyzicus is on the mainland to the south.

[11] Byzantium is on the west shore of the Bosphorus, Chalcedon on the east shore.

[12] Athens' port city.

[13] Chief magistrates of the demes.

[14] Possibly a departure from the normal mode of enrolling oarsmen. See Hamel 1998: 24. The word translated "sailors" is ambiguous, referring either to rowers (perhaps excluding slaves) or more generally to members of the crew (see Ballin 1978: 78–81).

[15] Son of Aristophanes of the deme Azenia. He is best known for being charged and acquitted seventy-five times for proposing unconstitutional decrees (Aes. 3.194).

[16] The mustering of sailors would have been conducted by the demarchs.

[17] For the importance of being first to have one's boat in readiness, see Dem. 51.4–5, 7.

ment, taking nothing from the public stores and, outdoing the other trierarchs, made it as fine-looking and resplendent as could be. Further, I engaged the best skilled seamen (*hypēresia*) [18] I could. [8] Not only, gentlemen, did I at that time spend so lavishly on the trierarchy, but I also contributed from the outset a large part of the special fund (*eisphora*) [19] that you voted was to be raised for the naval expedition. You see, you had resolved that the Council members and demarchs [20] would make up the list of those who were to advance the funds to pay the *eisphora* on behalf of the deme members and those who held property in a deme; [21] and because my property was visible, [22] my name was inscribed on the list of three separate demes. [9] Moreover, I did not offer any excuse to evade these services, claiming that I was already a trierarch and could not perform two liturgies simultaneously or that the laws did not allow it. No, I was the first to pay the *eisphora* in advance. And I was not reimbursed for my advance payments because at first I was abroad serving you as a trierarch, but later, after I returned, I found that others had already collected the money from those who had resources, and all the rest had nothing to give. [10] To show that I am telling you the truth, the clerk will read depositions from the men who collected the funds for paying the soldiers and from the magistrates in charge of fitting out the squadrons (*apostoleis*); he will also read out the wages I was paying month by month to the skilled sailors and marines (*epibatai*). From the generals I took only money for food, except for two months' wages in a period of one year and five months; further, he will read the names of the sailors whom I hired and how

---

[18] The term *hypēresia* has been controversial, but there are very strong arguments that it refers to sixteen "skilled seamen" (I take the phrase from Ballin's commentary): helmsman, boatswain, purser, bow officer, shipwright, piper, and ten deck hands (see also Gabrielsen 1994: 106). If this is correct, the "sailors" referred to earlier would be primarily rowers.

[19] Property tax paid by rich Athenians and metics in times of special need, usually during a war.

[20] The translation follows those editions that add the word *demarchs*.

[21] Lit. "those subject to the *egktētikon*," a tax paid for the right of holding property in a deme other than one's own.

[22] "Visible property" consists primarily of land, structures, animals, slaves, and the like, but not money.

much money each man got. The purpose is that from these depositions you can learn of my zeal, and you will know why Polycles refused to take the ship over from me when the period of my trierarchy had elapsed.

[WITNESSES]

[11] Gentlemen of the jury, you have heard from the depositions that were read out that what I have been telling you is true. And as for what I am about to say, you will all agree that it is true. It is agreed, after all, that the crew of a trireme is broken up, first, if nobody pays the wages, and second, if during its period of service the ship puts in at Piraeus. Very many men desert, and the rowers who remain by the ship refuse to re-embark unless somebody gives them extra money to cover their household expenses. I faced both of these situations, gentlemen of the jury, with the result that my trierarchy was more expensive. [12] For eight months I received no wages from the general, and then I brought the ambassadors back to Athens because my ship made the best time; then, when the order came from the Assembly to take the general Menon[23] to the Hellespont to replace Autokles,[24] who had been voted out of office, I put to sea and was quickly off. In place of the sailors who had left I hired others, offering them bonuses and advance payments; and to those of the original crew who remained, I gave something for them to leave at home for household expenses over and above what they had before. I was not unaware of the crew's needs at the time and how hard it was on each man, [13] but I was myself without resources, by Zeus and Apollo, in a way nobody would believe who wasn't really keeping track of my affairs. Pledging my plot of land as security, I borrowed thirty minas from Thrasylochus[25] and Archeneüs,[26] which I gave to the rowers. Then I put to sea, intending, as far as I could, not to fall short in executing any of the Assembly's commands. The Assembly heard about these events and not

---

[23] He was subsequently prosecuted by Apollodorus (Dem. 36.53). The charge, procedure, and outcome are unknown, but there is epigraphic evidence to show that he was not executed.

[24] He too was prosecuted by Apollodorus (Dem. 36.53).

[25] Possibly the same man whom Apollodorus mentions in 52.

[26] Nothing is known for certain about this man.

only praised me but called me to dine at the *prytaneion*.[27] A deposition and the Assembly's decree will be read out to you showing that I am telling the truth.

[DEPOSITION; DECREE]

[14] Now, when we arrived at the Hellespont, the period of my trierarchy had passed and the soldiers had been paid only two months' wages; another general, Timomachus,[28] arrived but did not bring new trierarchs to take over the ships. Many of my crew got discouraged and left the ship. Some went to fight on the mainland, while others, attracted by high wages, went over to ships from Thasos and Maroneia;[29] they got a large sum in advance and were also tricked by many verbal promises.[30] [15] They saw that I had exhausted my resources, that the city was not concerned, that the allies had no resources, that the generals could not be trusted, that the period of my trierarchy had elapsed and the ship was not sailing home, and that no new trierarch had come to the ship from whom they could expect help. To the extent that I had the ambition[31] to man the ship with good rowers, I suffered more desertion than the other trierarchs. [16] The others at least had the advantage that the men who had been assigned to their ship from the mustering-list[32] remained with the ship waiting for a safe return home

---

[27] A building that served as a sort of town hall. For an Athenian citizen, a dinner at the *prytaneion* was a mark of very high honor. In the *Apology* (37a), Plato represents Socrates as proposing meals in the *prytaneion* as an appropriate "punishment" for himself.

[28] The third of the generals prosecuted by Apollodorus in connection with events in the north Aegean. Apollodorus charged him with treason for betraying the Chersonesus to Cotys. Timomachus was tried *in absentia* and sentenced to death, but escaped into exile (Dem. 19.180, 36.53; Aes. 1.56 with scholion).

[29] Respectively, an island in the Aegean not far from the southern coast of Thrace and a city on that coast. Both were members of the Second Athenian League.

[30] This translates the Oxford Classical text, which here deviates from the manuscripts.

[31] Lit. "loving honor." On the approving attitude towards ambition for honor won by patriotic service, see K. J. Dover, *Greek Popular Morality in the Time of Plato and Aristotle* (Oxford, 1974), 230–233.

[32] Cf. 6.

when the general discharged them. But my men had confidence in their ability to row, and so went off where they could again get the highest wage, since in their minds immediate profit outweighed the fear that I would later catch them.[33] [**17**] This, then, was my situation when the general Timomachus ordered me to sail to Hieron[34] to escort the grain transports, but he supplied no money. Word also came that the Byzantines and Chalcedonians were once again conducting the boats to shore and forcing them to unload their grain. So I borrowed fifteen minas at interest from Archedemus of the deme Anaphlystus,[35] who happened to be at Sestus.[36] I also took 800 drachmas from Nicippus, owner of a merchant ship, as a maritime loan at 12½ percent interest, with the understanding that if the boat made it back to Athens I would return the principal together with the interest.[37] [**18**] I sent Euctemon,[38] the ship's purser (*pentēkontarchos*), to Lampsacus.[39] I gave him money and letters to foreign friends (*xenoi*[40]) of my father, and I instructed him to hire the best sailors he could. I myself stayed behind in Sestus and gave some money, as much as I had, to those original crew members who remained when the period of my trierarchy had elapsed; and I took on other rowers at full pay[41] during the time the general was preparing the expedition to Hieron. [**19**] But when Euctemon came back from Lampsacus with the sailors he had hired and the general gave the order to put out to sea, Euctemon sud-

---

[33] Apollodorus presumably means that he could arrest them for desertion, but Ballin (1978: 127) doubts that he had the legal authority to prosecute Athenians who had not been conscripted or foreign mercenaries.

[34] A town on the Asian (south) side of the Bosphorus.

[35] Otherwise unknown.

[36] A city on the north coast of the Hellespont. The Oxford Classical Text follows the mss, which put Nicippus, not Archedemus, at Sestus. For the change in word order (proposed by Boeckh) and other emendations, see Ballin 1978: 130.

[37] For a summary of what is known and contested about loans of this type, see Todd 1993: 337–340.

[38] Not otherwise known.

[39] A prospering commercial city on the northeast coast of the Hellespont.

[40] See 50.56n.

[41] Ballin suggests that here and at 35, Apollodorus means "payment of the wages contracted for at the end of each month," i.e., not cheating them of the balance of pay they had been promised.

denly fell sick and was in very bad shape. So I gave him his pay, adding provisions for his journey, and sent him home. I got another purser and set off to escort the grain transports; I stayed there forty-five days until the merchant boats left the Pontus, after the rising of Arcturus.[42] [20] I arrived at Sestus supposing that I would be sailing home. The period of my trierarchy had ended, the extension had already gone on for two months, and my successor had still not come to the ship. But when ambassadors from Maroneia came to the general Timomachus and asked him to escort their grain boats, he ordered us trierarchs to attach cables and tow the vessels to Maroneia, a long trip across the open sea.

[21] I have described all these events from the beginning for this reason: so you will know how much I spent, how burdensome was the liturgy I shouldered, how much I spent on behalf of Polycles when I served as trierarch beyond my term because he did not come to the ship, and how many dangers I myself faced from stormy weather and enemies. Then, after we escorted the grain-boats to Maroneia and reached Thasos, Timomachus together with the Thasians, sent food and peltasts[43] to Stryme,[44] intending to take the territory himself.[45] [22] The Maronites were arrayed against our ships, ready to fight at sea in defense of their territory; our soldiers were exhausted, since they had sailed a great distance towing the boats from Thasos to Stryme; and besides, the storm was still blowing, there was no harbor, and we couldn't disembark to prepare a meal since this was enemy territory and mercenaries and barbarian troops from the area were stationed around the wall. So it was necessary to ride at anchor all night on the open sea, with no food or sleep,[46] on guard through the night for an attack by the Maronite triremes. [23] Besides that, during the night at

---

[42] At the latitude in question, this important astronomical event, after which sailing became increasingly dangerous, occurred on September 16.

[43] Light-armed soldiers.

[44] A town somewhere on the Thracian coast.

[45] There is little clear information on the origins and outcome of the conflict between Thasos and Maroneia and the part in it played by Athens. Apollodorus does not even say how the sea battle he here narrates ended.

[46] Triremes normally were beached each night, permitting the crew to sleep more comfortably.

that time of the year—exactly the setting of the Pleiades[47]—we had rain, thunder, and strong wind; certainly you can imagine, gentlemen of the jury, how the soldiers lost heart and how many men again deserted me afterwards. The sailors from the original crew had endured great suffering but got little benefit—only as much as I could borrow to give to each man to supplement what they had got from me earlier, since the general didn't give them enough even for their daily subsistence. I had already done three months of extra service as trierarch, but Polycles still had not come to the ship. So I borrowed money and hired sailors to replace those who had deserted.

[24] Polycles is the only one of the successor trierarchs who has no excuse for not taking over the ship long before. You see, when Euctemon, the purser, fell sick and was sent home from the Hellespont, he heard that Polycles had been appointed to take over from me. Since he knew that the period of my trierarchy had expired and I was already serving beyond my term, he took my father-in-law Deinias[48] along and approached Polycles in the bazaar[49] in Piraeus. He told Polycles to join the ship as quickly as possible, since large sums were being paid each day in addition to what the general gave the ship for rations. [25] He told Polycles in detail of the wages given monthly to the skilled seamen and the marines and to the rowers he had himself hired at Lampsacus and those who came on board later to replace the deserters. On top of that there was what I had given each of the original crewmembers who asked me for money when my term had expired. He also told him how much I had spent on the boat each day. He knew this from experience because, as purser, he had done the buying and made the payments. [26] Euctemon told Polycles that I was using my own gear for the ship and had nothing from the city. "See whether you want to persuade him to sell you the gear, or get your own gear and sail off. I think," he said, "Apollodorus will be agreeable, since he owes money there and will want to pay it back from the price of the gear." When Polycles heard this from Euctemon and from my father-in-law

---

[47] About November 6.

[48] Deinias is also known from Dem. 36.15, 36.17, and 45.55. He was clearly a rich man, but besides these mentions in court speeches, nothing substantial is known about him.

[49] Lit, *deigma,* a place where merchants displayed their wares.

Deinias, he gave no answer to what they had said to him; they reported that he laughed and said, "The mouse has just got a taste of pitch: he wanted, you see, to be an Athenian."[50] [27] Since he paid no attention to what he heard from Euctemon and Deinias, another approach was made to him later by Pythodorus of the deme Acharnae and Apollodorus of the deme Leuconoë,[51] good friends of mine. They urged him to go join the ship, since he was the replacement trierarch. About the gear, they told him that everything I had was my own—none of it was public. [28] "If you want to use that gear," they said, "leave the money here and don't risk taking it there." They planned to pay off the mortgage on my land by paying Archeneüs and Thrasylochus the thirty minas.[52] As for the wear and tear on the gear, they were prepared to draw up a written note for Polycles, stating that they would guarantee on my behalf whatever other trierarchs guaranteed their replacements. Depositions will be read out to show that everything I am telling you is true.

[DEPOSITIONS]

[29] I think I have considerable evidence to show you that Polycles did not intend of his own accord to take over the ship from me, and that when he was forced by you and your decree to join the ship, on his arrival he refused to take it over. You see, by the time he came to Thasos it was the fourth month of my extended period of service as trierarch. I took witnesses along, as many citizens as I could, marines and skilled seamen, and I went up to him in the agora in Thasos and demanded that, as my replacement, he take the ship over from me and reimburse me for my expenditures during the extra time. [30] I was

---

[50] Polycles, scion of an old Athenian family, uses a proverbial saying to deride the son of a slave who rose to the status of metic (a resident alien) and was then made a citizen. Ambition, Polycles means, has led Apollodorus into a predicament, extravagant expenditures as trierarch, from which he now cannot extricate himself.

[51] Pythodorus is known from several inscriptions dating after this trial; it has been suggested that his grandfather had helped Apollodorus' father acquire Athenian citizenship. For Apollodorus of the deme Leuconoë, see Is. 7, which concerns a dispute over his estate.

[52] See 13.

prepared to give him an item-by-item account with witnesses standing by—sailors, marines, skilled seamen—so I could refute him on
the spot if he disputed me at any point. I had such a precise account
written down that not only were my expenditures themselves listed but
even where the money was spent and for what; also the price, and in
which currency, and what was lost in the currency conversion. All this
was recorded so that my successor could put me to a detailed test if
he thought I was foisting a false entry on him. [31] Further, I offered
to swear an oath confirming the calculation of my expenses. I made
this challenge, but he answered that he did not care *what* I said. In
the course of this exchange an aide came from the general ordering
me to sail—me, not Polycles, my successor, whose liturgy had already
started. Later in my speech I will tell you why he did this. At that point,
I decided to sail where the general ordered. [32] When I sailed back to
Thasos after towing the boats to Stryme, as the general had ordered,
I instructed the skilled seamen, marines, and rowers to remain on the
ship; I myself went to the house where Timomachus the general was
staying, with the intention of handing over the ship with a full comple-
ment of men to Polycles, in the general's presence. [33] I found Polycles there, together with the other trierarchs and their replacements
and some other citizens, and I went in and spoke to him right away in
front of the general; and I demanded that he take over the ship from
me and pay me back for my expenses, for what I had spent during my
extra period of service. And I asked him whether he would take over
the gear or if he had come to the ship with his own. [34] When I put
this challenge to him, he asked me why I was the only trierarch who
had his own gear and whether the city did not know that there were
some men who could provide gear for its ships, so the city did not have
to provide them herself. "Or," he asked, "are you so much richer than
the others that you have your own gear and are the only trierarch to
sport gilded ornamentation? [35] Who," he went on, "could put up with
your crazy extravagance? A corrupted crew, used to big advance payments, getting out of the usual chores of shipboard service, and bath-
ing in tubs, marines and skilled seamen coddled in soft luxury from
getting lavish wages paid in full?[53] You are teaching the army," he said,

---

[53] Polycles' language, as Apollodorus presents it, is indignant and not entirely
grammatical.

"evil habits and bear some responsibility for the other trierarchs getting worse soldiers: they're looking to get the same deal that your men
get from you. You should have been doing the same as the other trierarchs." [36] When he said that, I answered that I did not take the gear
from the arsenal, "Because *you* ruined it.[54] But if you wish, take over
the ship's gear; otherwise, get some for yourself. As for the sailors,
marines, and skilled seamen: if you claim I corrupted them, then when
you take over the ship, you get your own crew: sailors, marines, and
skilled seamen of the sort that will sail with you without pay. But do
take over the ship, since I'm not supposed to be trierarch any longer.
The period of my service is up, and I've served four months beyond my
term." [37] When I said that, he answered that his co-trierarch had not
reached the ship: "And I will *not* take over the trireme by myself, he
said."[55] Depositions will be read out to show that what I have been telling you is true, that Polycles first answered me in the agora by saying he
didn't care what I was saying and that in the house where Timomachus
was lodged Polycles declared he would not take over the ship alone.

[DEPOSITIONS]

[38] After these events, gentlemen of the jury, since he refused to
take over the ship and would not reimburse me for what I had spent
during the extension of my service, and the general was ordering me
to set sail, I approached Polycles in the harbor at Thasos; and in the
presence of the general, with my trireme fully manned, I said something that was not right, but to *his* advantage, and that my situation forced me to suggest: "Since you say, [39] Polycles, that your co-
trierarch has not come, I will recover from him, if I can, the expenses
incurred during the four months of my extra service. But take over the
ship first and serve as trierarch for your period of service, six months.
Then, if your co-trierarch comes during this period, you will hand
the ship over to him, having done your service; if he doesn't, nothing

---

[54] The text and meaning of this retort are obscure. Apollodorus may mean that
Polycles' willfully negligent attitude to liturgies somehow taints equipment associated with those services, or perhaps that Polycles did once turn in damaged gear
at the conclusion of a trierarchy.

[55] The sharing of trierarchical duties by two men is attested as early as the late
fifth century: see Gabrielsen 1994: 173–182.

terrible will happen to you if you do an extra two months' service. [40] Or, is it the case that after I have served extra time, after I have done the liturgy for both my period and my co-trierarch's period[56] on behalf of you and your co-trierarch, you, who have spent nothing, do not feel obliged to do the liturgy even for your own period or to reimburse my expenses?" When I said that, his response was that I was whistling in the wind.[57] The general ordered me to embark on my ship and set sail with him. Please read the deposition stating that this was his answer.

[DEPOSITION]

[41] I also want to mention some evidence, so you will know that I was blatantly mistreated. You see, Mnesilochus of the deme Perithoidae and Phrasierides of the deme Anaphlystus were at this same time the replacements for Hagnias and Praxicles.[58] Though Phrasierides did not join his ship, Mnesilochus went to Thasos, took over the vessel from Hagnias, and [42] paid back the sum Hagnias convinced him he had spent during the extra period of service. Mnesilochus also rented the gear from Hagnias and then himself served as trierarch. Later, representatives came from Phrasierides and reimbursed Mnesilochus for a portion of his expenses and for the remaining time, shared whatever expenses were needed for the ship.[59] Please read these men's deposition.

[DEPOSITION]

[43] Perhaps, gentlemen of the jury, you are eager to hear just why the general did not force Polycles to take over the ship when, as my successor, he traveled to it, and the laws on the matter are strict. I want to give you a clear explanation of the reason. You see, gentlemen of the

---

[56] Apollodorus has not until now acknowledged that he had a partner to share the liturgy.

[57] Lit. "telling tales."

[58] Mnesilochus is not otherwise known. Phrasierides, an ex-slave, appears at Dem. 23.302 and 49.43. Hagnias may be the man recorded by several inscriptions as performing various liturgies. Praxicles' name may appear on an inscription recording members of the Council of 367/6.

[59] The passage shows that a trierarch did not always serve in person.

jury, in the first place Timomachus wanted to make use of a trireme that was in all ways well equipped. [44] He knew that if Polycles took over the ship, he was likely to do a poor job as trierarch. He would not get the crew to serve[60]—the marines, the skilled seamen—since none of these men would stay with him. Besides, if he gave the order to set sail, without giving him any money, Polycles would not likely put out to sea as I would but would instead give him a hard time. Further, Polycles had lent Timomachus thirty minas on the condition that he not force him to take over the ship. [45] But I want to explain clearly why Timomachus got angry and insulted me and why he steadfastly refused to explain his actions, so that you will know that I did not at that time put a higher value on my convenience, nor on his power, than on the people of Athens and its laws; instead, I put up with being wronged in action and abused in words—which was much harder to bear than spending my money.

[46] While the fleet was delayed at Thasos, a dispatch boat came from Methone in Macedonia with a messenger and letters from Callistratus[61] to Timomachus asking him, as I learned later, to send his fastest trireme, so he could join Timomachus. At dawn the next morning Timomachus' servant came and ordered me to call the sailors to the ship. [47] When it was fully manned, Callippus the son of Philon of the deme Aexone[62] came on board and told the pilot to sail to Macedonia. When we arrived at a small Thasian trading post on the mainland across the way,[63] we disembarked and were having our meal, when one of the sailors approached me, Callicles son of Epitrephes of the deme Thria,[64] and said he wanted to discuss a matter that had to do with me. I asked him to continue, and he said that he wanted to show

---

[60] This translates a textual emendation.

[61] Callistratus son of Callicrates of the deme Aphidna was among the most important Athenian politicians for much of the first half of the fourth century. That Apollodorus mentions him without further identification shows that he could expect his audience to know whom he meant. His career is treated by Raphael Sealey, "Callistratos of Aphidna and His Contemporaries," *Historia* 5 (1956): 178–203.

[62] He is best known as the member of Plato's Academy who murdered Dion of Syracuse. See Plato, *Letter* 7.334a–b.

[63] Its precise location is unknown.

[64] Not surprisingly, this ordinary sailor is otherwise unknown.

his gratitude as much as he could for the help I gave him when he was in a tight spot. [48] "Do you know," he asked, "why we're making this trip and where we're going?" I answered that I did not know. "Then," he said, "I'll tell you. You should listen and think carefully what to do, as you are about to transport an exile whom the Athenians have twice condemned to death,[65] Callistratus, from Methone to Thasos, to his in-law Timomachus. That," he went on, "is what I heard from Callippus' slaves. If you use your head, you will not allow any exile to get on your ship. The laws forbid it, you know."[66] [49] When I heard this from Callicles, I went to Callippus and asked him where he was sailing and why. He laughed at me and made the sort of threats you can imagine, since you have some experience of Callippus' manner. So I said, "I hear you are sailing to Callistratus. Now, I will not transport any fugitive, and I will not go and get him. The laws do not permit taking on an exile: a man who does so is liable to the same penalties as those in flight. I am, therefore, sailing back to the general, to Thasos." [50] When the sailors got on board, I told the pilot to sail back to Thasos. Callippus protested and ordered him to sail to Macedonia, as the general had commanded. Poseidippos the pilot answered that I was the trierarch and subject to official scrutiny[67] and that he got his wages from me. He would sail where I had instructed—to the general in Thasos. [51] When we arrived at Thasos the next day, Timomachus summoned me to where he was staying, outside the city walls. I was worried that Callippus had denounced me and that I would be arrested,[68] so I did not obey the order in person, but instead I told the aide that if Timomachus wanted to discuss something with me, I would be in the agora and that I was sending my slave to him; if he had instructions for me, the slave would pass them on. [52] For these reasons, gentlemen of the jury, which I have told you, Timomachus did not compel Polycles to take over the ship; also, he wanted to use the

---

[65] There is no scholarly consensus on what Apollodorus means by "twice condemned."

[66] The only text tending to confirm the existence of such a law at Athens is Thuc. 1.137.2.

[67] The rendering of accounts (*euthynai*) to which all officials were subject at the conclusion of their term of service. The *euthynai* of trierarchs is mentioned at Aes. 3.19.

[68] For the disciplinary authority of generals in the field, see Hamel 1998: 59–63.

fastest ship. You see, he persuaded Thrasylochus of the deme Anagy-ros[69] to rent his office as trierarch of the ship on which Timomachus himself had sailed to Callippus, so that Callippus would have complete authority over the ship and would transport Callistratus. Timomachus himself came aboard my ship and sailed all around from place to place until he arrived at the Hellespont.

[53] When he had no further need of triremes, Timomachus put Lucinus of the deme Pallene[70] on board my ship as commanding officer with instructions to him to pay the sailors their daily wage, and he ordered me to sail for home. But when we had reached Tenedos[71] on our homeward voyage, Lucinus, to whom Timomachus had given the order, was not distributing money for food to the sailors. He said he didn't have the money but would get it from Mytilene. Since the soldiers had no money to buy food, and without food could not row, once again I took along witnesses from among the citizens [54] and approached this man Polycles in Tenedos, and I demanded that he take over the ship, since he was my replacement, and reimburse me for what I had spent during the prolongation of my service as trierarch. My purpose was to prevent him from claiming in his defense before you, that out of a spirit of rivalry (*philotimia*) I had refused to hand over the ship, intending to sail home on a well-operated ship and show off my expenditures to you. [55] When he refused to take the ship over and the sailors were demanding money to buy their supplies, I again approached him, with witnesses, and asked whether or not he had come with money to take over the ship. When he answered that he had come with money, I demanded that he make me a loan, with the ship's gear as collateral, so I could pay the sailors and bring the ship back to Athens, since he was refusing to take it over, though he was my successor. [56] To this demand he answered that he would not lend me any money whatsoever. So I borrowed money from Tenedian friends of my father, Cleanax and Eperatus,[72] and gave it to the sailors for their food.

---

[69] Probably not the same Thrasylochus mentioned in 28 but the far better known man, son of Cephisodorus, who tangled with Demosthenes on a number of occasions.

[70] Except for an inscription that apparently commemorates a liturgy, nothing else is known about this man.

[71] An island in the northeast Aegean.

[72] These men are not otherwise known.

Since Pasion was my father and had many foreign friends (*xenoi*) [73] and was trusted all around Greece, I had no lack of sources from whom to borrow money when I needed it. I will provide depositions to show that I am telling you the truth.

[DEPOSITIONS]

[57] The clerk has read you the depositions of as many of the bystanders as I could present, testifying that I tried on many occasions to pass the ship on to Polycles but that he refused to take it over. Further, I have given you enough evidence to show why he refused to take over the ship. I also want to have the laws on successor trierarchs read out to you, so you will know that though the penalties for not taking over a ship at the stipulated time are so severe, he had contempt not only for me but for all of you and for the laws. [74] [58] For his part, nothing was done for the city or our allies, since he did not go to the ship, as the law requires, and when he did go, he refused to take it over. I performed the liturgy for you, both during my assigned period and during that of my co-trierarch; and when the period of my trierarchy had expired and the general ordered me to sail to Hieron, I sent grain to the Athenian people [59] so you would have an abundant supply to purchase and there would be no shortfall due to any failure of mine. And all the other services the general wanted from me and from the trireme I did for him, not only spending my money but also putting my life at risk by joining the expedition. My personal affairs fell into such difficult straits in that time that you might feel pity hearing me speak about them. [60] My mother [75] was sick and close to death while I was abroad, so she could help me only a little in my deteriorating financial circum-

---

[73] A *xenos* in this context is a citizen of another city with whom an Athenian had a private social and commercial relation. This form of practical friendship has deep roots in Greek culture (it is a prominent feature in Homeric society) and often persisted for many generations.

[74] As there is no instruction to the clerk to read this law out, it is thought that there is a gap in the manuscripts.

[75] In keeping with a convention of courtroom speech, Apollodorus does not name her, but we know she was Archippe. We hear more about her in Dem. 45, written for Apollodorus' action against a man he charges with giving false testimony on behalf of Phormio, once the slave of Pasion (Apollodorus' father), whom she married after Pasion's death. At 45.3 Apollodorus condemns her marriage to

stances. It happened that on the sixth day of my return she saw me, called my name, and died; she was no longer in charge of her property, so she could not give me as much as she wanted.[76] Many times before she had sent for me, asking that I come to her myself if I could not come with my trireme. [61] And my wife, who means the world to me, was sick for much of my absence.[77] My children were small,[78] my fortune was pledged as security, and not only did my land produce no harvest but that year, as you all know, the wells dried up, so not even a stalk grew in the garden. When the year ended, my creditors came to get the interest due them, unless someone paid them according to the contracts.[79] [62] How do you suppose I felt when I heard about this, some of it from the reports of arriving travelers, and some from letters sent by my family? How many tears do you imagine I shed as I reckoned up my circumstances and longed to see my children and wife and the mother I had little hope of finding alive? What does a man find sweeter than these? Why would he want to go on living without them?

[63] Though my situation had come around to this, I did not put my own interests ahead of yours; instead, I thought I should rise above the loss of my money and the neglect of my affairs at home and my wife and my sick mother, so that no one could charge that I left my post or that my ship was of no use to the city. [64] In return for all this I now ask that you show the same consideration for me today as I did in being upright and useful to you; I ask you, remembering everything I have told you—the witnesses, the decrees I presented—to help me,

---

Phormio. Quite a different picture emerges from Dem. 36, a speech in Phormio's defense.

[76]There are difficult problems in sorting out the issues of inheritance and property control in this very rich, but dysfunctional family. See, for example, Davies 1971: 427–442.

[77]This comports with what is said by his brother-in-law at Dem. 59.2, but that speech was presumably written by Apollodorus too. Cf. Apollodorus' own generalization about what a man expects from various sorts of women at Dem. 59.2, though there his major point is that true Athenian wives produce legitimate Athenian citizens. A very different view of women is expressed in a speech against Apollodorus at Dem. 36.45.

[78]Two daughters are mentioned in other speeches. See Dem. 45.54, 45.85, 59.2.

[79]The particular property and the contractual terms of the loan are obscure. See Harrison 1968–1971, Vol. I: 262–267, esp. 266-267.

the victim of injustice, to take vengeance for yourselves and to exact from him what I expended on his behalf. Otherwise, who will be willing to compete before you for honor when he sees there is no gratitude for good, orderly citizens, and no punishment for the evil men running out of control? [65] The clerk will read out the law to you,[80] and also, item by item, the expenses I incurred during the period of my supplementary service when I served as trierarch in his place, and a list of deserters, how much each had when he absconded from the ship and where he went, so you will know that I am telling you nothing false now, nor did I before; and I think it is my obligation both to serve my liturgies impeccably during the time stipulated by the laws and to expose those who are contemptuous of you and the laws and refuse to obey them as wrongdoers, and to see them punished. [66] Be clear in your minds about this: you will not be punishing Polycles on my account more than your own; and you will not be showing your concern only in regard to past trierarchs but also for those to come, so that those accepting liturgies do not lose heart, and their replacements do not sneer at the laws but rather join their ships whenever they are assigned to do so. It falls to you to think about these things correctly and give a just verdict on them all.

[67] I would be glad to know what judgment you would have delivered on me, gentlemen of the jury, if when my period of service had expired and Polycles had not come to the ship, I had *not* served for an extra period when the general so ordered but had sailed away. Wouldn't you have been angry at me and thought that I had done wrong? So if you would have been angry with me in that hypothetical situation for *not* serving an extra period, you should certainly recover for me expenses I incurred on behalf of this man who did not take over the ship.

[68] The clerk will read out a deposition to show that Polycles failed to take over a ship not only from me but also from Euripides;[81] there was a contract between them that each would sail for six months, but after Euripides had sailed and completed his time, Polycles did not take the ship over from him.

[DEPOSITION]

---

[80] Again (see 57n), the manuscripts do not contain the expected instruction to the clerk to read the law to which Apollodorus alludes.

[81] There is no other trace of this man.

51. ON THE TRIERARCHIC CROWN

INTRODUCTION

On the Trierarchic Crown shares a subject with the preceding speech, 50, *Against Polycles,* a dispute concerning a trierarchy, but otherwise it is unlike the other speeches in this volume in several respects. It was written for delivery before the Council of Five Hundred (*boulē*), which was not a court but sometimes heard legal disputes. The nature of the proceedings is not certain: it might have been a formal or informal *diadikasia,* a hearing to decide between competing claims to something of value, normally an inheritance. In this case the speaker claims that he should be awarded a crown for meritorious discharge of his office.[1]

The fourth-century AD writer Libanius says in his summary of this speech that Apollodorus was the author and speaker (see pp. 12–15), but modern scholars have not accepted this attribution. The polish and vigor of the writing seem consistent with speeches unquestionably written by Demosthenes, and it was conjectured long ago that the speaker was Demosthenes himself.

For dating the speech we can probably rely on two references to the general Cephisodotus, one explicit in the first section, the other implicit in 17 ("better men" is a plural, but that can easily be an oblique reference to the one man who spoke in favor of the speaker). Cephisodotus led a naval expedition to the Hellespont in 359, and it seems very likely that that was the military action for which the triremes un-

---

[1] The city of Athens bestowed crowns of gold or ivy to acknowledge either excellence in an official duty (as here) or voluntary beneficence.

der discussion in this speech were being prepared and that this speech was delivered in that year.[2] The speech would thus be only some six years after Demosthenes began legal action against his guardians (see the Introduction to this volume).

51. ON THE TRIERARCHIC CROWN

[1] Members of the Council, if the decree (*psēphisma*) required that the crown be given to the man with the greatest number speaking for him, I would be foolish to demand that I receive it, given that only Cephisodotus has spoken for me, while many men have spoken for my opponents. But in fact, the Assembly directed the Treasurer (*tamias*) to give the crown to the first man to get his trireme ready, and that is what I did; for this reason I say that I should be crowned. [2] I am astonished that these men have neglected their triremes but enlist speakers, and I think they have missed the entire point when they suppose that you should be grateful not to those who accomplish the deed but to those who *say* they have. Their judgment of you is not the same as mine. And in this respect you would rightly feel friendlier to me, as clearly I think you are better men than they are. [3] Men of Athens, it was the right and honest thing for those who thought they should get the crown from you to show themselves worthy of the honor rather than abusing me in their speeches. But since they neglected that duty and did this instead, I will show that on both counts they are lying, in their self-praise and in their slanderous statement they have made against us to you—in both instances from the very actions, theirs and mine.

[4] You see, you had passed a decree providing that whoever failed to bring his ship to the pier before the last day of the month be imprisoned and handed over to a lawcourt, and you made this decree valid. I brought in my ship and for this reason received a crown from

---

[2] For Demosthenes' good relations (at the time) with Cephisodotus, see Aes. 3.51; but at Dem. 23.163–168 the speaker relates how Cephisodotus was nearly sentenced to death by an Athenian jury enraged at his dealings with Charidemus, a mercenary from Euboea whose relations with Athens were remarkably volatile.

you, but these men had not even launched theirs and consequently were liable to imprisonment. You would, then, certainly be doing the strangest thing if you were seen crowning the men who exposed themselves to such a penalty. [5] The gear that the city is required to provide to the trierarchs I acquired at my own expense, taking nothing from the public supplies, whereas these men used your gear and spent none of their own funds on them. Moreover, they could not even claim that they tested their ship before me, since before they even touched theirs, mine was manned, and you all saw my ship being tried out. [6] Further, I got the best crew[3] by paying by far the highest wage. Now if these men had a crew inferior to ours, that would not be terrible; but in fact they have hired a crew of no sort whatever, though they speak about having hired a larger one than I. But how do they have the right, after completing their crew later, to get the crown for now being the first to be ready?

[7] I think that, even if I said nothing, you would know that it would be most just for you to crown me. But I want to show this, that these men alone have no right to speak about the crown. What evidence will best make this clear? Their actions, since they looked for the man who would serve as trierarch for the lowest price and contracted the liturgy.[4] But it is surely unjust to shrink from spending money and then claim a share in the honors resulting from those expenditures. And it is unjust to blame the failure of the ship to be brought around on the man they hired, but on the other hand to order you to express gratitude to them for those services that *were* properly performed. [8] You should, men of Athens, examine what is right not only on the basis of these facts but also in light of how you yourselves acted when certain others did the same thing as these men. You see, when you were defeated in the sea battle against Alexander,[5] you regarded those trierarchs who leased their liturgies as the most to blame for what had

---

[3] *Hypēresia.* See Dem. 50.7.

[4] For this arrangement, whereby a man simply pays another man to perform the liturgy assigned to him, see also Dem. 21.80 and Gabrielsen 1994: 95–102.

[5] Alexander of Pherae defeated the Athenians at Peparethus, an island in the Aegean north of Euboea, in 361.

happened. And you convicted them of betraying the fleet and deserting their posts and sent them to prison.[6] [9] Aristophon[7] was the prosecutor, and you served as their judges. And if your anger had not been more restrained than their wickedness, nothing would have kept them from being executed. These men know that they have committed the same acts as those trierarchs, but instead of trembling in fear of what would properly be done to them in this body, they make speeches denouncing other men and demand crowns for themselves. But think how your deliberations will be viewed if you are seen judging some men worthy of execution and others—for the same reason—worthy of a crown. [10] And not only would you seem to be wrong if you do that but also if you fail to punish them for such actions when you have them in your power. After all, you should not be angry after allowing something of yours to be lost but rather at the time when it is still secure and you see that out of greed the men in charge of it are not taking proper care to preserve it. And none of you should disapprove of my speech because he thinks it harsh, but instead you should disapprove of the men who have committed this act, since it is because of them that my speech is harsh. [11] And I wonder why these men imprison and punish sailors who desert, each of whom gets only thirty drachmas, but you do not take the same action when trierarchs, men who get thirty minas for each naval expedition,[8] do not sail out with the others. If a poor man does the wrong thing by reason of poverty, will he be liable to the most extreme punishments, whereas, if a rich man[9] does the same out of greed, will he be forgiven? Where are equality and democracy to be found if you decide these issues this way? [12] Further, this too seems to me illogical, that if a man is convicted

---

[6] The procedure was an *eisangelia*. See the Series Introduction, p. xxvi, and for a detailed discussion of this case, including the difficult matter of the roles played by the Council and the Assembly, see M. H. Hansen, *Eisangelia* (Odense, 1975), 118–119.

[7] An important politician who in the course of his long political career was prosecuted seventy-five times for unconstitutional proposals but acquitted each time (see Aes. 3.194).

[8] Probably a reference to funds from which the trierarch is to pay out the sailors' wages.

[9] The Greek word (*plousios*) often has the connotation "filthy rich."

for making a proposal contrary to the laws, he loses one-third of his rights as a citizen,[10] but those whose crime is an act, not a word, pay no penalty. And, men of Athens, you will all agree that to show leniency towards such acts is to teach others to do wrong.

[13] Since I have come forward to speak, I want to describe the consequences of such events. You see, when someone who has been hired to take on a trierarchy sets sail, he plunders and pillages everybody and reaps the benefits for himself, but an ordinary Athenian pays the penalty for their acts: you are the only ones who cannot go anywhere without a herald's staff[11] because of the hostage taking[12] and plundering they contrive. [14] Consequently, if one truly looks into it, he will find that triremes like that sail out not on your behalf but against you. You see, the man acting as a trierarch for the city should not expect to grow rich from public property but to promote the city's interests from his private fortune, if there is anything you will need. Each of these men set sail with the opposite idea, and in fact by harming you they compensate for the mistakes brought on by their own moral failures.[13] [15] And none of this is illogical, since you have granted those who want to do wrong permission to keep their gains if they are not discovered, and to be pardoned if they are caught. Accordingly, those who do not care about their reputation can do whatever they want with impunity. We call those private citizens who learn by suffering "shortsighted"; what are we to call you who are not on your guard, though you have already suffered many times over?

---

[10]An allusion to prosecution for an unconstitutional proposal (*graphē paranomōn*). The "one-third" perhaps refers to loss of the right to serve as a magistrate. The translation deviates from the Oxford text, which is so punctuated as to mean "if a speaker is convicted a third time for making an unconstitutional proposal, he loses part of his rights as a citizen." Some scholars (perhaps rightly) regard this latter text as confirmed by Hyp. 2.11–12, but cf. Harrison 1968–1971, Vol. 2: 176, n. 2. For a broad treatment of the subject, see M. H. Hansen, *The Sovereignty of the People's Court in Athens in the Fourth Century B.C. and the Public Action against Unconstitutional Proposals* (Odense, 1974).

[11]A traditional means of appealing for protection from attack.

[12]For the legal taking of hostages in certain circumstances, see Dem. 23.83–84.

[13]For a nobler mode of correcting private deficiencies by public service, cf. Pericles as reported by Thuc. 42.3.

[16] It is worthwhile to say something about the men who have spoken on my opponents' behalf. You see, certain men suppose that they enjoy such broad liberty to do whatever they want and say whatever they want to you, that after joining Aristophon on that occasion [14] in bringing prosecutions, after bitterly denouncing those who leased out their trierarchies, they *now* urge that *these* men here be given crowns. They are proving themselves guilty in one of the two cases, either acting unjustly in bringing malicious suits then or now taking money to speak as advocates for my opponents. [15] [17] And they ask you to grant them a favor, as if we were discussing a gift, not a reward for victory, or as if it were fitting for you to do a favor, at the urging of these advocates, to men who neglect their responsibilities, instead of expressing gratitude, at the urging of better men, to those who do their duty as they should. [16] And then, they think so little of keeping a decent appearance, and they regard absolutely everything else as secondary to profit, so that they not only have the brass to make a public speech opposite to what they themselves have said earlier but even now contradict themselves: they say that the crown should belong to the trireme that has its own crew, [17] but they ask you to crown trierarchs who have rid themselves of the liturgy. [18] On the one hand, they say that no one got his ship ready before these men, but on the other, they say that we should be crowned together with them, though the decree does not provide for that. I am as far from agreeing to that arrangement as from contracting out my trierarchy: I would not tolerate the former, and I did not do the latter. They pretend they are speaking for justice but are more zealous in doing so than any of you would be without thought of reward, as if it were fitting for them to work for a fee [18] but not to declare an opinion. [19] Then, as if they were not part of a political community where, for that reason, any man who

---

[14] See above, 8–9.

[15] According to Dem. 46.26, payment to a co-speaker would be illegal.

[16] A difficult passage to translate, in part because the same word (*charis*) can mean either "favor" or "gratitude." As noted in the Introduction, "better men" may be an implicit reference to Cephisodotus.

[17] It is not clear what this means. Perhaps the implication is that the trierarch has properly recruited, paid, and therefore retained the same crew throughout.

[18] See 16n.

wants to may speak, they treat the government as a private priesthood, and they are dreadfully pained if someone speaks out for justice at your meetings, and they call him brash. They have come to be so blinkered that they suppose that if they call a man shameless if he has spoken a single time, they themselves will be regarded as gentlemen (*kaloi kagathoi*) for their entire lives. [20] But it is because of these men's political speeches (*dēmēgoriai*) that many things are in a worse state, and it is because of those who think they should oppose them and speak for justice that all is not lost. My opponents have procured men of this type to speak on their behalf, though they know that such severe defamation could be turned against themselves by those who choose to be critical; nevertheless they thought it right to speak and they dared abuse another man—these men who should have been happy not to be abused themselves.

[21] No one is more to blame for the injustice and audacity of these men than you, since you learn the character of individuals from the speakers, from men whom you know are doing this for a fee, instead of looking for yourselves. Yet it is certainly strange to regard *these* men as the most evil of citizens but to judge those who are praised by them as honest. [22] My opponents do everything on their own account, and all but sell public property with a herald,[19] and they direct you to crown or not to crown whomever they designate, setting themselves up as wielding greater authority than your decisions. But I advise you, men of Athens, not to make the ambition (*philotimia*) of those willing to spend their money on public service depend on the greed of speakers. Otherwise, you will be teaching everyone to be as frugal as possible in managing the responsibilities you assign, and as lavish as possible[20] in hiring men to tell shameless lies on their behalf.

---

[19] I.e., as if at a public auction.
[20] Or, following a different reading, "as many men as possible."

52. AGGAINST CALLIPPUS

❧❧❧

INTRODUCTION

This speech was written for delivery by Apollodorus, and in all
likelihood he was also its author. If so, this is the earliest of his surviving speeches. The court case arose from the banking activities of
Pasion, Apollodorus' father (see pp. 12–13). Lycon, a man from Heraclea, a town on the southeast coast of the Black Sea, had deposited
money with Pasion. Before leaving Athens on an ill-fated voyage, he
reviewed the account and left instructions for paying it out to a partner, a certain Cephisiades. Callippus, if we believe the speaker, at-
tempted to lay his hands on Lycon's money by abusing his position as
a consular representative (*proxenos*) of the Heracleans.[1] The narrative
suggests that Callippus saw his chances of getting the money in question as very much greater once Pasion died, for the arbitrator who felt
reluctance in ruling against a figure with considerable standing in the
city would be far less inhibited in acting against his son. This makes
it likely that the suit to which this speech responds came to court in
369/8, the year following Pasion's death (Dem. 46.13). This date, which
falls some five years before Demosthenes reached majority and began
legal action against his guardians, would of course preclude Demosthenic authorship. The style, moreover, seems to fit well with other

---

[1] A *proxenos'* function was rather like that of a modern diplomat from a foreign
country who deals mostly with individuals in matters of visas, passports, or difficulties encountered by his fellow citizens with the local authorities. In ancient
Greek practice, however, he would be a citizen of the city-state in which he oper-
ated, helping citizens of another state. Thus, Callippus, an Athenian citizen, was
expected to render assistance to citizens of Heraclea who were visiting Athens.

speeches attributed by scholars to Apollodorus.[2] It is a pity that the abundant evidence we have for Apollodorus' life does not reveal whether he was successful in persuading the jury.

Callippus' initial action against Pasion was a private suit for damages (14 and 16: *dikē blabēs*), but in the action against Apollodorus he adopted a different strategy, bringing instead a suit "for money" (14 and 16: *dikē arguriou*). This speech makes a number of interesting allusions to the practices of Athenian bankers[3] and the role of arbitrators.

For a discussion of this speech, see Trevett 1992: 96–97.

52. AGAINST CALLIPPUS

[1] There is nothing harder, gentlemen of the jury, than when a man who enjoys a good reputation and who is a skilled speechmaker dares to tell lies and has an abundance of witnesses available to him. You see, the defendant must no longer speak only about the issue but also about his opponent himself, arguing he should not be believed on account of his reputation. [2] For if you make it a habit to give greater credence to men who are good speakers and enjoy a good reputation than to those who are more limited in their ability, you will have established this habit against your own interests. So I ask you, if you have ever judged a case on its own merits, without favoritism for either side —either the prosecutors or the defendants—but with a view to the claims of justice, judge that way now. I will tell you what happened from the beginning.

[3] Now, Lycon of Heraclea, gentlemen of the jury, as my opponent himself says, was a client of my father's bank, just as the other merchants are. He was the guest-friend (*xenos*) of Aristonoüs of the deme Deceleia and of Archebiades of the deme Lamptrae, a sensible man.

---

[2]The prominence of directly quoted speech in the narrative has often been noted: see Victor Bers, *Speech in Speech: Studies in Incorporated Oratio Recta in Attic Drama and Oratory* (Lanham, MD, 1997), 197 (with references to earlier treatments). In one passage (31), readers hoping to find clarification of an important procedural point are frustrated, in Harrison's phrase (1968–1971, Vol. 2: 66, n.2), by "a notoriously slovenly speaker."

[3]See Paul Millett, *Lending and Borrowing in Ancient Athens* (Cambridge, 1991), passim, and Cohen 1992: 120.

When Lycon was about to sail to Libya, he arranged his account with my father in the presence of Archebiades and Phrasius and directed my father to give Cephisiades the money that he was leaving on deposit with him. The sum, as I will demonstrate in detail, was sixteen minas and forty drachmas. He said that Cephisiades was his partner and that he lived in Scyros[4] but was for the moment out of town on another trading journey. [4] Lycon directed Archebiades and Phrasius to show Cephisiades to my father and introduce him when he returned from his voyage. All bankers have a fixed procedure, whenever some private citizen deposits money with them and directs that it be given to a representative, first to write down the name of the man making the deposit and the sum of the account and then to write next to it "To be paid to so-and-so"; and if they know the man by sight to whom it is to be paid, it is customary to do only this: to write down the name of the man to whom it should be paid, but if they do not know the man by sight, to add in writing the name of the man who is going to introduce and point out the man who is to get the money. [5] But disaster struck Lycon: immediately after he sailed from Athens and was in the Argolic Gulf,[5] he was intercepted by pirate ships. His goods were taken to Argos, and he himself was hit by an arrow and died. Callippus, the man here, went at once to the bank and asked if they knew Lycon of Heraclea. Phormio, this man here, answered that they did. Callippus asked, "Did he do business with you?" to which Phormio responded, "Why are you asking?" "Why am I asking?" said Callippus, "I will tell you. He has died, and I happen to be the consular representative for the people of Heraclea. I ask that you show me the ledger so I can know whether he left any money. I am obliged to look after all the people of Heraclea." [6] When Phormio heard this, gentlemen of the jury, he immediately showed it to him. So he showed him the ledger, and Callippus—and no one else—read it and saw the entry, "Lycon of Heraclea. Sixteen hundred and forty drachmas.[6] To be paid out to Cephisiades. Archebiades of the deme Lamptrae will introduce

---

[4]An island in the Aegean Sea.

[5]I.e., somewhere in the body of water adjoining the Argolid in the northeast Peloponnesus.

[6]I.e., the same as sixteen minas and forty drachmas.

Cephisiades." Then Callippus went away in silence and said nothing about the matter for more than five months. [7] Afterwards, Cephisiades came home, went to the bank, and asked for the money; Archebiades and Phrasius were present, gentlemen of the jury, those men whom Lycon had introduced to my father and whom he directed to identify Cephisiades on his arrival; and other men were also present when Phormio, who is here, counted out and paid the sixteen minas, forty drachmas. The clerk will read you the depositions concerning all this to show that I am telling the truth.

[DEPOSITIONS]

[8] You have heard from the depositions, gentlemen of the jury, that everything I have told you is true. A long time later Callippus here approached my father in the city center and asked him whether Cephisiades, the man the notation designated as the one to whom the money left by Lycon of Heraclea was to be given, had returned yet. My father answered that he thought he had, but if Callippus wanted to go down to Piraeus, he would know for sure. "Pasion," Callippus said, "do you know what I will ask you?" [9] And by Zeus, Apollo, and Demeter, I will not lie to you, gentlemen of the jury, but will tell you what I heard from my father. "You can," Callippus said, "do me a favor at no cost to yourself. You see, I happen to be the consular representative for the men of Heraclea; and I think you might prefer that I got the money rather than a resident alien (*metoikos*), who lives in Scyros and is a good-for-nothing fellow. Now, the situation is like this. Lycon happened to be childless and he left no heir at home, as I have learned. [10] Besides, when he was wounded and taken to Argos, he gave the goods he had transported with him to Strammenus, consular representative for the men of Heraclea in Argos. Now, I am in the same position as Strammenus, and I think it right that I get their property here, since I regard myself as the right person to have it. So if Cephisiades hasn't taken the money, if he comes for it, tell him I am contesting his claim; if he has taken the money, tell him that, with witnesses present, I demanded that you produce the money or the man who took it; and if somebody wants to take it away from me, tell him he would be taking it from a man who is a consular representative." [11] To this my father replied, "Callippus, I want to do you a favor—in fact I would be crazy if I didn't—but in a way that will not detract

from my reputation or result in any loss. It's all the same to me to say this to Archebiades and Aristonoüs and to Cephisiades himself. But if they are unwilling to do it when I propose it to them, then tell them yourself." "Don't worry, Pasion," Callippus said. "If you want, you'll make them do it."

[12] That, gentlemen of the jury, is what Callippus here said to my father and what he repeated to Archebiades and Cephisiades at Callippus' request and to do him a favor: it is from this that this lawsuit has, in small steps, been contrived. I was willing to give Callippus whatever would constitute the most solemn pledge, swearing that I heard this from my father. [13] Cephisiades here, the man who demands that you believe he is telling the truth, let three years go by after my father spoke to Archebiades and Cephisiades' other friends and they said to pay no attention to Callippus or anything he said. [14] But when Callippus heard that my father was by then an invalid and could barely make his way to the city center and his eyesight was failing, he initiated a suit against him—not, by Zeus, for a sum of money (*dikē arguriou*), as in the present case, but for damages (*dikē blabēs*).[7] He complained that my father had injured him when he gave Cephisiades the money Lycon had deposited with him, after my father had promised that he would not pay it out without Callippus' consent. After he started the suit, he withdrew the complaint from the public arbitrator and challenged my father to submit it for arbitration by Lysitheides,[8] who was a friend of Callippus, Isocrates,[9] and Aphareus,[10] and an acquaintance of my father.[11] [15] My father agreed to having Lysitheides serve as arbitrator, and so long as my father was alive, despite his close relations with these

---

[7] Todd 1993: 280 n. 24 suggests that "perhaps the *dikē blabēs* would have been for penal damages and the *dikē arguriou* for simple restitution."

[8] Epigraphic and literary sources show that Lysitheides was a rich landowner with mining interests. For his services to the city, see Dem. 21.157, 24.11–14, and Isoc. 15.94. Isoc. 15.93 speaks of him as one of his first students.

[9] This is the famous orator.

[10] Poet and speechwriter, legally adopted son of Isocrates. See [Plut.], *Moralia* 839d; Isoc. 15.4–5, 145; Dem. 47.31–32.

[11] This passage, for which there is no parallel, shows that it was possible to drop a suit already in progress and turn to an unofficial arbitrator; but it also shows that there were rules even an unofficial arbitrator had to follow.

men, Lysitheides did not dare to commit any wrong against us. Still, some of Callippus' friends were so lacking in shame that they dared to testify that Callippus challenged my father to swear an oath, but he had refused to swear in Lysitheides' presence. They think, I suppose, they will persuade you that Lysitheides, a close friend of Callippus, who was acting as the arbitrator, would have refrained from immediately giving a judgment against my father, when my father was refusing to be a judge in his own case.[12] [16] To show that I am telling the truth and that these men are lying, first consider this evidence, namely, that Lysitheides would have given a judgment against my father and I would now be a defendant in a suit for recovery (*dikē exoulēs*),[13] not a suit for a sum of money (*dikē arguriou*). Further, I will present as witnesses those who were present on each occasion when my father and Callippus came together before Lysitheides.

[WITNESSES]

[17] Both from the evidence and from this deposition it will be easy for you to know that Callippus did not at that time challenge my father to swear an oath, that now that my father is dead he is telling lies about him, and that he is producing friends to casually give perjured testimony against me. Also, you will know that I was willing to give Callippus the pledge stipulated by law when someone with a complaint against a dead man brings a suit against his heir, [18] affirming that I believe my father did not agree to pay Callippus the money that Lycon had deposited, and that Callippus was not introduced to my father by Lycon, that Phormio stated on oath that he calculated the account for Lycon in the presence of Archebiades and was instructed to give the money to Cephisiades, that Cephisiades introduced Archebiades to him; [19] and that when Callippus first came to Phormio's bank to report that Lycon was dead and demanded to examine the ledger

---

[12]I.e., if he took an oath and that oath resolved the case in the arbitrator's mind. Presumably if Pasion refused to swear the oath, this would be like an admission of guilt and would cause the arbitrator to rule against him.

[13]By this procedure, a man unable to recover property awarded to him by a jury could, if successful in the *dikē*, seize the disputed property, employing violence if he deemed it necessary, yet be immune from a charge of assault (see Todd 1993: 377).

himself to see whether his guest-friend had left money; that Phormio did in fact immediately show him the ledger, and that when Callippus saw the entry directing that the money be paid out to Cephisiades, he went away in silence, making no protest nor pressing any claim on Phormio for the money. The clerk will read you both depositions on these matters and the law.

[DEPOSITIONS. LAW]

[20] Now please do pay attention, gentlemen of the jury. I will show that Lycon did not have anything to do with Callippus, since I think this has some bearing on Callippus' bragging when he claims that he was given this money as a gift from Lycon. Lycon lent forty minas to Megacleides of the deme Eleusis and his brother Thrasyllus [14] for a voyage to Ace. [15] Lycon [16] had a change of heart about making the voyage and sustaining the risk. He quarreled with Megacleides about the interest, complaining that he had been cheated, and he sued him, seeking to recover the loan. [21] During the long dispute over such a large sum, Lycon never made any appeal to Callippus but turned rather to Archebiades and his friends; and it was Archebiades who reconciled Lycon and Megacleides. To show I am telling the truth, I will present Megacleides himself as a witness.

[DEPOSITION]

[22] Gentlemen of the jury, Lycon clearly has so close a friendship with Callippus that he did not appeal to him for help with his affairs or ever stay at his house. And this one thing alone Callippus' friends have not dared to testify, that Lycon stayed with him, because they know well that evidence taken from the slaves by torture [17] would re-

---

[14] These men are not otherwise known.

[15] A Phoenician coastal town.

[16] The translation follows the manuscripts, but some scholars believe that it was the brothers who changed their minds.

[17] Attic law in principle admitted the testimony of slaves only if exacted under torture. There is, however, no certain evidence that this procedure was ever carried through, despite the numerous challenges and offers mentioned in the court speeches. It may be that the value of such evidence was essentially a rhetorical ploy. See Dem. 59.120, 124; Ant. 1.6; and M. Gagarin, "The Torture of Slaves in Athenian Law," *Classical Philology* 91 (1996): 1–18.

fute them if they told some lie like that. [23] But I want to tell you about a piece of evidence so powerful that it will make it clear to you, I think, that everything Callippus has said is false. Gentlemen of the jury, if Lycon was fond of Callippus and was close to him, as Callippus here maintains, and if Lycon wanted to give him a present in case something happened to him, [24] wouldn't it have been better for him to deposit the money with Callippus directly? If Lycon returned safe, he would recover the money rightly and honestly from a man who was his friend and consular representative, but if something happened to him, he would have given him the present directly, just as he wished? Or would depositing it with a bank be better? I think the first alternative is more just and more magnanimous. But in fact it is clear that Lycon took neither of these actions—consequently, you should take that as evidence—but instead left written and oral instructions that the bank was to give the money to Cephisiades.

[25] Consider this point also, gentlemen of the jury, that Callippus was a fellow citizen of yours and was perfectly capable of doing either harm or good, while Cephisiades was a powerless *metic;* it follows that my father would not have taken Cephisiades' side, contrary to justice, rather than do the right thing and side with Callippus. [26] But, by Zeus,[18] he might perhaps say that *privately* my father got more profit from the money and for that reason sided more with Cephisiades than with Callippus. And so, in the first place, he did wrong to a man who could do him twice as much damage as the profit? And, in the second place, he was greedy here but not in his special taxes (*eisphorai*) and liturgies and gifts to the city?[19] [27] And he did wrong to none of the foreigners (*xenoi*), but to Callippus? And although Callippus offered an oath to my father, so he claims, presuming him to be an honest man who told no lies, does he now speak about him as an evil man who erases entries from his deposit ledger? And if my father refused, so Callippus says, to take an oath and did not give the money back, would he not have been immediately condemned for that? Who, gentlemen of the jury, would believe this? [28] For my part, I think nobody will. Further, is Archebiades so shameless that he gives testimony against Callippus, a fellow deme member, a man active in politics, and not a

---

[18] As often, *hypophora* (an imagined objection) is preceded by an oath.
[19] See Dem. 59.2n for Phormio's lavish beneficences to the city.

man who sticks to private matters, that he says that we are telling the truth while Callippus is lying; and what's more, does he do so knowing that if Callippus wants to denounce him for giving false testimony [20] or simply administer an oath to him, he will be forced to take whatever oath Callippus orders him to take? [29] Then, will you believe that Archebiades would have perjured himself in order that Cephisiades, a *metic,* might get the money, or Phormio, whom Callippus here says expunged something in the deposit ledger? This is not in the realm of the probable, gentlemen of the jury. It is not right for you to condemn Archebiades for any wrongful act, or my father; after all, you know that my father was too ambitious (*philotimos*) to do anything wrong or shameful, and he was not on such terms with Callippus that in contempt for him, he would do him any injustice. [30] Callippus' power does not seem to be so slight that it is easily held in contempt: indeed, he is so strong that last year, after he initiated this suit against me and then challenged me to submit it to Lysitheides for arbitration, although he held me in contempt, I planned at least this aspect correctly: I referred the matter in conformity with the laws and handed it over to the magistrate. [21] But Callippus persuaded the arbitrator, a man legally designated to give his decision without swearing an oath, [22] over my protest that he must declare his decision in conformity with the laws —so that Callippus could say to you that Lysitheides, a gentleman (*anēr kaloskagathos*), had given a verdict about the matter. [31] You see, gentlemen of the jury, as long as my father was alive, Lysitheides would not have wronged him, with or without an oath, [23] since he cared about him. But he does not care about me, if he's not on oath, though perhaps with an oath he would not have done wrong—for his own sake. For that reason he gave his decision without swearing an oath. I will

---

[20] This legal action would be a *dikē pseudomarturiōn.*

[21] Apollodorus is very vague here, perhaps intending to deceive the jury. The formal step he reports having taken is not known from any other source.

[22] Presumably the arbitrator's decision went against Apollodorus.

[23] This seems to contradict what Apollodorus said in the last section about the legal necessity of the arbitrator taking an oath. It is unclear whether the first or second statement accurately reflects the legal requirement (see Harrison 1968–1971, Vol. 2: 66 n. 2 for discussion).

also offer as witnesses to the truth of these statements men who were present.

[WITNESSES]

[32] Gentlemen of the jury, you have heard from the witnesses what Callippus can do in violation of the laws and contrary to justice. But I ask you, for myself and for my father, to remember that I have presented witnesses, evidence, laws, and oaths to substantiate what I have said; and I show that, if some of the money belonged to him, Callippus could have proceeded against Cephisiades, the man who acknowledges that he took the money and still has it and still Callippus has taken pledges from me; [33] but he does not proceed against Cephisiades, although he knows that we do not have the money. So I ask you to acquit me. In doing that, you will, first, be giving a verdict that is both just and in accordance with the laws, and one that is worthy of yourselves and of my father. I would rather that you took all that is mine than that I pay it out as a victim of malicious litigation.

53. AGAINST NICOSTRATUS

〰〰〰

INTRODUCTION

Apollodorus delivers this speech and, despite the ascription to Demosthenes, is probably its author as well.[1] As we see in many other lawcourt speeches, the litigant narrates a chain of actions and reactions, often in the form of legal maneuvers, nearly all of which would be deemed irrelevant in a modern court. Apollodorus tells a dramatic story, complete with reported dialogue, of friendship betrayed: his neighbor Nicostratus and Nicostratus' brother Arethusius repaid Apollodorus' exceptional kindness by employing the courts to make common cause with his adversaries in earlier litigation, damaging his property, laying a legal trap for him, and assaulting him physically.[2]

The formal occasion of this speech is an *apographē*. The term literally means "list" or "inventory" and, by extension, the procedure in which a list of property is the centerpiece of the legal argument. In the variety of *apographē* exemplified here, a citizen acting as a voluntary prosecutor went to court to claim that items he has listed, which are owned by another individual, are liable to sale by the city's official "sellers" (*pōlētai*) to discharge their owner's debt to the state.[3] Until re-

---

[1] See pp. 12–15.

[2] M. Christ speculates that as Nicostratus worked for Apollodorus (4), the men's relationship was not precisely one of friendship and that Apollodorus' banking activities "may well [have been] at the roots of his dealings with Nicostratus" (1998, 176–177).

[3] See R. Osborne, "Law in Action in Classical Athens," *Journal of Hellenic Studies* 105 (1985): 44–47, 54–55.

cently it had been thought, on the basis of the second section of this speech, that a successful prosecutor (*ho apographōn,* "the one inscribing") in such a case was rewarded for his efforts with three-quarters of the proceeds of the sale of the denounced property, but new evidence suggests that he was entitled to only one-third.[4] If he failed, he was subject to a fine of one thousand drachmas.

The *apographē* at issue here involves human property, two slaves, whose sale would bring in some part of Arethusius' debt to the public treasury. He had been fined a talent in an earlier case, a public prosecution brought against him by Apollodorus for falsely attesting the serving of a summons (*graphē pseudoklēteia*). The legal core of the present speech is Apollodorus' attempt to refute Nicostratus' claim that he, not his brother, is the owner of the slaves.

The date of this speech cannot be precisely determined.[5] It followed some time after Apollodorus' service as a trierarch mentioned in 5, which can be dated to 368/7; the reference to other litigation at 14 is too vague to help.

The commentary by J. E. Sandys and F. A. Paley 1886–1896 is still useful.

53. AGAINST NICOSTRATUS

[1] Let the size of the *apographē* and the fact that I have brought the action in my own name serve as powerful proof in your eyes, gentlemen of the jury, that I am doing this not as a *sykophant* but because I was wronged and roughly treated by these men, and because I think I should seek revenge.[6] Surely, you see, I would not have instituted an *apographē* from a desire to engage in *sykophancy* over slaves worth two and a half minas—this is their value according to the assessment of my opponent himself—and run the risk of incurring a thousand-drachma fine and never again being able to indict anyone in my own

[4] See 53.2n.

[5] Trevett 1992: 32–33 favors 366 or 355.

[6] On the term *sykophant,* see the Series Introduction, pp. xxvi–xxvii. In Athenian lawcourts, anger toward one's opponent and a desire for revenge are commonly offered, without apology, as motives for prosecution.

name.[7] [2] And I was not so lacking in resources or friends that I could not find another man to enter the *apographē*. But I think the most terrible thing of all is to be wronged myself, yet put someone else's name forward on my behalf when I am the one who was wronged; and this would serve my opponents as proof that I am lying when I say that my hatred for them is the reason for my bringing the *apographē,* since they could have said I would never have put up another man to bring the action if I myself was really the one who had been wronged. If I show that the slaves I list belong to Arethusius, who is inscribed in my inventory as their owner, I will relinquish to the city the one-third reward[8] that the laws grant to a private citizen who enters an *apographē,* and I will be satisfied with merely getting revenge. [3] If I had enough time to tell you the story from the start, how many benefits my opponents got from me and how they have treated me in turn, I am sure you would all the more forgive my anger at them and look on them as the most impious of men. But in fact, even twice the time would not be enough. So I will tell you about the greatest and most blatant of their crimes and the origin of this *apographē* but leave many things out.

[4] Now then, Nicostratus[9] here, a man of my own age, was my neighbor in the countryside. I had known him for a long time, but when my father died[10] and I went to live in the countryside, where I live now, we then saw more of each other because we were neighbors and contemporaries. As time went by, we became really good friends; I felt so close to him that he never went without anything he needed from me; he, in turn, was helpful to me in looking after things and managing my affairs; and whenever I was away, whether, in public service acting as a trierarch or pursuing some private business, I would leave him in charge of everything in the countryside. [5] Now, it hap-

---

[7]A fine of a thousand drachmas was assessed on litigants who failed to get one-fifth of the jurors' votes. This was a considerable sum of money, and litigants sometimes looked for a friend to assume the risk of bringing a case.

[8]The manuscripts have "three-quarters," but an inscription of the mid fourth century makes it likely that one-third is the true portion of the reward paid a successful prosecutor. See Osborne 1985 (above, n. 3): 44–45.

[9]Aside from this speech, there is no certain evidence for Nicostratus' identity or career. See Davies 1971: 481 n. 1 and Trevett 1992: 126–127.

[10]The year of his death is known from Dem. 46.13 to have been 370/69.

pened that I was serving as trierarch off the Peloponnesus,[11] and from there I had to take the ambassadors elected by the Assembly to Sicily. I had to set off quickly and wrote Nicostratus a letter saying that to avoid delaying the ambassadors, I had put out to sea and so could not go home. I directed him to look after my affairs at home and manage them, just as in the past. [6] While I was away from home, three of Nicostratus' slaves ran away from his farm, two of whom I had given him myself, and one he had bought himself. Then, while chasing them, he was captured by a trireme, taken to Aegina, and there sold. When I completed my journey in my capacity as trierarch, Nicostratus' brother Deinon[12] approached me and told me of Nicostratus' misfortune. He said that for lack of the wherewithal for the trip he had not, on getting his brother's letters, set off to recover him; Deinon told me also that he heard his brother's condition was terrible. [7] When I heard this, I felt a deep sympathy for Nicostratus' bad luck, and I immediately sent his brother Deinon to him; I gave him three hundred drachmas for the trip. Nicostratus returned and came to me. First he embraced me and thanked me for providing his brother with travel expenses; he complained about his misfortune, complained of his own family,[13] and asked me to help him, just as in the past I had been a true friend to him. In tears, he told me he had been ransomed for twenty-six minas, and he asked me to contribute money to win his release.[14] [8] I felt pity for him when I heard this and saw the wounds left by the chains on his shanks, where I saw there were still scars—though if you ask him to show you the scars, he certainly won't want to do it.[15] I answered him that I had been his true friend in the past, and now too I would help him in his time of misfortune. I forgave the loan of three hundred drachmas that I gave his brother when he traveled to get him

[11] The liturgy is quite securely dated to 368.

[12] Not otherwise known.

[13] Presumably for refusing to help him.

[14] On ransoming of prisoners, see W. K. Pritchett, *The Greek State at War,* Vol. 5 (Berkeley, 1991), 245–297. Nicostratus must have promised to pay his captors the money later, counting on his friends to lend it to him.

[15] Presumably Nicostratus would have calculated that his disfigurement, both a humiliating mark of his time as a slave and ugly in itself, would win him far more contempt than pity from the jury.

and said I would contribute a thousand drachmas towards his ransom.[16] [9] I certainly did not make a verbal promise, without carrying it through; but since I was rather short of money because of my dispute with Phormio and because I was deprived by him of the inheritance my father left me,[17] I brought some cups and a gold crown that I happened to have from among my father's property to Theocles,[18] who was then operating a bank, and I ordered him to give Nicostratus one thousand drachmas. I gave him this money as a gift, and I acknowledge that I gave it.[19] [10] Not many days later Nicostratus came to me in tears and said that the foreigners, the men who had put up the money for his ransom, were demanding repayment of the remaining sum. The contract required that he give back the money within thirty days or owe double the amount; no one was willing to buy his farm, the one in my neighborhood, or give him a mortgage on the property with the property as collateral. That was because his brother Arethusius—who owns the slaves listed in the present *apographē*—said he would allow no one to buy the farm or use it as collateral, since money was owed to him as it was security for a loan.[20] [11] "Give me the outstanding balance," he said, "before the thirty days are up so the thirty drachmas I gave them are not lost, and I don't become liable to seizure. I will collect contributions," he said, "and when I am free of my debt to the foreigners, will give you back whatever you lent me. You know," he said, "that the laws provide that if a man ransomed from the enemy does not pay back the ransom to the man who has provided it, he is to become that man's property."[21] [12] When I heard him say that, I didn't

---

[16]Apollodorus agreed to join others in making an *eranos,* a collective, interest-free loan amounting to a gift. See Kapparis 1999: 231–232.

[17]See Dem. 36, 45, 46.

[18]Not otherwise known.

[19]I.e., Apollodorus is not claiming that this money is owed him.

[20]Evidently the jury is to believe that the farm in question belongs to Nicostratus but is now encumbered under the terms of a loan his brother has made him. This would be consistent with what Apollodorus says in 28. See Harrison 1968–1971, Vol. I: 267–268.

[21]A partial exception to the law instituted by Solon prohibiting enslavement for debt. There must have been the expectation that the debtor would eventually find the necessary money and resume his previous status.

suspect he was lying, so I answered him as a young man, a friend, would answer, not thinking I would be wronged: "Nicostratus, I was your true friend in the past, and now I have given you as much help as I could in your misfortunes. But since at the moment you cannot provide the whole amount, although I do not have the money on hand, since I do not have any myself[22]—I will lend you as much of my property as you wish to put down as security for a loan to cover your remaining debt, and you can use the money for a year, without interest, to pay back the foreigners. Then you can collect contributions, as you say you will, and pay off the mortgage for me." [13] When he heard this, he thanked me and asked me to do it as quickly as possible, before the day came when he said the ransom was due. Accordingly, I mortgaged my rooming house for sixteen minas to Arcesas of the deme Pambotadae,[23] whom Nicostratus himself had introduced to me, at an interest rate of eight obols per mina per month.[24] After taking the money, not only did Nicostratus show no gratitude for the favors he got from me, he started right in, plotting to cheat me of the money and make me his enemy—I was at a loss, being an inexperienced young man, as to how to deal with the situation—so that I would not work to recover the money for which the rooming house was mortgaged but would let Nicostratus have it. [14] First, he plotted against me, joining with my adversaries in law cases, and gave them a pledge of support. Next, when my cases against them were underway, he reported to them the arguments he knew I would be making; and he registered against me a summary fine of 610 drachmas payable to the public treasury, a fine for which I received no summons, for failure to produce certain articles.[25] He employed Lycidas the miller[26] to pursue the case. He listed his brother Arethusius here, the man who owns these slaves, as a witness to the summons, and some other man.

---

[22]Presumably he means that he neither has money with him at home nor on deposit at a bank or with some business associate.

[23]Not otherwise known.

[24]I.e., 16%.

[25]A procedure, not entirely understood, whereby a man laying claim to something might force its current possessor to surrender it. See Harrison 1968–1971, Vol. 1: 207–210.

[26]Not otherwise known.

And if I proceeded to a preliminary hearing (*anakrisis*) of the suits that I was bringing against my relatives who had wronged me,[27] they were prepared to denounce me[28] as a state debtor and throw me into prison. [15] Then, following up these actions, he[29] got a judgment of 610 drachmas against me, though I received no summons, and he listed false witnesses to the serving of a summons; and then, he broke into my house and carried off all the furniture, worth more than twenty minas, leaving nothing behind. I thought I should retaliate, so after discharging my debt to the public treasury, once I learned of the summary fine, I proceeded in accordance with the law for false witness against Arethusius, who admitted he had witnessed the summons. Then he entered my property at night and cut down all the cuttings grafted to the fruit trees and the vines trained on the trees and broke down the rows of olives planted around the garden beds. They acted with a ferocity worse than enemies in wartime would have done. [16] On top of that, in broad daylight they sent a little boy, a free Athenian (*astos*), onto my property—they are neighbors and their property adjoins mine—and instructed him to pluck the blossoms off my rose bush. Their purpose was that if I got angry and tied up or hit the boy, thinking he was a slave, they would indict me for assault (*hybris*).[30] They failed in this scheme, and I had witnesses to attest what had been done to me, but I did nothing wrong to them. At that point they instigated the most outrageous plot against me. [17] You see, I had already had the preliminary hearing (*anakrisis*) in my public suit against him for false attestation of a summons and was about to go to trial. He waited for me as I was coming up from Piraeus late at night; when I was near the quarries, he hit me with his fists and grabbed me around the waist and would have pushed me into the quarries if some men hadn't heard me shouting and come to the rescue. A few days

---

[27] His suits against Phormio and Stephanus (see the Introduction, pp. 13–14).

[28] *Endeixis,* lit. "pointing to," was the term used for a number of procedures. Here the threat is to denounce Apollodorus as barred from instituting a suit on the ground that he was a state debtor.

[29] Arethusius, according to the manuscripts, but some scholars believe either Nicostratus or Lycidas is meant.

[30] This passage shows that it would not count as *hybris* if the boy was a slave. See Todd 1993: 190.

later I went to trial on a day devoted to hearing a number of cases. By proving that he had lied about the summons being served and that he was guilty of the other crimes that I have mentioned, I convicted him. [18] During the assessment of penalty (*timēsis*), when the jurors wanted to punish Arethusius with death,[31] I asked them not to do such a thing on my account but instead agreed with the penalty they[32] proposed: one talent; I was not trying to keep Arethusius from being executed, since what he did to me deserved death, but as a son of Pasion, and being myself a citizen by decree, I did not want to be the killer of any Athenian. I will present witnesses to you that confirm that all I have told you is true.

[WITNESSES]

[19] I have explained, gentlemen of the jury, the wrongs they have done for which I instituted the *apographē*. Now I will show you that the slaves belong to Arethusius and that I listed them in the inventory as being part of his property. You see, he raised Cerdon, one of the slaves, from early childhood. I will present witnesses to you who know that he belonged to Arethusius.

[WITNESSES]

[20] I will present witnesses to you who know that Arethusius would collect wages on his account whenever Cerdon worked for someone; and that Arethusius would receive compensation for damages or, pay compensation if Cerdon ever did some damage, since he was his master.[33]

[DEPOSITION]

As for Manes, the other slave, Archepolis of the deme Piraeus gave him to Arethusius when he was unable to pay back a loan, either the

---

[31] In some law cases, as this one and the trial of Socrates, after a conviction, each side proposed a penalty, between which the jurors would have to choose. As there was no formal mechanism for the jurors to express their individual opinions before voting, this is probably a report of jury sentiment expressed by shouting.

[32] I.e., Arethusius and those speaking on his behalf, presumably including his brother.

[33] For the responsibility of master for slaves, cf. Dem. 55.31 and Lys. 10.19.

interest or the full principle. And I will present witnesses to the truth of what I say.

[WITNESSES]

[21] Furthermore, gentlemen of the jury, you will know from the following evidence that the men belong to Arethusius. You see, whenever the slaves bought the fruits of a harvest or contracted to harvest a crop or took up some other agricultural work, it was Arethusius who negotiated the purchase or arranged for their hire. And I will present you with witnesses of the truth of this statement also.

[WITNESSES]

[22] I have now presented all the testimony I have that the slaves belong to Arethusius. I also want to speak on the subject of the challenge that they made to me and I made to them. At the first hearing (*anakrisis*), they said they were prepared to turn the slaves over to me directly for torture,[34] wanting this offer to serve as testimony of a sort on their side. [23] I answered them before witnesses that I was prepared to go with them to the Council (*Boulē*) and to accept the slaves for questioning in conjunction with the Council or with the Eleven.[35] And I explained that if I were pursuing a private case (*dikē*) against them, and if they handed the slaves over to me, I would take them, but in reality both the slaves and the *apographē* belonged to the city. Accordingly, the slaves should be put to the torture by a public agent. [24] You see, I regarded it as improper for a man acting in a private capacity to interrogate state-owned slaves. I was not legally in charge of the torture, and it was not appropriate for me to judge what the slaves said; and I thought the officials or men chosen by the Council should have the answers recorded, and after sealing up whatever testimony the slaves gave, present it before the court, so that you could hear it and on that basis give whatever verdict seemed right to you. [25] If the slaves were tortured by me in private, my opponents would have contradicted all their statements; but if the examination were public, we would have

---

[34] The defendants may have hoped that by accepting the slaves for torture Apollodorus would implicitly acknowledge that they were the owners, but see Dem. 52.23n.

[35] A board of eleven officials that discharged a number of functions connected with public cases, including execution, most famously the execution of Socrates.

kept silent, and the officials or men chosen by the Council would have interrogated the slaves as long as they saw fit.[36] That was my wish, but my opponents refused to hand them over to the officials or accompany me to the Council. [To the clerk] Please call up the witnesses to the truth of what I am saying.

[WITNESSES]

[26] In many respects, then, to me they seem shameless in laying claim to your property, but the strongest argument by which I will expose them to you derives from your laws. When the jurors wanted to punish Arethusius with death, my opponents begged them to set a monetary fine and begged me to go along with that.[37] They agreed to join in paying the fine themselves. [27] But they have not only not paid what they pledged, they are even laying claim to what is yours. Yet the laws provide for the confiscation by the city of property that is put up as security for money owed the city, so it follows that if the slaves were their property, it would be right for those slaves to be confiscated by the city—assuming that the laws are of some use. [28] Before he was in debt to the treasury, Arethusius was acknowledged to be the richest of the brothers; but when the laws order his property to become yours, *then* Arethusius is portrayed as a poor man, with his mother claiming part of his property, his brothers other parts. If they wanted to behave honorably to you, they ought to have disclosed all of Arethusius' property and then claimed as their own any property if anyone listed it in an *apographē*. [29] If you consider that there will never be a shortage of people laying a claim on your property—they will fabricate orphans or heiresses and demand that you pity them, or they will speak of old age and poverty and taking care of their mothers, and sob away, using whatever words they hope will be most effective in fooling you, trying to cheat the city of what it is owed. If you look past all these ploys and vote for conviction, you will decide this case correctly.

---

[36] The interrogation of slaves was supposed to continue until, in the judgment of the examiners, they told the truth. If this procedure indeed took place, it probably gave rise to frequent disputes.

[37] See 18n.

54. AGITAINST CONON

INTRODUCTION

From antiquity[1] until the present day, *Against Conon* has been one of the favorite speeches of the Demosthenic corpus. Moderns are amused by its vivid portrayal of drunken brawling in an army camp and in the streets of Athens itself, as well as the other forms of shocking behavior the speaker describes. There is, moreover, much interest in the speaker's discussion of the choices available to a man contemplating a lawsuit and his account of an arbitration hearing.

If we are to believe Ariston, the speaker, there was no enmity between himself and Conon until he had the bad luck to find himself bivouacked near Conon's sons, who for no good reason directed what we can term frank anal aggression against Ariston's slaves. The hostilities continued and escalated when Ariston returned from military duty. This time (so we are told) Conon, the defendant, was not only an active participant in the abuse but took the lead. The actual charge is battery (*aikeia*), but Ariston repeatedly refers to *hybris*. That term, much studied in recent years,[2] may suggest maltreatment intended to diminish the victim's status, but in this speech, "assault" seems a sufficient

---

[1] If we can believe a fourth-century AD account by Eusebius, admiration for the work was first manifested by the plagiarism of *Against Conon* by Demosthenes' enemy Dinarchus in *Against Cleomedon for Battery*.

[2] The matter is highly controversial. Recent discussions include M. Gagarin, "The Athenian Law against *hubris*," in G. W. Bowersock, W. Burkert, and M. C. J. Putnam (eds.), *Arktouros: Hellenic Studies Presented to B. M. W. Knox* (Berlin, 1979), 229–236; N. R. E. Fisher, "The Law of *hubris* in Athens," in P. Cartledge, P. Millett, and S. C. Todd (eds.), *Nomos* (1990), 123–145; and Johnstone 1999, 58.

translation. The speaker offers no definitions of the term *hybris* and *aikeia*, only an indication that the former is the more serious offense. Perhaps the meaning of the words was so well known that a formulation in the form of a written law was unnecessary.[3]

Neither the date of the events Ariston describes nor the date of the trial can be confidently ascertained. In the third section, Ariston places the initial clash at Panactum two years before the trial, and a remark at Demosthenes 19.326 appears to point to 343 as a possible date and to exclude the period 355–346. This reasoning entails a date of either 355 or 341. But Demosthenes may be unreliable in that speech, and the military activity mentioned there may not be the sort described in this one.[4]

There are commented texts by Sandys 1896 and Carey and Reid 1985, and a translation by Carey 1997.

54. AGAINST CONON

[1] I was assaulted,[5] gentlemen of the jury, and at the hands of Conon, the man here, I suffered injuries so severe that for a very long time neither my family nor any of the doctors expected I would survive. But when I unexpectedly recovered and was out of danger, I initiated this private case for battery (*dikē aikeias*) against him. All the friends and relatives whom I asked for advice were saying that for his deeds Conon was liable to summary arrest (*apagōgē*)[6] as a cloak stealer, and to public suits for *hybris* (*graphai hubreōs*). But they advised me and urged me not to involve myself in greater troubles than I could handle; and also, not to be seen to complain more than a young man should about what was done to me. I have acted accordingly and, because of those advisers, have instituted a private case, but I would, with the

---

[3] For *hybris* as an undefined term, see Dem. 21.47. For a short general discussion of the matter of terminology, see Todd 1993: 61–62.

[4] In the earlier speech, Demosthenes says, "We go out with arms"; in *Against Conon* the term used is "guard duty." For more detailed discussion, see Carey and Reid 1985: 69, and Carey 1997: 84.

[5] Lit. "subject to *hybris*." See the Introduction.

[6] This would have been understood as a crime committed not to acquire a valuable object but to humiliate the victim.

greatest pleasure, men of Athens, have put him on trial on a capital charge. [2] You will all forgive this feeling, I'm sure, when you hear what I suffered. You see, shocking as the assault was, his brutality afterward was no less terrible. I say it is right, and I ask you all without distinction, first, to listen sympathetically to my account of what I suffered, and second, if it seems that I have been wronged and treated illegally, to help me—as is just. I will tell you from the beginning how each of the events happened, in as few words as I can.

[3] Two years ago I went out to Panactum[7] when we were assigned guard duty there. The sons of this man Conon pitched their tent near us—I wished they hadn't. You see, that is where the hatred and the clashes between us first began: you will hear what it started from. These men regularly spent the day drinking, starting right off at their first meal, and they went on doing this for as long as we were on guard duty. We, on the other hand, behaved while away from the city just as we are accustomed to do when here. [4] When the others had their dinner, these men were already drunk and abusive, mostly to the slaves who were attending us, but finally to us ourselves. You see, with the excuse that while they were cooking, our slaves were aiming the campfire smoke in their direction, or that every word our slaves spoke to them was an insult, these men beat them, emptied out their latrine buckets on them, urinated on them, and indulged in every sort of brutal and outrageous behavior. When we saw this, it bothered us, and at first we objected,[8] but when they mocked us and would not stop, we reported the matter to the general—all of us messmates going to him as a group, not I apart from the others. [5] He rebuked them and reprimanded them not only for treating us roughly but also for their general conduct in the camp. But far from stopping or feeling shame, as soon as it got dark that very evening, they burst in on us. They started with verbal abuse but ended up actually hitting me; and they raised such yelling and uproar at the tent that both the general and the tribal detachment leaders (*taxiarchai*) came and also some of the other soldiers; they kept us from suffering irreparable injury or doing the same in retaliation when attacked by these drunkards. [6] The business came

---

[7]To the northwest of Athens, on the border of Boeotia. For the chronology of these events, see the Introduction.

[8]This translates a textual conjecture.

to such a point that when we returned to Athens, we naturally felt anger and hatred for one another over what had happened. But by the gods, I really did not think that I should bring a suit (*dikēn lachein*) against them nor take any account of what happened, but instead, I simply resolved to take precautions in the future and to guard against getting near men like this. So first I want to present witnesses to the events I have mentioned and after that to explain what I suffered at this man's hands, so that you know that the man who ought to have condemned the first wrongdoings, this very man, was the first to commit crimes much more shocking.

[DEPOSITIONS]

[7] These are the events I thought I should ignore, but not long after, while I was taking a stroll, as was my custom, in the evening in the Agora with Phanostratus of the deme Cephisia, a man of my own age, Conon's son Ctesias came by, drunk, along by the Leocorion, near Pythodorus' shops.[9] He saw us, yelled out, and said something to himself, as a drunk will do, so you can't understand what he's saying, and then went up toward Melite.[10] There they were drinking, as we later learned, at the shop of Pamphilus the fuller: Conon here, a fellow named Theotimus, Archebiades,[11] Spintharus the son of Eubulus,[12] Theogenes the son of Andromenes, and many fellows whom Ctesias incited as he made his way into the Agora. [8] It happened that we encountered these men as we were turning away from the temple of Persephone[13] and were walking back, just about at the Leocorion. In the mêlée, one of them, a man I didn't know, rushed Phanostratus and pinned him down, and Conon here and his son and the son of Andromenes fell on me. First they pulled off my cloak, then tripped me and threw me down in the mud, jumped on me and hit me so hard

---

[9] The topography of this stroll is uncertain. Though it acquired some notoriety, the Leocorion cannot be securely located. A tentmaker named Pythodorus is mentioned at Isoc. 17.33. See Wycherly 1957: 191.

[10] The deme southwest of the Agora, taking in the Areopagus and the Pnyx.

[11] A man famous for his Spartan style beard and scowl. See Plut., *Life of Phocion* 10.

[12] In all likelihood, Spintharus' father is the prominent politician.

[13] Probably to the west of the Agora, towards the Acropolis.

they split my lip and made my eyes swell shut. They left me in such a state that I could not get up or speak. And as I lay there, I heard them saying many shocking things. [9] Generally it was filthy stuff, and I hesitate to repeat some of it before you, but I will tell you something that is evidence of Conon's insolence and indicates that the whole business came about at his instigation. You see, he sang out, imitating victorious fighting cocks, and his cronies urged him to flap his elbows against his sides, like wings. Afterward, passersby took me home, naked,[14] and these men went off with my cloak. When I got to my door, my mother and the serving women cried and shrieked and only with difficulty got me into a bath, washed me off all around, and showed me to the doctors. I will present witnesses of these events to show that I am telling the truth.

[WITNESSES]

[10] Now it happened, gentlemen of the jury, that Euxitheus of the deme Cholleidae, this man here, a relative of mine, together with Meidias,[15] met me on their way back from dinner somewhere. I was already near my house, and they accompanied me as I was carried to the bath and were present there when people were bringing in a doctor. I was in such poor condition that to spare me being carried a long way to my house from the bath, those who were present decided to take me to Meidias' house for that night, and so they did. [To the clerk] Take their depositions too, so you will learn that many men know how I was abused by these men.

[DEPOSITIONS]

[To the clerk] Also take the doctor's deposition.

[DEPOSITION]

[11] My condition then as the immediate consequence of the blows and abuse I suffered was as you hear, and all those who saw it right after have given you their testimony. Afterwards the doctor said he was

---

[14] Not to be taken too literally. In a military context a man without his weapons might be called *gumnos,* and here the speaker probably means that he was left wearing only his tunic.

[15] Neither man is otherwise known (the latter is not the defendant in Dem. 21).

not too worried by the swellings on my face and my cuts, but continuous fever followed and pains, terrible pains throughout my body, but especially in my sides and belly, and I lost my appetite. [**12**] And as the doctor said, if I hadn't spontaneously lost a great deal of blood—I was already suffering intense pain and in despair—I would have died from an abscess. But this loss of blood saved me. [To the clerk] Read out the depositions of the doctor and my visitors to show that what I say is true, that my illness, a result of the blows I suffered at their hands, was so severe that I nearly died.

[DEPOSITIONS]

[**13**] I think it has become clear in many ways that the blows I suffered were not ordinary or insignificant, but that I was in extreme danger because of abuse and brutality of these men, and I have instituted a suit far less severe than appropriate. But I suppose that some of you are wondering what Conon will possibly dare say in answer to this. I want to tell you in advance that I have learned he is prepared to turn the issue away from the assault and the deeds that were done and try to reduce it to laughter and ridicule. [**14**] He will say that there are many men in the city, sons of gentlemen (*kaloi kagathoi*), who play around as young men will, giving themselves nicknames; some they call "*ithyphalloi*," others "*autolēkythoi*,"[16] and some of them are in love with *hetairai*[17] and in point of fact his own son is one of them, and he is often getting into fights over a *hetaira*. And that's the way of young men. And Conon will paint me and all my brothers as violent drunks but also as hardhearted and sour. [**15**] Gentlemen of the jury, though I feel resentful about what I have been put through, I would be just as indignant and would consider myself as no less abused, if I may say so,

---

[16]Neither of these compound words bears an entirely transparent meaning. The straightforward sense of the first is "with erections," but it is very likely that the word was chosen for its association with various cults known to have been celebrated with raucous obscenity. The second element of the second word is "oil flask," but the force of the first element is less clear. Some scholars believe the word suggests "carrying one's own oil flask," i.e., impersonating a poor man and therefore not having a slave in attendance to carry the vessel and witness his owner's disreputable behavior; others believe that this word too carries a phallic connotation.

[17]Expensive and relatively elegant prostitutes.

if this man Conon comes across as telling the truth about us, and there is an ignorance so deep among you that whatever character someone claims for himself, or whatever a neighbor charges him with, you will believe him to be as described, and no benefit whatsoever comes to decent people from their daily lifestyle and practices. [16] You see, we have never been seen by anybody engaging in drunken behavior or treating people insultingly, and we think we are doing nothing hardhearted if we think it is right, for wrongs done to us, to seek justice in conformity with the laws. To this man's sons we concede the titles "*ithyphalloi*" and "*autolēkythoi*," and I pray to the gods that this business and all activities like it recoil on Conon and his sons. [17] You see, these are the men who initiate each other with the *ithyphallos* and do things of the sort that decent people are very embarrassed even to mention, let alone do. But what does this have to do with me? I for one, I am amazed if any excuse or pretext has been found in your court that would allow someone who is proven to have assaulted and beaten another to escape paying the penalty. To the contrary, to prevent escalating violence, the laws have anticipated pleas based on necessity.[18] For example—you see, because of this man I have been forced to do research and learn about these things—there are private suits for slander (*dikai kakēgorias*). [18] People say that these suits come about for this reason, that men who verbally abuse each other will not be incited to physical violence. Also, there are suits for battery (*aikeia*), and I hear that they serve this purpose, that a man who is getting the worst of it won't defend himself with a stone or anything else of that type but instead will wait for the legal process. Also, there are public suits for wounding (*graphai traumatos*) to prevent homicides when men are wounded. [19] In my view, there is provision for the least important of these acts, verbal abuse, to avoid the final and worst, homicide, from happening and to prevent the escalation by small steps from verbal abuse to blows, from blows to wounds, and from wounds to death; instead, the laws provide a legal action for each of these, instead of letting these actions be decided by the individual's anger or desire. [20] That is how it is in the laws, but if Conon says, "We are a group of fellows called the '*ithyphalloi* club,' and when we have love affairs, we punch

---

[18]A "plea of necessity" (*anagkaia prophasis*) might take the form, "Since X insulted me, I *had* to retaliate."

and we throttle whomever we want," then are you really going to laugh and let him go? I don't *think* so! None of you would have laughed if you happened to be there when I was being dragged around, stripped, and abused. I left my home in one piece and came back on a stretcher, and my mother rushed out when she saw me, and in the house the women were shrieking and crying so much, as if someone had died, that some of the neighbors sent people to us to ask what had happened. [21] In general, it is the right thing, gentlemen of the jury, that in your court there be no such excuse or impunity available for anybody that would make it possible for him to engage in abuse. Now, if someone *is* to have such excuse or immunity, it is right that those men who do something because of their youth win indulgence of that sort, but even for them, the indulgence should not mean escaping the penalty but that they pay a penalty milder than the expected one. [22] But when a man over fifty[19] is in the company of younger men, especially his sons, and not only does not divert them or stop them but in fact is himself their leader, initiates their action, and is the most repulsive of them, what penalty might he pay that would match his acts? For my part, I don't think even death would be sufficient. For in fact, if Conon had committed none of these acts, but merely stood by while his son Ctesias did the same things as he blatantly has done, he would deserve your hatred. [23] For if he trained his sons in such a fashion that they commit offenses in his presence—some of which are punishable by death—without fear or shame, what punishment do you think would be unreasonable for him to suffer? I think this is evidence that Conon had no respect for his own father, since if he had honored and feared *him,* he would have demanded the same from his own sons.

[24] [To the clerk] Please take the laws, both the one on assault (*hybris*) and the one on clothes-stealers. You will see that these men are in fact liable under both. Read them out.

[LAWS]

For his deeds, this man Conon is liable under both these laws, since he committed assault and stole a cloak. If we chose not to punish him by reference to these laws, we would rightly be seen as respectable

---

[19]The expression might remind the jury of the herald's call at meetings of the Assembly, "Which man over fifty wishes to speak, and then which man?" (Aes. 3.4).

people minding our own business, but he is evil all the same. [25] And if something had happened to me,[20] he could have been charged with homicide and the most severe consequences. The father of the priestess at Brauron,[21] at any rate, was sent into exile by the Areopagus, and rightly so, for inciting a crime though it was admitted that he had not touched the dead man—because he encouraged the assailant to strike him.[22] You see, if those who are present, instead of preventing men who have set their hand to committing a crime, whether in drunkenness or anger or for some other cause, encourage them, there would be no hope of survival for someone who fell in with brutal men, but they would have license to go on with their assault until they got tired. And that is just what happened to me.

[26] I want to tell you what they did during the arbitration meeting,[23] since from that you will observe their brutality. You see, they stretched things out past midnight, refusing to read out their depositions or to provide copies, just bringing our witnesses, one by one, to the stone[24] and putting them under oath and writing out irrelevant depositions—the boy was Conon's son by a *hetaira* and this and that had happened to him—things that, by the gods, gentlemen of the jury, everyone present criticized and found disgusting, and in the end they disgusted themselves. [27] Anyway, when they finally had enough of that business and let it go, for the sake of delay and to prevent the document holders from being sealed,[25] they issued me a challenge, stating

---

[20] A euphemism for "if I had died."

[21] Brauron, a town west of Athens, was the center of a cult of Artemis.

[22] There are obscurities in the precise legal status of this alleged precedent for judicial severity. Some scholars have thought the priestess' father was charged with *bouleusis* (lit. "planning") an intentional homicide, others that the charge was intentional wounding. M. Gagarin ("*Bouleusis* in Athenian Homicide Law," *Symposion 1988:* 96–97) argues that *bouleusis* was not a technical legal term for planning a homicide and that the charge was simply for homicide (*phonou*).

[23] Public arbitration, the only compulsory judicial duty at Athens, was assigned to men after their fifty-ninth birthday; litigants in private suits were required to submit to arbitration but did not have to accept the results. See *Ath. Pol.* 53.

[24] A stone marked the spot where the arbitration was conducted. See *Ath. Pol.* 55.5, with Thompson and Wycherly 1972: 88.

[25] These were vessels into which testimony, challenges, and the texts of relevant

their willingness to hand over slaves whose names they wrote down to testify about my wounds.[26] And I suppose that the majority of their arguments will center on this. But I think you should all consider this point, that if these men had issued the challenge to have the interrogation under torture actually take place, and if they had put trust in this means of proof, they would not have issued the challenge at night when the arbitrator's decision was already being announced and they had no excuse left. [28] Instead, they would have done so from the first, before bringing the suit, when I was lying wounded, not knowing whether I would survive, and I was declaring to all who came to visit that Conon was the first to strike me and had inflicted most of the abuse I suffered. He would have come to my house right away with many witnesses, and on the spot he would have offered to hand over his slaves and would have called in some members of the Areopagus. I say Areopagus, since if I had died, the trial would have taken place in that court. [29] If perhaps he was ignorant of this, and so did not prepare for such a great danger, although he had this means of proof available, as he will now say he did, then at least as soon as I got up from my sickbed and summoned him, at the first meeting before the arbitrator, he would have openly offered the slaves: but he did not take any of these steps. To show that I am telling the truth and that his challenge was issued as a delaying tactic, [To the clerk] read out this deposition, since it will be clear from this.

[DEPOSITION]

[30] So on the subject of the interrogation under torture, remember this, what time it was that he issued the challenge, his motive for doing it—to stall for time—the first opportunities he had to issue the challenge, when he clearly did not want to use this means of proof, as he neither proposed the challenge nor demanded an interrogation. But since he was proven at the arbitration to have done all the same things he is now proved to have done, and he was clearly shown to be

---

laws were sealed. *Ath. Pol.* (53.2–3) states that no material in these categories other than what had been sealed up at the arbitration could be adduced in court. The containers could not be sealed in this case until the new challenge could be included. For the archaeological evidence, see Boegehold 1995: 79–81, 222–226.

[26] On slave testimony, see Dem. 52.22n.

liable to all the charges against him, [31] he throws in a false deposition and has inscribed in it as witnesses the names of men whom I suppose you too will recognize if you hear them: "Diotimus son of Diotimus of the deme Icaria, Archebiades son of Demoteles of the deme Halae, Chairetius son of Chairimenes of the deme Pithus testify that while returning from dinner along with Conon, in the Agora they came across Ariston and Conon's son fighting, and Conon did not hit Ariston"— [32] as if you will immediately believe them and not take account of the truth, first, that Lysistratus, Paseas, Niceratus, and Diodorus, who have explicitly testified that they saw me being struck by Conon, having my cloak ripped off, and all the other abusive acts that I suffered, are men who did not know me and were present only by chance; that they would not have been willing to perjure themselves, unless they saw me suffering those insults. Further, if he had not treated me in this way, I myself would never have let off those who are acknowledged by these men themselves to have beaten me and would never have chosen to prosecute first a man who did not even touch me. [33] Why would I have done that? No, the man who struck me first and dealt me the worst abuse, he is the one I am suing, and whom I detest, and whom I am prosecuting. And everything I am saying is true and plainly so. But if Conon had not offered these witnesses, he certainly would have had no argument but would have been convicted on the spot, without saying a word. But as this man's drinking companions, men who shared in many acts of that sort, they naturally gave false testimony. If things are to be like this, if some people lose all shame and dare to give blatantly false testimony, and there is no advantage in telling the truth, then it will be a most shocking state of affairs. [34] But no, by Zeus, they're not like men of that sort![27] But many of you, I think, know Diotimus and Archebiades, and Chairetius, this man here who's turning gray, men who during the day wear sullen expressions and say that they follow Spartan fashion and wear light cloaks and thin sandals,[28] but when they get together and enjoy each other's company, they indulge in everything foul and disgusting. [35] And this is their sparkling,

---

[27] The oath, as often in Demosthenes, suggests that the speaker is quoting some imagined speech.

[28] See above 54.7n and Plato, *Protagoras* 342b, for a description of men who emulated Spartan modes.

young man's talk: "What, we're not going to testify for each other? Isn't that what pals and friends do? Really, what terrible charge will Ariston bring against you? Do some people say they saw him being beaten? We'll testify that he wasn't even touched. His cloak was pulled off? We'll say that others did this first. His lip was stitched? We'll say that your head or some other part of you was broken." [36] But I am presenting doctors too as witnesses. Gentlemen of the jury, this is evidence these men do not have. Aside from what they produce themselves, they have no witness to bring against us. By the gods, I could not tell you how ready they are to do anything at all. But so you know what sorts of acts they go around doing, [To the clerk] read them these depositions here, and [to the man in charge of the waterclock] you, stop the water.[29]

[DEPOSITIONS]

[37] Do you suppose that men who break into houses[30] and who beat people they encounter would hesitate to give false testimony for each other on a scrap of paper, these partners in viciousness, wickedness, shamelessness, and brutality so foul and extreme? You see, I think all that is part of their actions. Yet there are other things they have done, even worse than that, though we would not be able to find all their victims.

[38] I think it better to tell you in advance about the most shameless thing that, I hear, he is going to do. People say that he will gather his children around him and swear on their heads and will call down certain dreadful, cruel curses, so awful that the man who heard them and reported them to us was amazed. Gentlemen of the jury, these acts of daring are impossible to resist, since I suppose that the best men who are least likely to lie themselves are most susceptible to being fooled by men of this character. But you must believe what you see of their lifestyle. [39] I will tell you of Conon's contemptuous attitude towards things like this. You see, I have been forced to learn about it. I hear,

---

[29] A member of the jury chosen to discharge this function (*Ath. Pol.* 66.2). Evidence on the waterclock is assembled at Boegehold 1995: 77–78, 226–230.

[30] Lit. "digging through." This mode of burglary was made possible by the relative fragility of the houses. See Hyp., *In Defense of Lycophron*, Speech B, Fr. 1, for alleged wall digging for an amatory purpose.

gentlemen of the jury, that a certain Bacchius,[31] who was executed by
your court, and Aristocrates, the man with the bad eyes,[32] and others
of this sort, and Conon, the man here, were friends as young men and
had the nickname "Triballoi."[33] These men would regularly gather
offerings to Hecate[34] and also pig testicles, the ones used for purifica-
tion when there is going to be a public meeting, and dine on them
every time they got together, and they swore oaths and perjured themselves as casually as can be. [40] Conon, a man of this sort, is certainly
not to be believed when he takes an oath, far from it. Rather, the
man who of his own free will makes no oath, not even an honest oath,
and would not even dream of swearing an oath on his children's heads,
which is not sanctioned by your custom, but would suffer anything
rather than do that—if an oath is in fact necessary—he is more to be
believed[35] than a man who swears by his children, even going through
fire.[36] Thus, Conon, I, a man who in every respect would more properly be trusted than you, was willing to swear these oaths; and my purpose would not be like yours, to avoid punishment for my crimes, all
along committing any act whatever; rather, I would do it for the sake
of the truth and so as not to suffer further abuse, with the aim of not
losing my case because of Conon's perjury. [To the clerk] Read out my
challenge.

[CHALLENGE]

[41] That is what I was willing to swear to then, and now too I swear
by all the gods and all the goddesses, for your sake, gentlemen of the

---

[31] Not otherwise known.

[32] This may be the man named at Dem. 39.2.

[33] The name was taken from a Thracian tribe that in the Athenian view was
uncivilized and belligerent in the extreme.

[34] A goddess associated primarily with magic.

[35] Some editors believe that the formula "destruction on himself, his family, and
his house" has been omitted by the manuscripts just before the word "more to be
believed."

[36] The text and precise meaning of this phrase are uncertain. It might refer to
the ritual of burning victims as part of the oath taking, or it might be a metaphori-
cal expression indicating willingness to endure any consequences.

jury, and the sake of the spectators,[37] that I did suffer at Conon's hands the insults of which I accuse him. I was dealt those blows, and my lip was split so badly that it needed to be stitched, and for this abuse I am suing him. And if I am swearing honestly, may I reap many benefits, and may I never suffer such a thing ever again, but if I am perjuring myself, may I myself be completely ruined, as well as anything I possess or will possess. But I am *not* perjuring myself, not even if Conon explodes with indignation. [42] So I ask you, gentlemen of the jury, since I have explained all my legitimate claims and have added an oath to them, that just as each of you, if you are injured, would hate your assailant, that you feel the same anger at this man Conon for my sake; and I ask you not to regard any affair of this sort as a private matter, even if it should happen to another man, but no matter who the victim is, to help him and give him justice and hate those men who before they are accused[38] are brash and reckless but at their trial are wicked, have no shame, and give no thought to opinion or custom[39] or anything else, except for escaping punishment. [43] But Conon will beg and wail. Do consider who is more to be pitied, the man who suffers the sort of things I have suffered at his hands if I leave the courtroom with an added insult and do not attain justice, or Conon, if he is punished? Is it to your individual advantage that it be permitted to hit and commit assault or not? I, for my part, think not. Well, if you acquit Conon, there will be many men like that; if you punish him, fewer.

[44] There is much I could say, gentlemen of the jury, about how we have been useful to the city, ourselves and my father, as long as he was alive, serving as trierarchs[40] and as soldiers and doing what was assigned, and useful as neither Conon nor his sons have been. But

---

[37] Bystanders seem to have been common at Athenian trials and important to the process: see A. Lanni, "Spectator Sport or Serious Politics: *hoi periestēkotes* and the Athenian Lawcourts," *Journal of Hellenic Studies* 117 (1997): 183–189.

[38] The translation here follows a textual emendation ("charges," in place of the manuscripts' "wrongdoings").

[39] Probably a reference to Conon's shockingly unorthodox method of swearing (40), but perhaps instead a reference to his own character.

[40] See the Introduction to 50.

there isn't enough time, and the argument isn't about these matters. You know, if it happened that we were, admittedly, *more* useless than these men and *more* evil, we should not on that account be beaten or insulted.

I don't know what more I should tell you, since I think you understand everything that has been said.

55. AGAINST CALLICLES
FOR DAMAGE TO PROPERTY

〜〜〜〜〜〜〜〜〜〜〜〜〜〜〜〜〜〜〜〜〜〜〜〜〜〜〜〜〜〜〜〜〜〜〜〜〜〜〜

INTRODUCTION

We cannot date *Against Callicles,* and we know nothing about the people involved in this dispute beyond what is in the text, not even the name of the speaker. Nevertheless, the speech is interesting for its portrayal of a quarrel that flared between neighboring families over difficulties faced by Attic farmers working steep slopes subject to occasional torrential rainstorms. We have evidence in this speech both for the private exchanges of the neighbors, first cordial, then rancorous, and for their turn to litigation to settle, or perhaps to protract, the dispute.

The speaker assumes that the jury is familiar with the sort of terrain he describes and the precise meaning of various terms for gullies, ditches, roads, and walls. As we are not so well informed, there is some uncertainty about what the speaker claims has happened. A recent account reconstructs the events as follows:

The dispute in this speech centres on damage caused by runoff water,[1] allegedly because the defendant (the speaker) had built a wall impinging on the main outlet for the water, a . . . seasonal watercourse. Careful reading of the text (especially [sections] 10–11) suggests that the disputants had plots on either side of a large gully, which for most of its course coincided with a road. The speaker claims that in the past the field had been neglected. The implication

---

[1] All we know about the damage allegedly done by redirected rainwater is what the speaker says in 24. Callicles undoubtedly described damages more grave than the wetting of a small quantity of grain.

of his description of this neglect in . . . §11 is that during this time the [seasonal watercourse] . . . had begun to change its course and the speaker's father had built a field boundary wall, which also served to encourage the seasonal river to go back into its old bed. Both vines and figs were planted on the plot belonging to the speaker (. . . §13). Though the speaker tries to imply they are old, they may have been planted by his father. There were old grave memorials on the land as well. The speaker's trees may have been planted along the road, like those he alleges his opponent to have; that is, planted along the road/rema and then walled in when the trees were quite large.[2]

The speaker is defending himself in a *dikē blabēs,* a private action for recovery of damages. This was a popular category of legal action, employed in a broad variety of circumstances (in the Demosthenic corpus, see 33, 36, 41, 52 [Introduction], 56). Some scholars have argued that *Against Callicles* displays some special variants of the simple *dikē blabēs:* the allegation that the speaker's father had violated a specific law against obstruction of a natural watercourse that could cause damage to another's property, and a penalty that required the defendant, if he could not pay a fine of one thousand drachmas, to surrender to the plaintiff either the section of land where the obstruction was created or the entire plot. That fixed fine that the speaker mentions at 28 is very puzzling, for the case at hand would seem to be an *agōn timētos,* that is, one in which there was no fixed penalty and the jurors would select between the penalties proposed by each side in the litigation: see 1, 2, 28, 34, and 35 (with notes). For discussion of this point, see H. J. Wolff, "The *dikē blabēs* in Dem. 55," *American Journal of Philology* 64 (1943): 316–324, MacDowell 1978: 136–137, Todd 1993: 134 and 280–281.

There is a commentary by Sandys and Paley, Vol. 2, 1896. Two recent books discuss the speech as evidence for the litigation culture of fourth-century Athens: Christ 1998, 174–176, and Johnstone 1999, 46–47.

---

[2]Lin Foxhall, "Cultivation Techniques on Steep Slopes," in Graham Shipley and John Salmon (eds.), *Human Landscapes in Classical Antiquity* (London, 1996), 47–48.

55. AGAINST CALLICLES FOR DAMAGE TO PROPERTY

[1] Gentlemen of Athens, it turns out that there is nothing harder than having a wicked, greedy neighbor; and that is just what has now happened to me. You see, in his desire to get his hands on my property,[3] Callicles has abused me with malicious litigation (*sykophantōn*).[4] First, he got his cousin to dispute the ownership of my property. [2] But after Callicles was plainly shown to be in the wrong, and I survived their plotting, he then got from arbitrators two judgments by default:[5] one was in his own name for one thousand drachmas, the other he got by talking his brother, Callicrates here, into bringing a suit. So I ask all of you to listen and pay attention, not because I am myself good at speaking but so that you may learn from the facts themselves that I am plainly the victim of malicious litigation.

[3] I have one answer, men of Athens, to everything they say, and it is a just answer: my father enclosed this field shortly before I was born, and while his neighbor Callipides, the father of these men, was still alive and of course had more accurate knowledge than these men do; Callicles was already a grown man at this time and living in Athens. [4] During all these years, no one ever came forward with a complaint or blamed my father, though clearly in those days too there were many rainstorms.[6] And there was nothing to keep someone from complaining right from the start if my father harmed anyone by enclosing our property. But no one asked him not to do it or made a formal protest for the more than fifteen years that my father lived after that—and

---

[3] The word here translated "property" (*choria*) sometimes carries the more specific meaning "field" or "farm."

[4] See the Series Introduction, pp. xvi–xvii.

[5] "Judgments by default" (*dikai erēmoi,* lit. "deserted cases") could be awarded by arbitrators, magistrates, or juries against parties who did not appear for the relevant proceeding. It is curious that the speaker does not explain his absence, especially if the case at hand was an appeal from the first arbitrator's award or the one thousand drachmas was specifically a penalty for non-appearance (see Harrison 1968–1971, Vol. 1: 250–251).

[6] It is important to realize that in Greece, rain is infrequent but often torrential when it does come.

their father Callipides lived just as long. [5] Really, Callicles, back then, when you saw the ditch[7] being walled off, you certainly could have complained right away, going to my father and saying, "Tisias, why are you doing this? You're walling off the ditch? But then the rain will flood *our* property." That way, if my father had agreed to stop, there would have been no dispute between us; but if he shrugged off the complaint and later a problem like this arose, you would have the men present at that conversation to serve as witnesses.

[6] Then, by Zeus, you should have proven to everybody that there *was* a ditch,[8] so you could have shown—not just by making speeches but in fact—that my father was doing wrong. Well, not one of them thought it worthwhile to do any of that, because in that case you would not have got the judgment by default against me that you did get, [7] and you wouldn't have profited by malicious litigation. Instead, from his own exact knowledge, my father would have shown what the circumstances were and would have easily refuted these conniving witnesses.[9] I suppose you all look down on me as young and inexperienced. Still, gentlemen of Athens, I present their own deeds as the strongest witnesses against all these men. Why, after all, did no one get depositions or bring a complaint or protest even once but instead were content to overlook the wrongs done to them?

[8] I think, then, that I have said enough in answer to their shamelessness. But, men of Athens, I will try to explain to you still more clearly so that you will know that my father did nothing wrong in walling off his property or in anything else and that everything these men have said against me is a lie. [9] In fact, they themselves acknowledge

---

[7]The Greek word, *charadra,* is translated "ditch" to suggest that it was created, or at least modified, by human agency. It may also be translated "seasonal watercourse" or "gully." It would be dry most of the year but could become the bed of a fast-flowing river in times of heavy winter rains.

[8]Clearly the exact boundary of the ditch is at question, not the existence of *any* watercourse in the area. See 10.

[9]The words "if you at that time brought in a witness and got him to make a deposition" are excised in some editions, including the Oxford Classical Text. If they are genuine, that witness probably would be the subject of the sentence, not the speaker's father.

that the property belongs to us, and once this fact is admitted, if you saw the property you would know for sure that I am the victim of malicious litigation. For this reason it was I who wanted to turn the matter over to knowledgeable, impartial arbitrators, not these men, as they are now trying to claim. This point too will soon be clear to everyone. Please, gentlemen, by Zeus and the gods, do pay attention. [10] You see, there is a road between my property and theirs, and there is a hill that surrounds our properties. As it happens, when rainwater runs off the hill, it is sometimes carried into the road, sometimes into the fields; and the part of the water that flows into the road continues down the road if there's no obstruction, but where there's some blockage, then it is forced to overflow into the fields. [11] And indeed, gentlemen of the jury, after a heavy rain it happened that the water flowed into this field. The field was neglected at that time: it was not yet owned by my father but by a man who was altogether disgruntled with the place and more an urban type. Two or three times the water came in and damaged the fields and cut more and more of a path in the ground. It was in fact because my father saw this happening—so I hear from people who know about it—and because the neighbors were grazing animals on the field and passing through it, that he built this dry wall.[10] [12] And I will provide you, men of Athens, knowledgeable witnesses of the truth of what I say and also proofs much more powerful than witnesses. Now, Callicles says that by walling off the ditch, I do him an injury. But I will show that this is my farm, not a ditch.[11] [13] If it is not agreed that the land is our private property, then we would perhaps be guilty of building something on public land; but the fact is that they do not dispute our ownership, and there are trees, vines, and figs planted on the land. Really, who would think it a good idea to set these plants to grow in a ditch? Nobody, of course. Who would bury his ancestors there? I don't suppose anybody would do that either. [14] But both of these things, gentlemen of the jury, were done. In fact not only were the trees planted before my father enclosed the farm with

---

[10]I.e., a wall made of stones fitted together but not held in place by mortar. For a general description of the sort of trouble neighboring farmers could make for each other, see Plato, *Laws* 843–846.

[11]I.e., not a strip, serving when dry as a public road, between two properties.

the dry wall but the ancient monuments were there before we acquired the land. Really, what argument could be more compelling than these facts, gentlemen of Athens? The facts give clear proof. [To the clerk] Now, please take all the depositions and read them out.

[DEPOSITIONS]

[15] You have heard the depositions, gentlemen of Athens. Don't you think they attest explicitly that the property is full of trees and that there are some memorials on it and other things that you find on most other properties; and also that the farm was enclosed while these men's father was still alive; and that neither they nor any other neighbors opposed it? [16] It is also worth hearing, gentlemen of the jury, about the other things Callicles has said. First, consider whether any of you has ever seen or heard of a ditch running along a road. I don't think there is a single such ditch in the whole country.[12] Why would anyone dig a ditch that would carry water coming down the public road into his private property? [17] Second, who among you, whether you live in the countryside or in town, by Zeus, would put up with water flowing down the road getting onto his property or house? Just the opposite: don't we all normally block it up and divert it with a wall if it comes in under pressure? So this man, then, thinks I should let the water from the road on to my property and then once it has passed his property, should direct the flow back onto the road. But then the neighbor farming the next piece of land will complain. In fact, *everybody* will be able to make the same complaint as these men make. [18] And this too: if I hesitate to direct the water onto the road, I guess I would have to be downright intrepid to let the water out on the adjoining property. Considering that I am being sued for a fixed amount (*dikai atimētoi*) because water running off the *road* came down on this man's property, what will happen to me, by Zeus, at the hands of those who suffer damages from water flowing from *my land* onto their land? If I won't be allowed to discharge water that comes onto my land into either the road or other properties, gentlemen of the jury, by the gods, what is there left for me to do? Surely Callicles won't make me drink it up, will

---

[12]This passage shows that paths and drainage channels normally coincided in the Attic countryside.

he? [19] Having had this treatment from these men, and many other terrible things besides, I would be happy simply not to owe any additional penalties [13]—never mind getting legal satisfaction. If there *were* a ditch to take water up again past my property, perhaps I would be in the wrong if I didn't let the water come onto my land—there are, to be sure, recognized drainage ditches on some other properties. The farmers highest up take the water in these ditches, as they take the water draining from the houses,[14] and likewise other farmers take the water from them. But no one gives me water in this way, and no one takes any from me.[15] So how could this be a ditch? [20] I suppose water flooding in has, in the past, damaged the property of many men who didn't take precautions against it, and now it has damaged this man's property. What's most outrageous of all is this: Callicles puts up a huge stone wall because water flows onto his property, then sues me on the grounds that my father, when this happened to *his* property, did wrong by building an enclosing wall. But if all who suffer damages from flooding in that area prosecute me, my fortune would not be enough, even if multiplied several times over. [21] Now, these men are different from the others to this extent: even though they have suffered no damages, as I will soon show you clearly, while the others have endured many substantial losses, these men alone have the nerve to bring a suit against me. And yet anyone else would have *more* right than they to do this. If my opponents have suffered any damages at all, they have done it to themselves, and they are just engaging in malicious litigation. The others, if nothing else, at least are not guilty of that. But to keep me

---

[13] The translation makes more explicit than the text what must be a reference to the thousand drachmas he has already been assessed by the arbitrator (2).

[14] Although the word *cheimaroi* normally refers to heavy winter rain, the speaker is most probably not referring to rainwater: archaeologists have found few, if any, gutters and downspouts meant to direct rainwater from the roof of ancient Greek houses. He presumably means instead the drainage of excess water from the house itself. Many Greek houses of the period have drains leading from the inner court to streets or alleys.

[15] This switch to the first person, even though he has been describing drainage systems *not* found on his property, is one of the speech's (possibly false) naïve stylistic turns (cf., for example, the joke in 18, the confession at the end of 21, the repetition of "narrower" in 22).

from getting everything confused as I talk, [to the clerk] please take my neighbors' depositions.

[DEPOSITIONS]

[22] Isn't it terrible, gentlemen of the jury, that these men, who have endured damages so great, bring no complaint against me—neither do any of the others who have had bad luck, but instead they put up with their fortune, while this man here engages in *sykophancy*? You will soon learn more clearly from the depositions that Callicles himself did wrong, first in making the road narrower by extending his wall so as to bring the trees on the road into his own property, then by throwing rubble out into the road, which made it higher and narrower. [23] I will now try to explain to you that he has brought such a serious charge against me, though he suffered no significant loss or injury. Now then, my mother was a friend of these men's mother before they started to try to hound me in the courts (*sykophantein*). They would visit each other, as you would expect women living as neighbors in the countryside to do and whose husbands, while alive, were friends. [24] My mother went over to their mother's place, and their mother wailed over what had happened and showed her the damage. This is how we learned everything about it, gentlemen of the jury. I am telling you what I heard from my mother. If I tell the truth, may everything turn out well for me, but if I'm lying—the opposite. She said—I swear it—that she saw and heard from their mother that the barley had got wet; and my mother herself saw it being dried out, and it did not amount to three *medimnoi;* and the wheat came to about half a *medimnos.*[16] And my mother said that a jar of olive oil had fallen over but wasn't damaged.

[25] Gentlemen of the jury, this is the extent of what happened to them; for *this* I am a defendant in a *dikē atimētos* for one thousand drachmas. Say my opponent had repaired an old wall, this too would not be something to be charged to my account—a wall that did not fall down or suffer any damage. The upshot is that if I agreed with them that I am responsible for everything that happened to them, well, *that* is what got wet. [26] Why do I need to say anything more, when, from the start, my father did no wrong in enclosing his property, and

---

[16] A *medimnos* is about 52 liters.

my opponents never complained over such a long stretch of time, and our other neighbors never made a complaint against me, even though they had often sustained dreadful losses, and you are all accustomed to direct water from your houses and properties onto the road and not, by Zeus, let water from the road flow into your property? It is clear from these facts that I am, plainly, the victim of *sykophancy* and that I am guilty of nothing, and they did not sustain the damages they complain about. [27] But so that you know that they threw rubble on the road, and that they narrowed the road by bringing their wall forward, and further that I offered an oath to their mother and summoned my own mother to swear to the same oath, please [to the clerk] take the depositions and the summons.

[DEPOSITIONS. CHALLENGE]

[28] Then, could there be men more shameless than these men or more blatant in their *sykophancy?* After they brought forward their wall and covered up the road with rubble, they sue other people for damages, and on top of that, bring a suit with a fixed penalty (*dikē atimētos*) for one thousand drachmas, these men who did not lose altogether even fifty drachmas? And consider, gentlemen of the jury, how many people have happened to sustain losses to their farms from floods, whether in Eleusis [17] or elsewhere. And still, Earth and Gods, these people will not think it right to recover their losses from their neighbors! [29] For my part, though I am the man most entitled to be angry when the road got narrower and higher, I keep my peace. But these men are so superior, so it seems, that they maliciously prosecute (*sykophantein*) the men they have wronged. But, Callicles, if you may enclose your own property, certainly we had the right to enclose ours. If my father did you wrong by enclosing his land, then you are likewise wronging me by now enclosing yours. [30] It's obvious, after all, that with your wall being built of large stones, the water blocked by those stones will come back on my property, whenever by chance and unexpectedly it knocks down my wall. But I will still not complain against them for that reason but will put up with my luck and try to

---

[17] A town in Attica, west of Athens, surrounded by a plain, subject to flooding by the Cephisus river.

protect my interests. I think, you see, that a man who protects his interests is being sensible, but in litigating against me, he is both very wicked and unbalanced by some disease.[18]

[31] Don't be surprised, jurors, by his fervor, not even if he has dared to bring false accusations against me, considering that before this, he persuaded his nephew to dispute ownership of my property, and he brought in nonexistent contracts, and just now he himself got another such arbitrator's judgment against me by default by indicting Callarus, one of my slaves. You see, on top of their other foul acts, they have hit on this tricky maneuver: they are suing Callarus in an identical action.[19] [32] But really, what slave would enclose his master's property if his master hadn't ordered him to do it? But since they have no other complaint against Callarus, they sue him over my father's building a wall fifteen years before he died. If, on the one hand, I abandon my fields and sell them to these men, or if I exchange the fields with them for other properties, Callarus is in no way guilty; on the other hand, if I don't wish to give up my property to them, then they are suffering the most grievous losses at Callarus' hands, and they look for an arbitrator who will award the properties to them and a settlement through which they will get the property. [33] Well, gentlemen of the jury, if those who plot and bring malicious litigation are bound to win the advantage, there's no use talking. But if you hate men like this, and you vote for what is just, seeing that Callicles lost nothing and was not wronged in the slightest either by Callarus or by my father—then I don't know what more I must say. [34] But so that you know that prior to this, with designs on my property, he set up his nephew and that now in his own name he has won a judgment against Callarus in this other suit—with malevolence towards me, since I value this man— and Callicrates[20] has again initiated another suit against Callarus, testimony on all these matters will be read out to you.

---

[18] The suggestion that one's opponent is suffering from a mental disorder, and not just moral depravity, is very unusual in Attic lawcourt speeches.

[19] Harrison 1968–1971, Vol. 1: 174 interprets the passage to mean that a slave could be sued in his own person, but see Todd 1993: 187 n. 35.

[20] The Oxford Classical Text follows the suggestion that a reference to Callicles' brother (mentioned at 2) was omitted by the copyists.

[DEPOSITIONS]

[35] By Zeus and the gods, gentlemen of the jury, do not abandon me, an innocent man, to my opponents. It is not the penalty that matters so much to me, though it would be hard for all men of small means; no, it's that they will expel me, completely, from the neighborhood (*deme*) by their *sykophancy*. To prove that we did nothing wrong, we were prepared to turn the matter over to knowledgeable, fair, impartial arbitrators; we are prepared to swear the customary oath, for we think that in this way we would be offering you, who are bound by an oath as well, the most powerful argument. [To the clerk] Please take my challenge and the remaining depositions.

[CHALLENGE. DEPOSITIONS]

56. AGAINST DIONYSODORUS
FOR DAMAGES

〰〰

INTRODUCTION

Although a "Demosthenes" is called up to speak at the very end of this speech, its style has struck most scholars as falling well below Demosthenes' standard of composition. Some technical characteristics also tell against Demosthenic authorship: hiatus, that is, the occurrence of a vowel at the end of a word and at the start of the following word; and the frequency of three short syllables in a row, contrary to Demosthenes' usual practice, which is referred to as "Blass's law." Perhaps another Demosthenes is meant, but the appearance of the name suggested to some compiler or bookseller that the famous orator Demosthenes was, or could be represented as, the author.

Like Demosthenes 55, this is a suit for damages (*dikē blabēs*), and like Demosthenes 32–35, this speech was delivered in the course of a *dikē emporikē,* literally a "case involving trade," though the phrase seems to be restricted to litigation over maritime commerce. As in Demosthenes 32, 34, and 35, the transactions in question involve the lending of money to men who own or rent ships. Interest on the loan was calculated for the period of the journey, generally two or three months, not for an entire year; thus the rates of which we hear, ranging from 12½ percent to 30 percent, were very high indeed, if one recalculates them as annual percentages. Collateral for the loan was the ship itself, hence it was common for scholars to employ the now obsolete English-law term "bottomry," which refers to the ship's keel. The high interest rates and the obligation to present the ship intact for the creditors' inspection reflect the inherent riskiness of sea voyages in this period. If a ship was lost at sea by shipwreck or piracy, the lender could recover neither principal nor interest. Since risk of total loss was shared by the borrower, who might lose his ship, if not his life, and the lender, and thereby reduced for both parties, the transaction resembles insurance as well as investment.[1]

Grain is the only cargo mentioned by the speaker, though it is quite possible that the ship was carrying other commodities as well. If we had no evidence besides this speech, we could see that Athens took strenuous measures to protect the flow of grain into Attica. Demosthenes 35.50–52 presents a "severe" law, enforced by "dreadful penalties," prohibiting Athenians or metics (resident aliens) from engaging in, or promoting by means of loans, the transport of grain to any port but Athens.[2] The speaker emphasizes the stipulation of Athens as the only allowable destination by repeated references to the contract he and the creditor have drawn up. It is virtually certain, then, that none of the parties to this case were Athenian or metics, since the speaker would not have passed up the opportunity to accuse Dionysodorus and his partner Parmeniscus of violating such an important law. Darius, the speaker, never identifies himself as an Athenian. Neither, presumably, did Pamphilus, his partner in making the loan, who probably made a very short opening speech. Perhaps Darius did most, or even all, of the speaking for the partnership because he spoke better Attic Greek than Pamphilus: jurymen were probably not very tolerant of other Greek dialects.[3]

The very existence of a written contract that serves as the required basis for legal action is a hallmark of the *dikai emporikai.* Scholars have suggested that many aspects of the *dikai emporikai,* such as the requirement of written contracts and the detention of convicted defendants and failed prosecutors until they paid what was owed (see Dem. 33.1

---

[1] See Signe Isager and Mogens Herman Hansen, *Aspects of Athenian Society in the Fourth Century B.C.* (Odense, 1975), 200–212; G. E. M. de Ste. Croix, "Ancient Greek and Roman Maritime Loans," in H. Edey and B. S. Yamey (eds.), *Debits, Credits, Finance and Profits: Studies in Honour of W. S. Baxter* (London, 1974), 41–59; Paul Millett, "Maritime Loans and the Structure of Credit in Fourth-Century Athens," in P. D. A. Garnsey, M. K. Hopkins, and C. R. Whittaker (eds.), *Trade in the Ancient Economy* (London, 1983), 36–52; and Cohen 1992: 165–166.

[2] See also Dem. 34.37 and Lyc., *Against Leocrates 27.*

[3] Plato represents Socrates as complimenting the jury for its toleration of non-Attic dialects of Greek (*Apology* 17d), but this is probably ironic.

and below, 56.4), reflect both the predominance of metics and foreigners in maritime trade and Athens' compelling interest in protecting its grain supply.

The speaker claims that he and his partner had made a bottomry loan, for a period of one year only, of three thousand drachmas to the defendant and his partner for the exclusive purpose of bringing grain from Egypt to be sold in Athens. He alleges that the defendant colluded with Cleomenes, a Greek enjoying great power in Egypt at this time, to sell the grain in Rhodes, where they could sell it at a higher price than at Athens. The defendants, if we can believe the speaker's account, maintained that damage to the ship had rendered it unseaworthy, forcing them to sell the grain in Rhodes; they offered the plaintiffs principal and interest proportionately adjusted for the part of the voyage they had been able to complete. The speaker argues that the defendants' claim is fraudulent, for the ship continued in service after discharging the grain in Rhodes; commentators have found it especially suspicious that the speaker offers no witnesses to the ship's condition.

56.7 shows that the speech must have been delivered after Cleomenes acquired his command in Egypt in 323/2. The ambiguity of a participle in that section, however, makes it possible that the speech was delivered soon afterwards, or as late as the date of Cleomenes' death in the latter part of 323 and late 322, when the Macedonians suppressed the democracy and a speaker was therefore unlikely to use the expression "your democracy" (50).[4]

There is a Greek text of this speech, together with introduction and notes, in Sandys 1886 and Carey and Reid 1985.

56. AGAINST DIONYSODORUS FOR DAMAGES

[1] Gentlemen of the jury, I[5] am a partner in making this loan. We, who have chosen to engage in maritime commerce and entrust that which is ours to other men, know this fact well: the man who borrows

---

[4] See Carey and Reid 1985: 201–203 and Usher 1999: 256 with n. 40.

[5] The *hypothesis* (summary) of the speech written by Libanius (fourth century AD) that appears in the manuscripts identifies Darius as the speaker. The name suggests a Persian origin. There is no certain reference to this Darius elsewhere.

the money enjoys a complete advantage over us. You see, he gets the agreed-upon amount of cash in hand, and on a small tablet that he has bought for two brass coins and a very little scrap of paper, he leaves a promise that he will do what is just. For our part, we do not just *say* we will give the money: we *give* it to the borrower on the spot. [2] In what, then, do we place our trust and what security do we take when we put our money at risk? We have you, gentlemen of the jury, and your laws, which require that whatever agreements one man voluntarily makes with another be binding. But I think that there is no value in the laws or any contract if the man who takes the money is not very honest and does not either fear you or feel ashamed before the man who lent him the money. [3] Neither applies to Dionysodorus, the man here. No, he has become so brazen that he borrowed three thousand drachmas from us, with his ship as collateral, on condition that he sail back to Athens; and then, although we should have recovered the money during last year's sailing season,[6] he took the ship to Rhodes, unloaded the cargo and sold it, thus violating the contract and your laws. Next, he sent the ship from Rhodes to Egypt and then back to Rhodes, but to us here in Athens, who lent him the money, he has never, up to the present time, returned the money or presented the security. [4] This is the second year that he has been using our money, holding on to the loan, the business, and the ship that is our collateral for the loan. Nevertheless, Dionysodorus has not hesitated to come before you, clearly with the intention to penalize us with the one-sixth fine[7] and put us away[8]—on top of depriving us of our property. So we ask and beg all of you, men of Athens, to help us if you think we have been wronged. I want first to tell you about the beginnings of the contract, since that way you will find it easiest to follow along.

[5] You see, men of Athens, Dionysodorus, here, and his partner

---

[6] Roughly, early spring until early autumn.

[7] I.e., a fine, payable to the defendant, of one-sixth the amount sought by the prosecutor if the latter failed to get one-fifth of the jurors' votes. Details of this fine are obscure (see Harrison 1968–1971, Vol. 2: 183–185 and Carey and Reid 1985: 208–209).

[8] The translation attempts to suggest the speaker's euphemism: he calls the prison "the dwelling place." For this unusual feature of the *dikai emporikai,* see the Introduction, pp. 93–94.

Parmeniscus approached us in the month Metageitnion[9] last year and said they wanted to borrow money on the security of the ship on which they would sail to Egypt and from there to Rhodes or to Athens; they agreed to pay interest up to their arrival at either of these markets.[10] [6] We answered, gentlemen of the jury, that we would make the loan with the prospect of no market other than Athens, and so they agreed that they would sail here. On these terms they borrowed three thousand drachmas for a roundtrip voyage, and they wrote out the contract with these terms. In the agreement Pamphilus[11] here was named as the lender, and I was an outside partner in the loan. Now, first, the clerk will read out the actual contract.[12]

[CONTRACT]

[7] In keeping with this contract, gentlemen of the jury, Dionysodorus here and his partner Parmeniscus got the money from us and sent the ship from here to Egypt. Now, Parmeniscus sailed with the ship, but Dionysodorus remained here. They were all, gentlemen of the jury—you should know this—servants and henchmen of Cleomenes, who was ruling in Egypt.[13] Ever since he took over the office,[14] he has done great damage to your city and even more to the rest of the Greeks, working the retail grain market and manipulating prices—Cleomenes himself and these men along with him. [8] Some of them, you see, would dispatch the product from Egypt; some would sail with the cargoes; others would remain here and sell off the goods. Then, tracking the market prices, those at home sent letters to those who were abroad, so that if grain was expensive here, they would

---

[9] Late August/early September in the Attic calendar.

[10] I.e., at whichever of the two ports Dionysodorus and Parmeniscus elected to terminate the loan period.

[11] An Egyptian metic of this name, perhaps the same man, is mentioned at Dem. 21.163.

[12] It was standard procedure to have witnesses to a written contract, but the speaker never produces them to confirm his account of the terms.

[13] Cleomenes was a Greek on whom Alexander the Great bestowed great influence in Egyptian affairs. He may even have been appointed satrap of Egypt. Aristotle (*Oeconomica* 2.1352b) describes his manipulation of the grain market.

[14] The interpretation of this phrase is controversial: see the introduction to the speech.

send it here, and if it was cheap, they would ship it to another market. This was the principal way the price of grain was manipulated,[15] from letters and plots of this sort. [9] Now, when they sent the ship from Athens, grain prices were fairly high. For that reason they accepted the clause in the contract requiring them to return to Athens and not sail to any other market. But later, gentlemen of the jury, when the convoy of ships from Sicily landed and the price of grain was gradually falling, and these men's ship was on the way to Egypt, Dionysodorus here immediately sent a man to Rhodes to tell his partner Parmeniscus about the situation at Athens, since he knew perfectly well that the ship had to put in at Rhodes. [10] So, in the end, Parmeniscus, this man's partner, after he got the letter Dionysodorus had sent, learned from it what the prevailing prices were in Athens and offloaded the grain in Rhodes and sold it there. He showed contempt for the contract, gentlemen of the jury, and for the penalties which they themselves wrote into the contract, which would apply to themselves if they violated it in any respect; and they also showed contempt for your laws, which require ship captains and the men who accompany and supervise the cargo to sail to the agreed-upon market or else be subject to very great penalties.[16] [11] As soon as we learned what had happened, we were astounded and went in extreme agitation to the architect of the whole plot, indignant, as was natural; and we complained that though it was explicitly specified in the agreement that the ship would never put in anywhere but Athens, and we had lent the money on this condition, he had exposed us to the suspicion of those who wanted to blame us and say that we too had participated in shipping the grain to Rhodes; and we complained that they had not even brought the ship back to Athens, their agreement to do so notwithstanding. [12] When we got nowhere speaking to him about the contract and what was right, we demanded that we at least be given the principal and interest agreed on from the start; but Dionysodorus treated us insultingly, refusing even to give us the interest stipulated in the contract. "If you want," he said, "to take the interest prorated for the part of the voyage

---

[15] Either by interpreting the verb that appears in the manuscripts or by emending the text, some scholars have understood the speaker to have a more specific meaning: "Such manipulations raised the price."

[16] These laws are nowhere else attested.

that was completed, I will give you interest for the period up to our putting in at Rhodes. I won't give you more than that." He was making up laws for himself and rejecting our claims based on the contract. [13] When we said we would not agree to any of this, reckoning that if we did, we would be admitting that we too had shipped grain to Rhodes, he pressed more and more. He approached us with many witnesses, saying that he was ready to return the loan and the interest prorated for the leg of the voyage to Rhodes. He wasn't intending to repay these sums any more than before; rather, he figured that we would refuse to accept the money because of the suspicion that attached to taking it. What followed made this clear. [14] You see, gentlemen of Athens, some of your fellow citizens were by chance nearby at the time; they advised us to take what was offered and let the disputed sums be judged by a court, and pending the judgment, not to accept the interest for the Rhodes leg of the journey as full payment. We agreed to this, gentlemen of the jury, fully aware of our rights under the contract but thinking we should settle for a bit less and reach an agreement that would not make us appear overly litigious. But when he saw us ready to meet him halfway [17] Dionysodorus said, "In that case, take back the contract." [15] "Take it back? That's the last thing we would do! We *will* agree to void the contract with a banker as witness up to the point of whatever sum you pay back, but we will not cancel the whole contract until we have had a judgment on the sum in dispute. After all, what legitimate claim would we have, what plea could we advance in litigation, if we have to go to an arbitrator or to court, once we have canceled the contract that contains our legal remedy?" [16] That is what we said, gentlemen of the jury, and we demanded that Dionysodorus here not disturb the contract and not make null and void what these men themselves agreed to as binding. As to the sum of money that he agreed was due, we demanded that he pay it back to us, but as for the disputed amount, we offered to have the matter adjudicated by one or several of the traders in the market. [18] Dionysodorus said he would not listen to any of this, but because we would not release him

---

[17] The meaning of this phrase is obscure. It may instead mean "ready to attack" or "calling his bluff" (so Carey and Reid).

[18] This is the offer referred to just below as a challenge. The text and interpretation of this sentence are, however, somewhat uncertain.

from the contract as a whole once we got back the money he was offering, he has for two years now been holding onto our money, and he
has been using it. [17] And what is most shocking of all, gentlemen of
the jury, is that Dionysodorus himself is making maritime loans with
our money; he is not lending it at Athens or for shipments to Athens
but to Rhodes and to Egypt; and he thinks he is not obliged to perform any of his duties to us, who lent him money for shipping to your
market. To show that I am telling the truth, the clerk will read you the
challenge we made him concerning these matters.

[CHALLENGE]

[18] This was the challenge, gentlemen of the jury, that we issued
to Dionysodorus here many times over and posted on the notice
boards over a period of many days.[19] He said we were utterly naïve if
we thought he was foolish enough to go to an arbitrator when it was
plain that the arbitrator would rule against him and require him to return the money, when he could take the money with him to court;
then, if he could fool you, he would leave the court with another man's
money; otherwise, he would return the money at that point. This is
how a man acts if he does not trust justice but instead wants to put
you to the test.

[19] You have heard what Dionysodorus has done, gentlemen of the
jury. I suppose you were astonished hearing again of his brazenness
and the basis for his confidence in coming here. It certainly is brazen
if a man borrows money at the market in Athens and [20] writes into
the contract an explicit stipulation that the ship is to sail back to your
market or pay back twice the amount borrowed, and then fails to
bring the ship to Piraeus, fails to return the money to his creditors, off-
loads and sells the grain in Rhodes, and having done all this, still dares
to look you in the face! [21] Hear what he says in response. He says
that on the voyage from Egypt the ship sprang a leak,[20] and for this
reason was forced to put in at Rhodes, and there the grain was off-

---

[19]In general, notices were posted at the statues of the eponymous heroes of the
ten Athenian tribes in the Agora (cf. Dem. 24.23), but perhaps notices concerning maritime cases were displayed in the port.

[20]The verb literally means "be broken," but the supposed damage was not severe enough to prevent its making port. We cannot be sure just what Darius has

loaded. The proof of this, he says, is that he rented boats leaving Rhodes and sent some of the cargo here. This is one part of his defense; here is the second. He says, you see, [22] that some other creditors agreed to accept the interest due up to the time when he put in at Rhodes. So, it would be outrageous, he says, if we do not agree to the same terms they did. The third point he adds to these is that the contract requires him to return the money if the boat is undamaged, but the boat did not make it safely back to Piraeus. Gentlemen of the jury, hear the claims we make in answer to each of these points.

[23] First, when he says that the ship sprang a leak, I think it's clear to everyone that he is lying. After all, if the ship suffered this mishap, it would not have made it safely to Rhodes and would not have been seaworthy afterwards. In fact, it clearly did make it safely to Rhodes and then was sent back again to Egypt and is still now sailing everywhere—except to Athens. It is certainly strange that when the ship is obliged to put in at the market in Athens, he says it sprang a leak, but when it comes to offloading the grain at Rhodes, then—the same ship is clearly seaworthy.

[24] "Why," he asks, "did I hire other boats, transfer the cargo, and then send it here?"[21] Because, gentlemen of Athens, he was not in charge of all the cargo, nor was his partner: The men on board in charge of cargo sent their goods here on other boats from necessity, I think, because these men had prematurely ended the voyage. That part of the cargo that was theirs, however, Dionysodorus and Parmeniscus did not send here in its entirety but picked out that part whose price had gone up. [25] Otherwise, why on earth, once you hired other boats, as you say they did, didn't you transfer the ship's entire cargo but instead left the grain in Rhodes? Because, gentlemen of the jury, it was to their advantage to sell the grain there, since they were getting word that prices here had fallen. On the other hand, they sent you the rest of the goods, those from which they expected to turn a profit. The conclusion is that when you talk about the renting of the boats, you

---

in mind; he may well be stating the matter with deliberate vagueness. "Sprang a leak," borrowed from Sandys' commentary, seems appropriately ambiguous.

[21] Darius is "quoting" Dionysodorus, but these words are of course only Darius' prediction of what his opponent will argue.

are not giving evidence that the ship sprang a leak but that you made a profit.

[26] On those matters, then, what I've said is sufficient. Now, about the lenders who they say agreed to take interest from them for the journey up to their arrival in Rhodes, this has nothing to do with us. If someone relinquished something you owe him, he is not a victim of wrongdoing, nor is the man who persuaded him to do so. But we relinquished nothing to you, and we did not agree to the trip to Rhodes, and there is nothing in our view that outweighs the contract. [27] What does this contract say? What itinerary does it specify? From Athens to Egypt and from Egypt to Athens. Otherwise, it requires payment of twice the amount. If you have completed this itinerary, you have done nothing wrong, but if you have not and have not returned the ship to Athens, it is your obligation to pay the penalty specified in the contract. This is a requirement no one but you yourself imposed. So show the jurors either that the contract is not valid or that you are not obliged to comply with all its provisions. [28] If some men have relinquished something and have somehow or other been persuaded to accept the interest due for the trip as far as Rhodes, does this mean you do us no wrong, when you have cheated us by breaking our contract and bringing the ship to Rhodes? I do not think so. These jurors are not now judging agreements made by others but rather the agreement you yourself made with us in a written contract. As for the remission of interest, if it really happened as these men contend, it is plain to all of you that it was to the advantage of the lenders. [29] You see, they lent them money for a one-way trip from Egypt to Athens. Once they reached Rhodes, where my opponents brought the ship to port, it made no difference to them, I suppose, if they relinquished part of the interest but recovered the principal in Rhodes and invested it in a return voyage to Egypt; it actually was much more profitable to do that than complete the voyage to Athens. [30] Weather conditions for the trip to Egypt are, after all, always favorable[22] and they could invest the same money in two or three trips; but if they came here, they would

---

[22] The translation accepts a conjecture, but the manuscripts present two different adjectives, one meaning "short," the other, "risk-free." In fact, none of these would make a true statement.

have to remain through the winter at Athens, waiting for the sailing season. So those lenders made additional profit and did not give anything up to them, whereas we cannot even recover the principal, not to mention the interest.

[31] Do not let this man trick you by making comparisons to what was done with the other lenders, but pull him back to the matter of the contract and the requirements of the contract, since I still have this point to explain to you; and Dionysodorus also insists on the same point when he says that the contract requires that the principal be returned if the ship makes it safely to port. [32] We agree that this is required. I wish you would tell me, Dionysodorus, whether you are speaking about a ship that has been lost or about one that is intact, for if the ship was ruined and is lost, why are you quarreling about the interest and demanding that we take the interest up to the ship's arrival in Rhodes, seeing that we have no right to get either the interest or the principal? But if the ship is safe and not lost, why don't you return the sum you wrote in the contract? [33] How, gentlemen of Athens, can you most surely ascertain that the ship is safe? Most of all, from the very fact that the ship is on a voyage, a fact, moreover, that these men themselves report. You see, they demand that we take the principal and a portion of the interest because, they imply, the ship is safe, although it has not completed its entire voyage. [34] Consider, gentlemen of Athens, whether it is we or they who are complying with the requirements of the contract. They failed to sail to the designated market but instead went to Rhodes and Egypt; and after they violated the contract, despite the ship being safe and *not* ruined, they suppose that they deserve remission of interest when they have made a lot of money for themselves by exporting grain to Rhodes, hanging onto our money and using it for the last two years. [35] What happened is the most outlandish thing. They tried to give us back the original principal, claiming the ship was safe, but then they still think it right to deprive us of interest, as if the ship were ruined. But the contract does not have one provision for the interest and another for the original principal; [36] no, the same requirements apply to both and the same action does too. [To the clerk.] Please read the contract again.[23]

---

[23] The fragmentary quotations may not be authentic.

[CONTRACT] . . . *from Athens to Egypt and from Egypt to Athens.*

You hear, gentlemen of Athens, it says, "From Athens to Egypt and from Egypt to Athens." Read the rest.

[CONTRACT] *If the ship safely reaches Piraeus . . .*

[37] Gentlemen of Athens, judging this case is very easy, and there is no need for many words. That the ship was saved and is now safe has been admitted by these men themselves, since otherwise they would not be offering to return the original principal and a portion of the interest; but the ship has not been brought back to Piraeus. For this reason we who lent the money assert that we have been wronged, and we are litigating about *this,* that it did not sail to the designated market. [38] Dionysodorus claims he did nothing wrong for this very reason, that he is not obliged to pay all the interest since the ship did not sail to Piraeus. What does the contract say? Not, by Zeus, what you say it says, Dionysodorus. Rather, it says that if you do not pay back the loan and the interest, or if you do not produce the security plain to see and free of any encumbrance,[24] or if you do something else contrary to the agreement, it orders you to pay twice the sum. [To the clerk.] Please read just this part of the contract.

[CONTRACT] *If . . . they do not present the security plain to see and free of any encumbrance,[25] or if they do anything contrary to the contract, let them pay twice the sum.[26]*

[39] Have you exhibited the ship anywhere in plain view since the time you took the money from us, acknowledging yourself that it was safe? Or did you, in the period after you took the money, sail to the market of the Athenians, given that the contract explicitly says that you are to put in at Piraeus and exhibit the ship to the lenders, plain

---

[24] A formula meaning that the borrowers were obliged to exhibit the ship, which served as security for the loan, to show that it was intact and to demonstrate that no other creditor had a claim on it.

[25] I.e., not subject to a claim by any other creditor.

[26] The omission of the requirement to repay the amount owed, a violation that Darius has mentioned (e.g., at 20), has caused scholars to question the authenticity and/or the completeness of this quotation of the contract.

to see? [40] This too is an important issue, men of Athens. Look how he exaggerates. The ship sprang a leak, this man says, and for that reason he brought it in at Rhodes. Well, it was later repaired and made seaworthy. Then why, *sir*,[27] did you dispatch it to Egypt and the other markets but have not yet, up to this day, brought it to Athens, to us, the lenders, to whom the contract orders you to present the ship plain to see and free of encumbrances, which is what we have repeatedly demanded and challenged you to do? [41] But you are so brave—or rather shameless—that though by the contract you owe us double damages, you suppose you have no obligation to pay us the accrued interest, and instead tell us to accept the interest up to Rhodes, as if what you stipulate has more authority than the contract; and you dare to argue that the ship did not make it safely back to Piraeus. For this act the jurors would be justified to sentence you to death. [42] Who is more responsible, gentlemen of the jury, for the ship not returning safely to Piraeus? We who lent money specifically for a trip to Egypt and back to Athens, or Dionysodorus and his partner, who borrowed money on the condition that they sail back to Athens but then put in at Rhodes? And many things make it clear that they did this of their own free will, not because they were forced to. [43] After all, if this was truly an unintended misfortune, that the ship sprang a leak, then afterwards once they repaired the ship, they would not have rented it for trips to other markets but would have instead sent it to you, thereby putting right that unintended misfortune. But in fact, not only did they not correct what happened, they committed far greater offenses on top of the first ones, and they have come into court making a farce out of the business, thinking it will be in their power, if you vote against them, to pay only the original sum and the interest. [44] So do not, men of Athens, give in to men like this and let them have it both ways,[28] so that if they succeed, they get what belongs to other men, but if they cannot fool you, they give back what they owe. No. Give them the penalties stipulated in the contract. It would be outrageous if these men had written into the contract a double penalty against themselves in case they violated any of its provisions, while you show them greater

---

[27] The normally deferential word, literally "O best [of men]," is sarcastic.

[28] Lit. "ride at two anchors," i.e., to make oneself secure.

lenience—and to top it off, especially when you have been wronged no less than we have.[29]

[45] Our claims can be stated briefly and are easy to remember. We lent Dionysodorus here and his partner three thousand drachmas for a voyage from Athens to Egypt and from Egypt back to Athens. We have not recovered the principal or the interest; they have retained and are using our money for the second year now. They have not yet even now returned the ship to your market, and they have not presented the ship to us plain to see. The contract requires that if they do not present the ship plain to see, they are to pay double damages, and the money can be exacted from one or both parties to the contract.[30] [46] With these claims we have come before you, asking that we recover what is our own with your help, since we cannot get it from the debtors themselves. This is the argument on our side. For their part, they do acknowledge that they borrowed the money and have not given it back, but they contend that they are not obliged to pay the interest stipulated in the contract but only the part as far as Rhodes—interest that they did not write into the contract and did not persuade us to accept. [47] Now if, men of Athens, we were pleading our cases in a court in Rhodes, these men might have had an advantage over us, since they brought grain to the Rhodians and sailed the ship to their market. But since we have in fact come before Athenians, and we contracted a voyage to your market, we do not think we should be defeated by men who have wronged both you and us.

[48] Apart from these matters, men of Athens, do not fail to realize that in judging one case now you will be making law for the whole market, for many whose business is maritime commerce are in attendance, watching to see how you will judge this case.[31] If you think that contracts and mutual agreements should have force and you will show no tolerance for those who violate them, then those who lend their own money will do so more readily, and your market will flourish as a result. [49] If, however, ship captains will be allowed to write con-

---

[29] I.e., by not receiving the benefit of having the grain delivered to Athens.

[30] I.e., from either Dionysodorus or Parmeniscus, singly or together.

[31] The translation "will judge" follows the future tense found in one manuscript. On the important role of the spectators, see Dem. 54.41n.

tracts that stipulate putting in at Athens but then take their ship to other markets, claiming that their ship has sprung a leak and offering pretexts like those Dionysodorus here uses, and if they are allowed to prorate the interest according to whatever itinerary they say they have completed, rather than the interest conforming to the contract, then nothing will prevent *all* the contracts from being revoked. [50] After all, who will be willing to risk his own property when he sees that contracts are void, and that arguments like those prevail, and that the pleas of wrongdoers are given priority over justice? Gentlemen of the jury, do not allow it. This business brings no advantage to your democracy[32] nor to those who have chosen to engage in commerce, men who bring the greatest benefits to both the general public and to those individuals who do business with them. For this reason you should be concerned for them.

I have said everything I can, so I ask one of my friends to speak in my support. Step up, Demosthenes.[33]

---

[32] *Plēthos,* a word that literally means "mass" but is a standard way of referring to the democracy. As noted in the Introduction, this has been taken as evidence for the date and authorship of the speech.

[33] See the Introduction.

57. APPEAL AGAINST EUBULIDES

❖❖❖

INTRODUCTION

This speech and *Against Neaera* (Dem. 59) revolve around the issue of Athenian citizenship. The stakes were very high: it is no rhetorical exaggeration when in the opening section the speaker equates conviction with ruin, for he was to be sold into slavery if he lost the case (though at 65 it appears that an unsuccessful appellant might be expected to escape from Attica before that happened).

A man named Euxitheus came before an Athenian court to present an appeal (*ephesis*) of the decision of his deme, Halimus, to strike him from its official register of deme members (*lēxiarchikon grammateion*). Although the trial arises from an appeal, the deme takes the role of prosecutor, represented by Eubulides and four other elected deme officers, an exception to the general rule that prosecution in the Athenian judicial system lay in the hands of volunteers.[1] Euxitheus had been removed from the register in the course of a review (*diapsēphisis*) in which the status of each member was confirmed by the vote of all members present. He claims that he meets the requirement of citizenship—descent from an Athenian mother and father—and that Eubulides,[2] the man responsible for his expulsion, acted out of personal enmity. The procedure and penalties relevant to this case are known from internal evidence, *Ath. Pol.* 42 and the *hypothesis* (summary) of the speech provided by Libanius (fourth century AD).[3] This hypothesis

---

[1] Another unusual feature: there was no penalty for unsuccessful prosecution.

[2] Eubulides is known from an inscription to have served as a member of the Council in the same year that the *diapsēphisis* was enacted.

[3] See also Is. 12, which also concerns the denial of citizenship during the same review, but where the procedure is rather different.

also supplies the speaker's name: the man has left no trace except for this speech. If we believe Euxitheus, the evidence against him was flimsy and mean-spirited: his father's dialect and his mother's humble employment, selling ribbons and working as a wet-nurse.

This case arises from a *diapsēphisis* that was conducted in 346/5 and mandated by a decree of the Assembly that had been proposed by Demophilus, possibly in the wake of an influx of Athenians (or pretend Athenians) expelled from Thrace a few years earlier by Philip II of Macedon.[4] The speech is likely to have been delivered about a year later. Most scholars believe it is an authentic speech by Demosthenes, though perhaps one to which he did not apply "the finishing touch," as the nineteenth-century scholar Friedrich Blass put it.

For a general treatment of the place of demes in Athenian society and government and discussion of some individual passages in this speech, see David Whitehead, *The Demes of Attica, 508/7–ca. 250 B.C.* (Princeton, 1986), and Nicholas F. Jones, *The Associations of Classical Athens* (Oxford, 1999). The speech is translated in Carey 1997.

57. APPEAL AGAINST EUBULIDES

[1] As Eubulides has made many false accusations against us, and made defamatory statements that are neither fitting nor just, I will try, gentlemen of the jury, by telling what is true and just, to show both that we have a share in the city[5] and that I myself have been treated badly by this man. I ask all of you, gentlemen of the jury, and I beseech you, and I implore you, to take account of the enormity of the present trial and the shame that comes to those ruined by a conviction, and to listen to me in silence,[6] preferably, if possible, with more goodwill toward me than toward him, since it is natural to show greater goodwill

---

[4]See Hansen 1999: 95. The main sources for this review of the deme rolls are Aes. 1.77, 86 and Plut., *Life of Pericles* 37.4.

[5]The phrase is tantamount to "be citizens." As often, the speaker switches from first-person singular to plural. The plural is not arrogant but a way of referring (imprecisely) to the speaker's wider circle, usually his family.

[6]For appeals to the jurors both for silence and to shout, see V. Bers, "Dikastic *thorubos,*" in P. Cartledge and D. Harvey (eds.), *Crux: Studies Presented to G. E. M. de Ste. Croix on His 75ᵗʰ Birthday* (Exeter, 1985), 1–16.

to those who are in danger; but if not, with at least an equal measure of goodwill. [2] I happen, gentlemen of the jury, to feel confident about your part in this matter[7] and about my belonging to the city and to have great hopes of doing well in court; but on the other hand, I am fearful of the city's current keen excitement over the disenfranchisement of citizens. Since many men have been rightfully expelled from all the demes, we who are the victims of plotting are tarnished by their disgrace, and each of us is in a trial that touches on those men's guilt and not just our own individual circumstances, with the inevitable result that we are afraid. [3] Although this is the situation, I will tell you first what I regard as just. You see, I think you should be angry at those who are exposed as aliens if they have secretly and against your will taken part in your sacred communal rites without having asked you or persuaded you to grant them the privilege; but you should help and save those unlucky people who demonstrate that they are citizens, reflecting that the most pitiable things would befall the victims of injustice, if because of your anger over this matter, we who should rightfully be in your company exacting the penalty will instead be among those who pay the penalty and would join in being the victims of injustice. [4] Now I think, gentlemen of the jury, that Eubulides and all those who are now bringing accusations in disenfranchisement proceedings should tell precisely what they know and bring no hearsay evidence into such a trial. After all, this practice was long ago so emphatically judged wrong that the laws do not even permit hearsay evidence to be included in testimony, not even in trivial cases. And reasonably so, since when some men are plainly lying when they claim to know something, why should we believe someone who speaks of what he himself has no personal knowledge? [5] Further, when a man is not permitted to harm anyone else by passing on what he says he has heard, even if he takes responsibility for it, how can it be proper for you to believe someone who cannot be held to account? Since Eubulides, knowing the laws rather too well,[8] makes the accusation unjustly

---

[7] The translation here follows the manuscript reading, "in respect to you," not a conjecture, "in respect to ourselves," adopted by the Oxford Classical Text.

[8] This is one of a number of passages showing that great familiarity with the law could be presented in a negative light. Someone often involved in litigation may be thought to have ulterior motives for prosecuting and possibly resemble a *sykophant*.

and for his own advantage, I am forced to speak first about how I was abused among the members of the deme. [6] I ask, gentlemen of Athens, that you not yet regard the expulsion voted by the deme members as evidence that I do not belong to the city. After all, if you believed that the deme members could decide all cases rightly, you would not have allowed appeals to be brought before you. The fact is that because you thought something like this would happen as a result of ambition, envy, personal hatred, and other reasons, you established this recourse to your courts, gentlemen of Athens, for those who had been treated unjustly, and by means of applying this procedure honorably, you have rescued all those who have been wronged. [7] So first I will tell you in what way the deme members handled the review of citizens (*diapsēphisis*). I take it that this constitutes "speaking to the specific point,"[9] to reveal everything that happened to a man unjustly victimized by political strife, contrary to the decree.

[8] You see, gentlemen of Athens, as many of you know, Eubulides,[10] this man here in court, indicted the sister of Lacedaemonius[11] for impiety but did not get one-fifth of the votes.[12] I testified honestly at that trial but in opposition to Eubulides, and because of animosity over that event, he attacked me. He was serving on the Council, gentlemen of the jury, and in charge of both the oath and the documents for summoning members of the deme, so what does he do? [9] First, when

---

[9] For some reason, the speaker repeatedly protests that he is sticking to the point. This may reflect a requirement, perhaps adopted not long before the date of the speech, that litigants in private cases (*dikai*) swear to speak to the issue when addressing the court (*Ath. Pol.* 67.1). In general, speakers in Attic lawcourts very often strayed without apology into what a modern judge would declare irrelevant material.

[10] Eubulides was a prominent figure (see the Introduction). That he was not barred from participating in the prosecution of Euxitheus despite his failure in an earlier public case to get one-fifth of the jury's ballots shows that Athenian law sometimes imposed the penalty of only partial *atimia* (loss of citizen rights) for unsuccessful prosecution: see Hansen 1976: 63–64.

[11] Probably the man whose brother's service as an arbitrator is mentioned at Dem. 59.45. Nothing more is known about the charges against the woman.

[12] Normally, a woman with Athenian citizenship could not be prosecuted in her own name.

the deme members were called together, he wasted the day in making speeches and introducing decrees. It was not by chance that he did this; rather, he was plotting to hold the *diapsēphisis* in my case as late as possible. And this he managed to do. Seventy-three of us deme members were sworn in, and we did not start on the *diapsēphisis* until late in the afternoon; consequently, it happened that when my name was called, it was already dark. [10] My name was around the sixtieth, and I was last of all the men called that day. By then the older deme members had left for the countryside, since, gentlemen of the jury, the deme is thirty-five stades [13] from the city and most of the members live there, so the majority had gone off. Those who remained numbered not more than thirty, and among this group were all those whom Eubulides had set up. [11] When my name was called, Eubulides leapt to his feet and immediately began slandering me, over and over, and shouting, as he has been doing just now. He offered no witness to support his charges—no member of the deme or any other citizen—yet called on the deme members to strike me from the rolls. [12] I demanded that the meeting be adjourned to the next day because of the lateness of the hour and because I had no one to help me, and the business had caught me unawares; the purpose of my demand was that he be able to make all the accusations he wanted and to put forward any witnesses he had, and I would be able to make my defense before all the deme members and put forward my own people as witnesses. And I was willing to accept whatever verdict was given in my case. [13] He paid no attention to my proposal but immediately put the vote to those members of the deme who were present; he offered me no chance to defend myself, and he produced no reliable proof. His accomplices jumped up and cast their ballots. It was dark, and each of them took two or three ballots from Eubulides and threw them into the urn. The evidence for this is that though there were not more than thirty men who voted, the ballots numbered more than sixty, which stunned us all. [14] I will provide witnesses that I am telling the truth: that the vote

---

[13] About four miles south of the city. This is the only extant reference to the location of a deme assembly, and it is not clear why the meeting was not held in a place more convenient to a majority of the men who attended. For discussion see Jones 1999: 87–88.

was not submitted to all the deme members, and the tally was larger than the number of men who had voted. Because of the late hour and my failure to ask anyone to stay, it happens that none of my friends or other Athenians were present to serve as witness on these matters; instead, I will have recourse to the very men who have wronged me as my witnesses. I have written down for them things they will not be able to deny. [To the clerk] Read this.[14]

[DEPOSITION]

[15] Gentlemen of the jury, if it had happened that the members of Halimus had conducted the vote on all the deme members that day, it would have made sense for the voting to run late, so they could accomplish everything your decree had mandated before leaving. But when more than twenty deme members remained who had to be voted on the next day, and when in any event it was necessary for the members to reassemble, what did Eubulides find so difficult about postponing the vote to the next day and having the deme members vote on my case first? [16] The reason was, gentlemen of the jury, that Eubulides knew very well that if I were given the floor and all the deme members were on hand and the vote were fairly conducted, his accomplices could do nothing. When I speak about my family, if you want to hear about it,[15] I will tell you what motive these men had for their plot. [17] But now, what do I think is a just claim and what am I prepared to do, gentlemen of the jury? To demonstrate to you that I am an Athenian on both my father's and my mother's side and to present witnesses to this fact whom you will agree are honest. Also, to refute their insults and accusations. If I seem to you, once you have heard these things, to be a citizen victimized by a conspiracy, then save me. If not, do whatever seems to you the pious thing to do.[16] I'll start with this. [18] You see, they slander my father, when they say he spoke like a for-

---

[14] This challenge probably followed the procedure known as *exōmosia*, whereby people in court were called on to give testimony or swear that they had no knowledge of the matter. See C. Carey, "The Witness' *Exomosia* in the Athenian Courts," *Classical Quarterly* 45 (1995): 114–119.

[15] More often than most speakers, Euxitheus defers (or pretends to defer) to the jury's desire to hear certain material (see n. 6).

[16] I.e., in accordance with the jurymen's oath.

eigner.[17] They leave out the fact that he was captured by the enemy during the Decelean War[18] and sold into slavery, then taken to Leucas,[19] where he fell in with Cleandrus the actor,[20] and after a long interval returned safely to his family; so they accused him of speaking with an accent, as though we should be ruined on account of his bad luck. [19] But I think I can demonstrate to you, from these very facts, that I am an Athenian. So, I will provide witnesses first that he was captured and returned safely; then, that on his return he got a share of his uncles' property; and further, that no one ever accused him, not among the deme members, not among his fellow phratry members, not anywhere else, of being an alien on the ground that he spoke with an accent. [To the clerk.] Please take the depositions.

[DEPOSITIONS]

[20] You have heard, then, about my father's capture and how it came about that he was rescued and brought back here. Now, gentlemen of the jury, to prove that he was a fellow citizen of yours — for this really and truly was the case — I will call my father's living relatives.[21] [To the clerk] Please call first Thucritides and Charisiades. You see, their father Charisius[22] was the brother of my grandfather Thucritides and my grandmother Lysarete — my grandfather married his half-sister

---

[17] From what Euxitheus goes on to say in the next sentence, it seems that his father had acquired a West Greek dialect.

[18] The Decelean War (413–404) is one period of what we call "The Peloponnesian War." It got its name from the continuous Spartan occupation of Decelea, a town in Attica.

[19] An island off the coast of Acarnania in the Ionian Sea.

[20] His name is found on an inscription recording his membership in the guild of actors, "The Artists of Dionysus."

[21] Here begins an unusually detailed presentation of a family tree. For specifics, consult Davies 1971: 93–95 and the chart accompanying Carey's translation (1997: 214–216, adapted from W. E. Thompson, *American Journal of Philology* 92 [1971], 89–90). Davies writes (93): "We have to do with a family of small means, whose members lacked the luck or ability to escape from their inherited position," but Ober 1989: 223 believes that the speaker's appeal for sympathy for his poverty is belied by his report (64) that he had dedicated arms to Athens.

[22] An inscription lists him as one of the Archons in the first half of the fourth century.

from a different mother—and Charisius is my father's uncle. [21] Then call Nikiades. His father Lysanias was the brother of Thucritides and Lysarete, and the uncle of my father. Next call Nicostratus.[23] His father Nikiades was my grandfather's and grandmother's nephew, and my father's cousin.[24] Please call up all these men and stop the waterclock.

[WITNESSES]

[22] You have heard, men of Athens, from my father's relatives, who testify and swear that he was an Athenian and was related to them. None of them, surely, standing alongside men who would know that he is lying, calls down curses on himself.[25] [To the clerk] Please take also the deposition of my father's relatives on the female side.[26]

[DEPOSITIONS]

[23] These living relations of my father, on both the male and female side, have testified that he was an Athenian on both sides and rightly had a share in the city. [To the clerk] Please call the members of my phratry (brotherhood) and then members of my genos (clan).[27]

---

[23] Known from epigraphic evidence to have been one of the Treasurers of Athena in 340/39 and a member of the Council in 335/4.

[24] Because Euxitheus speaks of four first cousins at 67, most scholars believe that the name of one cousin has been omitted by the manuscripts, but W. E. Thompson (above, n. 21) has argued that Lysarete's mother was, like her daughter, married twice, and that she had one or more children with her first husband; one of those children, in turn, had a child who in Attic kinship terminology would count as Euxitheus' maternal, but not paternal, cousin.

[25] I.e., bring down on his head the ruin with which a deponent curses himself for potential perjury when he takes the witness's oath.

[26] I.e., the relatives of his father's mother, who would testify that she too was an Athenian.

[27] The *phratries* (roughly, "brotherhoods") were social and political units of great antiquity that survived Cleisthenes' reorganization of Attica in the last decade of the sixth century BC. Within a phratry there were smaller kinship units called *genē* (clans). Among their functions was the maintenance of a registry to which members would add the names of their legitimate sons. As part of Cleisthenes' reorganization of Attica in 507, in which the principle of locality supplemented kinship, recognition of citizenship also required registration in a deme, a village or urban quarter assigned to one of the ten tribes (*phylai*) that replaced the original four tribes.

[WITNESSES]

Take the depositions of the deme members and of my relatives that my fellow phratry members elected me an official of the phratry (*phratriarch*).

[DEPOSITIONS]

[24] You have heard the testimony of all the appropriate people, members of my phratry, members of my deme, and members of my genos. From them you can learn whether a man who had these people to vouch for him was an Athenian (*astos*) or an alien. You see, if we for protection looked to one or two men, we would be subject to some suspicion that these witnesses were set up. But if my father, during his lifetime, and now I, have clearly passed muster with all the affiliated groups, as each of you has—namely, phratry members, relatives, deme members, *genos* members—how could I manage to rig all these pseudo-relatives? [25] Now if my father was rich and blatantly giving money to these men to talk them into declaring themselves his relatives, the argument that he was not an Athenian (*astos*) might arouse some suspicion. But being poor, if he presented as his relatives the same men as those he listed as giving him a share of their property, then it is surely crystal clear that he is in truth related to them. If he were related to none of them, they certainly wouldn't have given him a share in their *genos* and also given him money. No, he *was* their relative, as the facts have made clear and as has been confirmed by testimony. Furthermore, he was selected for a magistracy by lot, was approved at his review,[28] and held office. [To the clerk] Please take this deposition.

[DEPOSITION]

[26] Does anyone of you suppose that the deme members would have allowed that man to hold office among them if he were an alien and not a citizen and would not have prosecuted him? Well, not one person prosecuted him or accused him of anything. And in fact there were compulsory *diapsēphisis* procedures, where the deme members had to swear on sacrificed animals when their deme register was lost

---

[28] Lit. "having been subject to *dokimasia*." The speaker does not specify which offices his father discharged and leaves implicit the point that his citizenship could have been challenged at one of these proceedings but evidently was not.

during the administration of the *demarch*[29] Antiphilus, father of Eubulides, and they drove out some of the members. But nobody spoke about my father or brought any charge against him. [27] Yet every man's life ends at his death, and it is right that his children always have to defend themselves against any charge the man incurred while alive.[30] But it is really outrageous if someone comes forward[31] to judge the children on charges no one brought against a man while he was alive. If no account of these matters had ever been tested, we might grant that the matter of his citizenship slipped by unnoticed. But if there was discussion, and they conducted the *diapsēphisis,* and no one ever accused him, it is certainly right that I would be counted an Athenian on my father's side, since he died before there was any dispute about his ancestry. I call witnesses to these matters also, to show that this is true.

[WITNESSES]

[28] Further, my father had four children from the same mother as mine. When they died, he buried them at his ancestral tombs, which belong to those who share his *genos.* No member of that *genos* ever said he could not, or prevented him from doing so, or sued him. Now, really, who would permit people not in the *genos* to be buried in their ancestral tombs? [To the clerk] Take this deposition attesting the truth of my statements.

[DEPOSITION]

[29] That is what I have to say about my father's being an Athenian, and I have provided witnesses who were confirmed as citizens by these self-same men, to testify that he was their cousin. It is clear that for all the time he lived here, my father was never challenged as an alien; no, he found protection with those who were his relatives, and these people took him in and gave him a share of their property as one of their own. [30] He was clearly born at a time when if he was an Athe-

---

[29]A man selected by lot to serve for one year to preside at deme meetings and look after the deme's list of members.

[30]This remark, made in the context of a dispute over hereditary citizenship, could apply to a wide range of offenses. It illustrates well the concept of the family, future unborn generations included, as a collective legal agent.

[31]The Greek is *ho boulomenos,* "the man who wishes [to bring a prosecution]."

nian (*astos*) on either side of his family, he was entitled to be a citizen (*politēs*), since he was born before the archonship of Eucleides.[32] Now I will speak about my mother—for they have slandered me in her case too—and I will call witnesses to what I say. Still, men of Athens, he has slandered me about the Agora,[33] not only in violation of the decree but in violation of the laws that command that the man is liable to a charge of slander if he insults a male or female citizen about his work in the Agora. [31] We do acknowledge that we sell ribbons and do not live in the style we would like. And, Eubulides, if you take this as a sign that we are not Athenians, I will show you the exact opposite, that an alien is not permitted to work in the Agora. [To the clerk] Please take and read first the law of Solon.

[LAW]

[32] [To the clerk] Take also the law of Aristophon.[34] You see, men of Athens, you thought Solon enacted such a just and democratic law that you voted to restore it.

[LAW]

It is fitting for you to help the laws, not by thinking that workers are aliens but by thinking *sykophants* are wicked, because, Eubulides, there is another law, dealing with idleness, one to which you, who slanders us who work, are liable.[35] [33] But such a great misfortune en-

---

[32] Pericles' citizenship law of 451/0 stipulated that one could be a citizen only if both parents were Athenian. Apparently because the rule had been neglected during the Peloponnesian War, it was reinstated in 403/2, during Eucleides' archonship, but not made retroactive.

[33] There is no other evidence for this curious prohibition of a rather innocuous form of slander (*kakēgoria*). In Athenian law the truth of the allegations was evidently not a sufficient defense, as it would be in modern laws on libel and slander. See Todd 1993: 260. In Lys. 10, the only surviving speech from a prosecution for slander, we hear that accusations of homicide, desertion of one's station in the hoplite phalanx, and physical abuse of parents counted as defamatory speech.

[34] Aristophon of the deme Azenia, who moved the restoration of this Solonian law, was an important politician of the late fifth and early fourth centuries. See Dem. 18.162, 19.21, 20.148; Aes. 1.64, 158, 23.139.

[35] Lysias is reported to have written two speeches for actions involving this law (*graphē argias*).

velops us now that he is permitted to defame me in irrelevant matters and do anything whatever to keep me from getting what I deserve. Perhaps you will criticize me if I talk about the way *he* does business as he goes about the city, and rightly so: what need is there to speak of what you all know? But do consider this. You see, for my part, I regard our working in the Agora to be a very strong indication that the charges he brings against us are false. [34] You see, many people who knew that woman who is, as he says, a notorious ribbon-seller, could properly give testimony and not only testimony based on hearsay evidence; and if she was an alien, they ought to have examined the duties paid in the Agora and should have shown whether she was paying the alien tax[36] and where she was from. If she was a slave, the man who bought her should have come forward to testify against her, and if not he, then the man who sold her; if not he, then some other man should have testified, either that she was a slave or that she had been set free. But in fact, he showed none of these things; but only hurled abuse, so it seems to me, of every sort. This is the *sykophant*'s game: to allege everything but prove nothing. [35] He also has said this about my mother, that she was a wet-nurse. We do not deny that this happened when the city suffered misfortune and everybody was doing badly. I will tell you clearly how and for what reason she was a wet-nurse. None of you, men of Athens, should take this in the wrong way, since even now you will find that many Athenian women (*astai*) are wet-nurses; if you wish, I will identify them for you by name.[37] Now, if we were rich, we would not be selling ribbons, nor would we be in such dire straits. But what does this have to do with our ancestry? Nothing, in my opinion. [36] No, gentlemen of the jury, do not dishonor the poor—being poor is trouble enough for them—or those who choose to work and get a living by honest means. Instead, once you have heard us out, if I show that my mother's relatives are the sort of people free men should be, and they deny under oath these slanders cast upon

---

[36] The officials in charge of collecting these duties were known as *agoranomoi* (*Ath. Pol.* 51.1).

[37] This is presumably only a rhetorical offer. If the speaker actually did name living, respectable Athenian citizen women, it would be an exception to the observed practice.

her, and they—people whom you will acknowledge as credible—testify that they know she is an Athenian (*astē*), cast your vote for justice. [37] Now, my grandfather, men of Athens, my mother's father, was Damostratus of the deme Melite. He had four children; from his first wife he had a daughter and a son, whose name is Amytheon; with Chaerestrate, his second wife, he had my mother and Timocrates. They had children: Amytheon had a son named for my grandfather Damostratus, as well as Callistratus and Dexitheus. Amytheon, my mother's brother, was among those who fought and died in Sicily,[38] and he is buried in the public tombs: this too will be attested. [38] His sister married Diodorus of the deme Halae, and they had a son, Ctesibios, who died in Abydus, on campaign with Thrasybulus;[39] of these, still living is Damostratus, Amytheon's son, my mother's nephew. Apollodorus of the deme Plotheia married the sister of my grandmother Chaerestrate. Their son is Olympichus, and they had a son, Apollodorus, who is living. [To the clerk] Please call them.

[WITNESSES]

[39] You have heard these men testifying and swearing the oath. Now I will call a man who is related to my mother on both sides, together with his sons. You see, Timocrates, my mother's brother, from the same father and mother, had a son, Euxitheus, and Euxitheus had three sons. All these men are living. [To the clerk] Please call those of them who are in Athens.

[WITNESSES]

[40] [To the clerk] Please take the depositions of my fellow phratry and deme members related to my mother, men who have the same ancestral tombs.

---

[38] Athens' great campaign against Syracuse began in 415 and ended in utter defeat two years later.

[39] This could refer to one of two men of that name. The more likely possibility is Thrasybulus of the deme Collytus, who is known to have commanded forces in the area of Abydus (on the Asian coast of the Hellespont) in 387. Less likely is the illustrious democratic hero of the resistance to the coup d'état of the Four Hundred (411) and the civil war against the Thirty (404/3).

[DEPOSITIONS]

I have demonstrated that as regards my mother's descent, she was an Athenian (*astē*) on both the male and female side. My mother, gentlemen of the jury, was first given in marriage by Timocrates, her brother from the same father and mother, to Protomachus, and had a daughter; subsequently, with my father, she had me. You should hear how it came about that she married my father. I will give you a clear account of all the charges Eubulides makes concerning Cleinias[40] and my mother working as a wet-nurse. [41] Protomachus was a poor man. Because he stood to win the inheritance of a rich *epiklēros*,[41] Protomachus wanted to marry my mother off, and he persuaded my father Thucrites, an acquaintance of his, to take her. My father married her in a ceremony[42] in which her brother, Timocrates of the deme Melite, gave her away, and both his uncles and other men witnessed the ceremony. Those men in that group still alive will give you their testimony. [42] Later on, when my mother had two babies, my father went away on campaign with Thrasybulus; because she was without means, she was forced to serve as a wet-nurse to Cleinias the son of Cleidicus. Doing that brought no advantage, by Zeus, to me in the danger that would come, since this work as a wet-nurse is the source of all the slander about us; but perhaps she did this both under the compulsion of the poverty that beset her and as a way of adapting to it. [43] Now it is plain, men of Athens, that my mother's first husband was not my father, but Protomachus, and that he had children with her and gave their daughter in marriage. Protomachus is dead, but he bears witness by his actions that my mother was an Athenian (*astē*) and a citizen (*politis*). [To the clerk] To show that what I say is true, please call first the sons of Protomachus; next, those who were present when my father

_____

[40] This Cleinias may have been related to the family of Alcibiades. See Davies 1971: 14.

[41] A woman "attached" to an inheritance but not truly an heiress in her own right, since only males could inherit. By marrying an *epiklēros,* a man would become the trustee of the property, pending the maturity of sons from that marriage. As the heiress' closest male relative, Protomachus was obliged either to marry her himself or to find a husband for her. He chose the former course.

[42] This ceremony, in Greek *egguēsis,* consisted simply in the bride's legal guardian declaring that he was granting her to the groom.

married my mother and men close to him in his phratry, for whom he gave the marriage feast for my mother; then Eunicus of the deme Cholargus, who from Protomachus received my sister in marriage; and then my sister's son. Call these men.

[WITNESSES]

[44] I would certainly suffer most pitiably of all people if despite all these many relatives here testifying under oath that they are related to me—and no one claims that any of them are not citizens—you vote that I am an alien. [To the clerk] Please take the depositions of Cleinias and his relatives. These people certainly know who my mother was when she nursed him. You know, the oaths do not demand that they attest what I'm saying today but what they have known all along about a woman thought to be my mother *and* Cleinias' wet-nurse. [45] You know, if the wet-nurse is a humble thing, I do not run away from the truth. We did nothing wrong, after all, if we were poor, but only if we were not citizens: and the present trial now is not about our luck or our money but about our descent. Poverty forces free men to do many servile, humble things: and it would be more in keeping with justice if they will be pitied for that, men of Athens, than if they are pushed further into ruin. I have heard that owing to the city's misfortunes at the time, many Athenian women (*astai*) became wet-nurses, servants, and grape harvesters, and many Athenian women (*astai*) rose from poverty to riches. But I'll turn to that subject soon. [To the clerk] For now, call the witnesses.

[WITNESSES]

[46] That I am an Athenian (*astos*) on both my mother's and father's side you have all learned from the testimony just given and from what was earlier presented concerning my father. It remains for me to speak to you about myself—I think what I have to say is perfectly straightforward and most in accord with justice—that I, an Athenian on both sides (*astoi*), the heir to both my estate and line of descent, am a citizen. Nevertheless, by providing witnesses I will demonstrate all the pertinent facts: that I was introduced to my phratry[43] and en-

---

[43] An Athenian would be introduced to his phratry sometime in childhood, perhaps even in infancy.

rolled in my deme,[44] I was chosen by the deme members themselves to draw lots with men of the best lineage for service as priest of Heracles,[45] and that, after passing the scrutiny (*dokimasia*), I served in office. Please call them.

[WITNESSES]

[47] Isn't it terrible, gentlemen of the jury? If I had drawn the lot for priest when I was selected to participate in the drawing, I would have been required in my own person to sacrifice on behalf of the deme members, and Eubulides would have been required to sacrifice along with me, but as it is, these same men do not allow me to sacrifice with them? Thus I have been clearly acknowledged, men of Athens, all along, by all my current accusers, as a citizen. [48] After all, Eubulides would not have allowed this alien or metic (resident alien),[46] as he now says I am, to serve in magistracies or to be selected to draw lots for the priesthood alongside him. He too, you see, was among those selected to draw lots. And as my enemy from long before, he would not have waited until this opportunity now, which no one anticipated, if he had known such a thing about me then. [49] But he did *not* know it, and that is why until now, while he was a member of the deme with me and participating in the lottery for the priesthood, he saw none of these things; but only when the whole city was filled with anger at the men who had outrageously jumped into the demes, did he *then* start to plot against me. On that earlier occasion a man who was certain of the truth of his assertion should have acted. But the present occasion is the time only for a personal enemy or a man who wants to play the *sykophant* to come forward. [50] Now please, gentlemen of the jury, by Zeus and the other gods, let no one shout, let no one get angry at what I am about to say. I think of myself as an Athenian, just as each of you

---

[44] Deme enrollment took place when the boy was eighteen.

[45] Insistence on choosing priests from aristocratic families for this cult suggests the reality or pretense that the cult was very old, even though the demes in their classical configuration dated only from the late sixth-century reforms of Cleisthenes.

[46] Neither would be an Athenian citizen, but it is peculiar that this possibility is first mentioned here.

does; I thought my mother was, from the start, the woman I have been describing to you, and I was not pretending to be her son while really the son of another woman. And the same thing, men of Athens, goes for my father. [51] So if you rightly take it as a sign of people being aliens that they are exposed as hiding the identity of their true parents and pretending they are someone else's children, then surely the opposite should show that I am a citizen. I would not, after all, claim to have a share in the city, while inscribing myself as the son of an alien woman and man. Instead, if I knew this was the case, I would have searched for people to claim as my parents. But I did not know any such thing, and so, sticking with my real parents, I claim my rightful share in the city. [52] Further, I was left an orphan,[47] and they say that I am well off and that some of my witnesses are paid to testify that they are my relatives. They simultaneously criticize me for the disgrace of poverty and slander me in regards to my descent, *and* they say that with my riches I have bought everything. [53] So which claims should be believed? Certainly it was open to these people who testified on my behalf to inherit all my property if I was in fact illegitimate or an alien. So then, they *chose* for a small payment to run the risk of a suit for false witness (*pseudomarturia*) and to perjure themselves—rather than receive everything, risk free and without subjecting themselves to utter destruction?[48] This is impossible. Instead, I think that, being my relatives, they did the right thing in helping one of their own. [54] They are not just doing this because they were persuaded,[49] but right away when I was a baby they introduced me to the phratry,[50] to the shrine of our ancestral Apollo, and to the other sacred places. I certainly could not, when a boy, bribe them to do that! No, my father, while still alive, himself swore the customary oath when he introduced me to the phratry members, that he knew that I was an Athenian (*astos*) born of an Athenian woman (*astē*) betrothed to him, and this has been presented

---

[47] The Greek word *orphanos* means only "without a father" and does not necessarily imply that the "orphan" is a child.

[48] In taking an oath, a man would call "utter destruction" down on himself if he violated the oath.

[49] In Greek rhetoric, "persuaded" often implies "paid" or "bribed."

[50] See above, 47 with note.

in testimony. [55] So I am an alien? Where did I pay the tax on met-ics?[51] Who in my family ever did so? Did I go to some other deme, and when I could not persuade them to enroll me, did I inscribe myself here? Where did I do any of the things that men improperly made citizens are seen doing? Nowhere, but quite simply, the deme of my father's grandfather, my grandfather, and my father is the deme in which I too am clearly a member. Now, how could anyone show you more plainly that he has a share in the city? [56] So let each one of you, men of Athens, think how he would show that his relatives were the same from the start using another method than I have: by having them give testimony under oath.

Feeling confidence in myself for these reasons I have turned to you for refuge. After all, men of Athens, I see that the courts hold greater authority not only than the voters of the deme Halimus who have ex-cluded me but even than the Council and the Assembly—and rightly so, since your decisions are in all matters the most just.[52]

[57] You who are members of the large demes, think about this too, that you have deprived no one of the opportunity to accuse or defend—and may you all enjoy many blessings for dealing with this business in a just manner—because when men were asking for postponements, you did not take away the opportunity to prepare. By that policy you have exposed the *sykophants* and those who lay plots in pursuit of pri-vate enmity. [58] You deserve praise, men of Athens, just as those who wrongly use a good and just procedure deserve blame. You will not find that more terrible acts happened in any other deme than ours. These men struck from the rolls some full brothers but not others, and they excluded men who were old and poor but retained their sons. If you wish, I will provide witnesses to these acts too. [59] But the most aw-ful thing of all that these conspirators did was this—and by Zeus and the gods, let no one be annoyed if I show that those who have wronged me are wicked men, since I think that in revealing their wickedness to you I am speaking precisely on the subject of what happened to me.[53]

---

[51] Amounting to twelve drachmas a year, not an onerous sum.

[52] Arist., *Politics* 1274a4–5: [Some blamed Solon] for "making the court all-powerful."

[53] See 7n.

Now then, these men, gentlemen of Athens, divided among themselves some aliens who wanted to become citizens, Anaximenes and Nico-stratus,[54] and they took money from them, each of them getting five drachmas. Eubulides and the others of his group would not deny on oath they knew about this business, and they did not now[55] strike them from the rolls. Now, what do you think these men would *not* do in private matters, seeing that they dared to do that in a public matter?[56] [60] Gentlemen of the jury, the men who conspire with Eubulides have ruined and saved many men for money. Even before—I will speak to the issue, men of Athens—when he was serving as demarch, Eubulides' father Antiphilus, as I have mentioned, contrived to get money from certain men; he claimed that he lost the public deme register, and thus he persuaded the men of the deme Halimus to conduct a *diapsēphisis* of their deme; he prosecuted and expelled ten of the deme members, all but one of whom the court restored to membership. All the older men know this. [61] It is very unlikely that they left on the rolls any who were not Athenians, seeing that they expelled true citizens, whom the court restored. And yet, although he was an enemy of my father, Antiphilus did not then make an accusation against him and in fact did not even vote that he was not an Athenian. How do we know this? Because absolutely all the deme members voted that he was. But why should we talk about fathers? This man here, Eubulides himself, when my name was put on the register and all the deme members, under oath, cast their ballots about my case in the proper way, neither made an accusation nor voted against me. You see, on that occasion too they voted unanimously that I was a member of the deme. And if they say I am lying about this, any one of them who wants may give testimony during my allotted time. [62] If, gentlemen of the jury, you think these men have a strong point in arguing that the deme has now voted to expel me, I show that four times before, when they voted in a pious fashion, in the absence of any conspiracy, they voted that I and my father were fellow deme members: first, the time when my father underwent his scrutiny (*dokimasia*); then at my own scrutiny; then

---

[54]Nothing else is known about these naturalized Athenians.

[55]I.e., in the *diapsēphisis* by which Euxitheus was expelled from the deme.

[56]Some understand the contrast to be between individual and collective action.

in the earlier *diapsēphisis,* when these men made the register disappear; and finally, when they voted to select me for the lottery for the priesthood of Heracles, along with others from the best families. All this too has been attested.

[63] But if I must mention my service as *demarch,* which caused some to be angry at me, because I quarreled with many of them when I exacted payments, many for sacred lands[57] and for other things they stole from public property, I would like you to hear about it—but perhaps you will regard this as off the point. In this matter too I can produce evidence that they have conspired. You see, they have expunged from the oath the phrase "will vote with my most honest judgment and without favoritism or enmity."[58] [64] This business became notorious, and also that those men whom I made reimburse the public treasury conspired against me: they committed the sacrilege of stealing the arms—this *will* be said—that I had dedicated to Athena and erased the decree that the deme members voted in my honor.[59] And they have become so shameless that they have been going around saying that *I* did this to help my defense. Who among you, gentlemen of the jury, would convict me of such extreme insanity that just to have evidence of such significance for my case I would commit acts worthy of execution and do away with the inscription that brought me distinction? [65] And they surely would not say that I contrived the most outrageous act of all. You see, my luck had just turned bad when immediately, as if I were already in exile[60] and a ruined man, some of them came to my small house in the country at night and tried to carry off what was inside. That is how great a contempt they had for you and the laws. If you want, we will call those who know these facts.

[66] I have many other things to show, things they did and lies they told, that I would gladly tell you, but since you regard them as off the

---

[57] Presumably rent payments were at issue.

[58] Cf. the phrase "I will listen to both sides impartially" in the jurymen's oath found in the manuscripts of Dem. 24.149–151. Presumably the speaker means the oath taken by the deme members before voting in a *diapsēphisis.*

[59] An expression of gratitude of the type found in profusion among the surviving inscriptions.

[60] See the Introduction for the possibility of evading slavery by preemptive self-exile.

point,[61] I will omit them. But remember those things I have told you
and see with what an abundance of just claims I have come before you.
Just as you interrogate candidates for *thesmothetēs,* so will I in the same
way interrogate myself.[62] **[67]** "Sir, who was your father?" "My father?
Thucritus." "Are there relatives who will testify for him?" "Certainly.
To start, four first cousins,[63] then a cousin's son, then the men who
married the female cousins, then phratry members, then clan members
sharing a cult of Ancestral Apollo and Household Zeus,[64] then those
who shared the same tombs, then deme members to attest that he
often passed scrutiny (*dokimasia*) and served in magistracies, and who
themselves clearly confirmed him as a citizen at the *diapsēphisis.* How
could I more properly or honestly show you the facts about my father?
I will call these relatives for you, if you wish. Now hear the facts about
my mother. **[68]** My mother is Nicarete, the daughter of Damostratus
of the deme Melite. Which relatives will testify for her? First a nephew,
then two sons of another nephew, then a cousin's son, then the sons of
Protomachus, who was my mother's first husband, then Eunicus of the
deme Cholargus, who married my sister, Protomachus' daughter, then
my sister's son. **[69]** Further, her relatives' fellow phratry members and
also their fellow deme members have given the same testimony. What
else do you need? After all, there has already been testimony that my
father married in accordance with the laws and held a wedding feast
for his phratry. Besides, I have demonstrated that I myself participated
in everything appropriate to free men. The result is that you would
honorably and properly abide by your oaths if you cast your ballot
for us. **[70]** Further, gentlemen of the jury, when you interrogate the
nine archons you ask whether they treat their parents decently. Well,

---

[61] Perhaps the jury and spectators shouted the speaker down at the trial, im-
pelling him to omit some of what he was going to say, and this event motivated a
revision when the speech was published.

[62] The *thesmothetai* were the six Archons who administered the popular courts.
On this passage, see Adele Scafuro, "Witnessing and False Witnessing," in A. L.
Boegehold and A. C. Scafuro (eds.), *Athenian Identity and Civic Ideology* (Balti-
more, 1994), 165–169.

[63] See 21n.

[64] Lit. "Zeus of the Courtyard," so called because a small statue of Zeus stood
in the courtyards of many Athenian houses.

I was left orphaned by my father, and I beg and beseech you: by this trial give me back the right to bury my mother in our ancestral tombs, and do not prevent me from doing so. Do not make me an outcast from my city, do not deprive me of so many family members, and do not utterly destroy me. Rather than leave them behind if I cannot be saved by them, I would kill myself, so they could at least bury me in my fatherland.

58. AGAINST THEOCRINES

INTRODUCTION

Acting, he says, to avenge his father, a man named Epichares[1] brought a denunciation of the sort called an *endeixis* against his father's enemy, Theocrines.[2] The father was debarred from bringing the prosecution himself: he had been disenfranchised (*atimos*) ever since Theocrines had successfully prosecuted him on a charge of unconstitutional action (*graphē paranomōn*[3]) (30). Epichares' father pressured his young and inexperienced son to institute litigation (2) and coached him in some detail (5). The specific complaint in Epichares' *endeixis* is that Theocrines had himself brought two prosecutions, despite his being a state debtor (*opheilōn tōi dēmōsiōi*) and therefore prohibited as *atimos* from doing so.

Our sources for the procedure of *endeixis* are not extensive, and there has been disagreement among scholars as to some of its features,

---

[1] As in the case of some other trials, it is not the text itself that provides the speaker's name, but the *hypothesis* by Libanius. It is possible that Libanius was simply guessing that, like many Greeks, the speaker bore his grandfather's name (see 67), a man about whom there is some independent evidence if he is indeed Epichares of the deme Cholleidae. Even if that was the speaker's name, his identification is problematic, as it is a common name (Osborne and Byrne 1994 list eighty-five men called Epichares).

[2] Aside from this speech, Theocrines has left no trace in our evidence.

[3] By a *graphē paranomōn*, a public action charging that a decree (*psēphisma*) was contrary to the laws. Formally, the charge was directed against the decree, which would be nullified if the action succeeded, but the man who proposed it was also in jeopardy.

especially how it relates to *apagōgē*.[4] Etymology suggests translating *endeixis* as "pointing to" and *apagōgē* as "taking away," but neither these translations nor the more idiomatic (and technical sounding) "indictment" and "arrest" are very informative. The most comprehensive study of these procedures to date, that of M. H. Hansen,[5] argues that they are "two phases of the same type of process." *Endeixis* and *apagōgē* did not, in Hansen's view, differ according to whether the prosecutor himself or state officials arrested the alleged offender; the real differences were (1) that only *apagōgē* required the claim that the person or persons arrested had been caught in the criminal act, (2) that an *endeixis* might require a summons, but an *apagōgē*, by its very nature ("summary arrest") did not, and (3) that the prosecutor in an *endeixis* (but not an *apagōgē*) might have had the option to agree to bail for the defendant. But there is no scholarly consensus on these points, and much remains uncertain about these procedures.

The authorship of this speech has been controversial since antiquity. Callimachus, the great Alexandrian poet and scholar of Greek literature (third century BC), listed the speech in his catalogue of speeches by Demosthenes, but Dionysius of Halicarnassus (first century BC–first century AD) believed it was written by Dinarchus, the last of the canonical Attic orators. This was a deduction from the speaker's invective against Demosthenes for withdrawing his support (42) and Dinarchus' unquestionable hatred for Demosthenes (see Din. 1, *Against Demosthenes*). Harpocration, a lexicographer of the first or second century AD, straddled the fence, attributing the speech to either Demosthenes or Dinarchus. Libanius (fourth century AD) concludes his summary of the speech (the *hypothesis*) with the declaration: "Many regard the speech as belonging to Dinarchus, but it does not differ from Demosthenes' speeches."[6] Scholars of the modern period have for the most part doubted that either Demosthenes or Dinarchus could be the

---

[4] Other relevant speeches: Ant. 5; And. 1; Lys. 6; Dem. 25, 26.

[5] Hansen 1976: esp. 1–24. For a summary of the case at hand, see 137–138.

[6] In fact, the stylistic features intensively studied in the nineteenth century, relative indifference to hiatus and runs of three short syllables, suggest the contrary (see the Introduction to Dem. 56).

author. Arnold Schaeffer, the great nineteenth-century Demosthenic scholar, thought it was written by someone "second rate."[7] The frequent inelegance of the Greek challenges the translator and appears to confirm Schaeffer's judgment.

The speech is dated to 341 or 340, a few years after the archonship of Lyciscus (28) but probably before Demosthenes' ascendancy in guiding Athenian policy toward Philip.

58. AGAINST THEOCRINES

[1] Gentlemen of the jury, our father suffered a misfortune in his public life, thanks to Theocrines here, and owed the treasury ten talents; then this sum was doubled,[8] leaving us no hope of salvation. For this reason, giving no weight to my youth or any other consideration, I thought I must bring this *endeixis* to punish him, with your help. [2] You see, gentlemen of the jury, my father, whom I have obeyed in everything, has been complaining to all his acquaintances that I might let the opportunity pass by when, because he is still alive,[9] I could take vengeance on this man, and by making my inexperience and youth a pretext, allow him to be robbed of everything, while Theocrines illegally indicts many of the citizens and pursues them in malicious prosecution,[10] though it is not his right to do so. [3] So I ask you all, men of Athens, and I beg you to give me a friendly hearing, first because I am in court helping my father and obeying him, and second because I am young and inexperienced and would be content if I am able, with your goodwill, to expose this man's deeds. [4] Besides that, gentlemen of the jury, I have been betrayed—you will be told the truth—by men we trusted because of their hatred for Theocrines. When they learned what happened, they said they would join me in the litigation, but they

---

[7] *Demosthenes und seine Zeit,* Vol. 3 (Leipzig, 1858), 279–280.

[8] See *Ath. Pol.* 48.1, with the commentary by P. J. Rhodes.

[9] Once the father dies, the speaker would inherit his father's *atimia* (disenfranchisement) as a state debtor; then his diminished status would bar him from prosecuting Theocrines.

[10] Lit. "acting as a *sykophant*" (see 53.1n).

have now abandoned me and have reached a settlement with Theocrines in this matter, with the outcome that there is now no one who will speak on my side, unless one of my own relatives helps out.

[5] Now, Theocrines here was liable to many *endeixeis,* and clearly in violation of all the laws dealing with them. But the most recent of his acts is, we find, the denunciation (*phasis*[11]) concerning the boat; accordingly, my father wrote this into the *endeixis* he gave me. The clerk will read you first the law concerning those who initiate a *phasis* but instead of carrying them through, make an illegal settlement. I suppose that it is fitting for me to start my speech at this point. Then the clerk will read the specific *phasis,* which Theocrines brought against Micon.[12] [To the clerk] Read it.

[LAW]

[6] This law, gentlemen of the jury, explicitly stipulates the terms on which those who choose to do so must enter indictments (*graphai*) or *phasis* actions or do any of the things included in the law. The terms are as follows, as you have heard in the law itself: if a prosecutor does not get a fifth of the votes, he pays a penalty of one thousand drachmas and, Theocrines, if he does not bring the prosecution, he pays another thousand. The purpose is that no one engage in *sykophancy* or, with impunity, make a profit by abandoning the city's interests. I contend that Theocrines is subject to this *endeixis,* because he initiated a *phasis* against Micon of the deme Collytus but did not prosecute him; instead, he accepted a bribe and let the matter go. [7] And I think I will also demonstrate this clearly. And yet, gentlemen of the jury, Theocrines and his band have left no stone unturned in approaching witnesses, sometimes threatening, sometimes bribing them not to testify.

---

[11] The *phasis* procedure (lit. "showing") was a denunciation for certain actions, including importing grain to any destination but Athens (cf. Dem. 56), the maltreatment of orphans, or the illegal possession of state property. A successful prosecutor, who did not need to claim any personal injury from the offense, would be awarded one-half of the fine imposed by the court. For that reason, it was a procedure particularly attractive for *sykophants.* Evidence for *phasis* is scanty, consisting mainly of this speech and a scene in Aristophanes' comedy, the *Acharnians.*

[12] Micon's identity is quite uncertain. See Davies 1971: 57–58f.

Nevertheless, if you want to help me, as is right, and if you order these men—or rather, join me in forcing them—either to testify or to swear that they know nothing about it, and if you do not permit them to jabber away, the truth will be discovered. [To the clerk] First read the *phasis* and then the depositions.

[*PHASIS*]

[8] Gentlemen of the jury, Theocrines summoned Micon and presented this *phasis,* and Euthyphemus, the market supervisors' clerk,[13] received it. The *phasis* was displayed for a long time before their meeting place[14] until Theocrines took a bribe and, when the archons called him to the *anakrisis* (preliminary hearing), let the *phasis* be erased. To show that I am telling the truth [to the clerk], call Euthyphemus, who served as secretary to the board.

[DEPOSITION]

[9] [To the clerk] Now read the deposition given by those who saw the *phasis* publicly displayed.

[DEPOSITION]

[To the clerk] Call the market supervisors and Micon himself, whose boat was the subject of the *phasis,* and read out the depositions.

[DEPOSITIONS]

[10] You have heard, gentlemen of the jury, from those witnesses who were in the best position to know about it, that Theocrines denounced Micon's boat, that the denunciation was displayed for a long time, and that when summoned to the preliminary hearing, he did not respond and did not carry through with the prosecution. And from the law itself you will readily learn that he is liable not only to the thousand-drachma fine but also to summary arrest (*apagōgē*)[15] and the other procedures that this law stipulates for the man who engages in *sykophancy*

---

[13]Men selected by lot to supervise the grain trade. See *Ath. Pol.* 51.4.
[14]I.e., the office of the market supervisors.
[15]Summary arrest: see the Series Introduction, p. xxvi, and the Introduction to this speech.

against the merchants and ship owners. [11] The man who made this law, with the intent that corrupt merchants not go unpunished and that the others not have difficulties, simply forbade men from bringing *phasis* actions if they lacked the confidence to demonstrate to you that the violations alleged in the *phasis* had in fact occurred. And if a *sykophant* acts in violation of that rule, he is subject to *endeixis* and *apagōgē*. [To the clerk] But read the law itself, since it will explain this business better than I can.

[LAW]

[12] You hear, gentlemen of the jury, what the law orders to be done to the *sykophant*. Accordingly, if Micon has done any of the things that Theocrines in his *phasis* accused him of doing and Theocrines has abandoned the matter and reached a settlement with the man, he does all of you wrong and deservedly owes the thousand drachmas. But if, on the other hand—men of Athens, let Theocrines choose between the alternatives—Micon sailed to a legitimate market, and Theocrines denounced him for that and summoned him, then he brings a malicious accusation against the ship owners and has violated not only the first law read out but also the one read out just now, and he has testified against himself that his speech and his actions are corrupt. [13] After all, who would relinquish the opportunity to act justly and claim a portion of the reward in accordance with the law and would instead want to reach a settlement and, for only a small additional profit, make himself liable under the laws, when he could, as I was just saying, get half of the value of the denounced property? No one, gentlemen of the jury, unless he knew he was guilty of engaging in *sykophancy*.

[14] These then are two laws that the man who indicts others for unconstitutional action [16] violates. There is also a third law, which stipulates that any volunteer from among the citizens may enter an *endeixis* against anyone in debt to the state, or to Athena, or to any of the other gods, or to any of the Eponymous Heroes. I will show that Theocrines is a debtor belonging to that category, as he has not paid the seven hundred–drachma fine to his tribe's Eponymous Hero that was assessed at his *euthyna*. [17] [To the clerk] Please read this part of the law.

---

[16] Lit. brings a *graphē paranomōn*.

[17] The rendering of accounts to which all officials were subject at the conclusion of their term.

[LAW]

[**15**] [To the clerk] Stop. You, Theocrines, do you hear what it says? ". . . or to any one of the Eponymous Heroes." [To the clerk] Now read the testimony of the tribe members.

[DEPOSITION]

Theocrines, gentlemen of the jury, would probably not have respect for many men or for those like Micon who spend most of the time sailing, seeing that he did not feel shame before his fellow tribe members or fear them while he managed their public business so badly that they convicted him of theft or when he was in debt to the state, though he knew very well that the laws forbade his bringing an indictment until he paid the fine. He was, thereby, doing violence to the laws in the belief that other men who owe fines should have no share in public life, but that *he* was above the law. [**16**] Now, he will say that it was his grandfather, not he, whose name is inscribed on the list of state debtors,[18] and he will talk at length about it, claiming that it is *that* man instead. I cannot say for certain which of the two it is; but if it is his grandfather, as Theocrines will say, I think it is all the more just that you convict him, if this is so. [**17**] For if his grandfather has long been in debt to the state, and the law provides that he is his grandfather's heir, and he has long been bringing indictments, although it was wrong for him to do so;[19] and if for this reason he will think that he should be acquitted, namely, that he is a third-generation scoundrel, then he will not be saying what is just, gentlemen of the jury. [To the clerk] Now, to show that Theocrines himself admits that this was the fine, and that it was set by the tribe members in his name and his brother's, and that it is wrong for those who wish to be true to their oaths to reject this *endeixis,* please take the decree that Scironides[20] proposed at the tribal assembly. [**18**] Theocrines came forward and admitted that he was a state debtor, and he said, in the presence of tribe members, that he would

---

[18] That would, of course, mean that grandfather and grandson shared the name Theocrines.

[19] This shows that disenfranchisement (*atimia*) could be inherited. The same argument would, of course, apply to the speaker, whose father has been disenfranchised (see note on 58.2).

[20] Not otherwise known.

pay the fine—when he saw us coming forward wanting to make copies of the names written on the list.

[DECREE]

Men of the tribe Leontis, you would have had much higher praise for those who forced Theocrines to pay back the seven minas than for Theocrines himself.[21] [19] There is a fourth law—yes, I admit that I have done extensive research on most of this man's deeds—according to which Theocrines here owes five hundred drachmas, as his father did not pay the supplementary fine he owed for claiming that Cephisodorus' slave was a free woman;[22] instead, he settled things with Ctesicles the speechwriter (*logographos*),[23] who was involved on his adversaries' side, so that he neither paid the fine nor had his name posted on the Acropolis.[24] [20] So I think that right now Theocrines owes the money just as much, according to the law. You see, if Ctesicles the metic makes a deal with him, one bad man with another, that someone who by law owes an extra fine not be turned over to the official collectors, this would cause the city to be cheated of fines that are set by the laws. No, rather, it is fitting for legal opponents in private suits to make whatever mutual arrangements with each other they agree to among themselves, but in public matters they must arrange things as the laws require. [21] [To the clerk] Please read both the law that requires that a man convicted of illegally asserting that a slave is a free

---

[21] An obscure passage. The translation follows the Oxford Classical Text editor, who believes that the speaker is addressing the men of the tribe Leontis, making a rueful reference to their voting on some occasion to honor Theocrines with an official laudation. The editor acknowledges that such an address to a portion of the jury is unusual but notes the apostrophe to the proposer of a law at 56.

[22] Even if Theocrines' father did no more than make a symbolic declaration that the woman was not a slave, he was liable to prosecution by the man who claimed to be her rightful owner. It is curious that along with the defrauded owner, the state treasury stood to profit from a successful prosecution. At the end of the next section, Epichares explains the additional fine. Cephisodorus is not otherwise known. (For details, see Harrison 1968–1971, Vol. I: 178–179, 221.)

[23] Like Lysias, Isaeus, and Dinarchus, a metic (see 20) and speechwriter. It is likely that the speaker hopes to excite prejudice against Theocrines by associating him with a man who falls in both these categories.

[24] I.e., as a state debtor.

person pay to the public treasury one-half of the assessed value of the slave, and Cephisodorus' testimony.

[LAW] [DEPOSITION]

[To the clerk] Read also that law that stipulates that the man is in debt starting from the day he is fined, whether his name is posted or not.

[LAW]

[22] What other proof, gentlemen of the jury, is it right for an honest prosecutor to present that Theocrines here is correctly named in an *endeixis* and that he is liable in the *endeixis* not only for the thousand drachmas for which he is indicted but for many other fines? For my part, I think there is no other way. After all, Theocrines should not be expected to acknowledge on his own that he is in debt to the state treasury and to agree that he is properly indicted but rather to present exactly the opposite argument and bring in all sorts of accusations, claiming he is the victim of a conspiracy, that he has fallen into this situation because of the indictments he has brought for illegal actions (*graphai paranomōn*). [23] This is the last refuge for people who are proved wrong in the relevant matters, to devise accusations and excuses that will make you forget the matter at hand and turn your attention to arguments extraneous to the charge. Gentlemen of the jury, I would have kept my peace if I had seen this written in the laws that have been read out: "This is binding in the case of *sykophants,* unless Theocrines has been indicted and wishes to bring charges against Thucydides,[25] or Demosthenes, or any other politician." But in fact, I do not see any of these excuses listed in the laws as a mitigating factor, and it is not a new excuse that you are hearing for the first time and should pay attention to; no, it has been put forward countless times by men on trial. [24] I hear from the older men, gentlemen of the jury, that it is not fitting in general to forgive anyone who broke the law, but if anyone should be forgiven, it should not be chronic villains or those who betray the laws for money—that would not be reasonable—but those who, from lack of experience, involuntarily violate some provi-

---

[25]Not otherwise known. He is, of course, not the historian with whom he shared a name.

sion of the written laws. Certainly nobody would say Theocrines belongs to that category; on the contrary, there is nothing in the laws with which he is *not* familiar.[26] [**25**] For that reason you must watch him, keeping your eye not on my words or those that he will utter. It is not right, after all, that those who sit here to defend the laws concentrate on long speeches and accusations but rather on matters that all of you could easily follow and by means of which you will show everyone in the city that you have judged this *endeixis* in a manner worthy of the laws. So ask him plainly,[27] "Theocrines and all who engage in the same activities as he does, what do you say? Do you think it right that we, men sworn to judge according to the laws, vote contrary to those laws because of your speeches? [**26**] When Micon, the man against whom Theocrines here initiated a *phasis* but did not pursue it, has given us his testimony and made himself legally responsible for his testimony, and when the clerk agrees that he accepted the *phasis* from him, and in the deposition that was read out a little while ago he too has made himself responsible? Further, when the market supervisors, though reluctant, nonetheless gave the same testimony as Micon and the clerk? And on top of that, when men who saw the *phasis* posted and went to the Archons have testified, as you heard a little earlier?" No, that would not be right, gentlemen of the jury.

[**27**] The defendant's habits and lifestyle will certainly not lead you to suppose that the depositions that have been read out are false, since Theocrines will demonstrate his character far more clearly from his habits than through his words. What has he *not* done that an evil *sykophant* would do? Isn't it true that on account of Theocrines' baseness his brother, while serving as a *thesmothetēs* and turning to Theocrines for advice, gained such a bad reputation that at the confidence vote on magistrates (*epicheirotonia tōn archōn*) he was not only suspended but caused the dismissal of the entire board?[28] And if they had not begged and supplicated and promised that Theocrines would no longer approach the board and if you had not been persuaded to return their

---

[26]Cf. 57.5n.

[27]Though heckling by the jury and spectators was probably a common phenomenon in the courts (see 57.6n), jurors could not formally make requests; thus these "scripts" that a speaker suggests to the jury should not be taken literally.

[28]For this procedure, whereby any Athenian citizen could propose the expulsion from office of any magistrate, see Hansen 1999: 220–221.

crowns,[29] wouldn't his colleagues on the board have suffered the worst possible disgrace? [28] I do not need to provide you with witnesses for this, since you all know that the *thesmothetai* in the year of Lysiscus' archonship[30] were removed from office by vote of the Assembly because of Theocrines. You should remember these events and assume that this man is the same man now as he was before. Indeed, not long after his removal from office, his brother died a violent death, and *this* was the attitude Theocrines took towards him: he sought out the perpetrators, and when he learned who they were, he accepted money to settle the case.[31] [29] His brother was serving as a Sacrificer (*hieropoios*)[32] when he died, and Theocrines illegally assumed this position, though he was not selected by lottery to fill the position or to be the alternate.[33] He went around complaining bitterly about what had happened to his brother, saying that he would summon Demochares to the Areopagus—right up to the moment that he settled with the guilty parties. What an honest man, so trustworthy, so immune to bribery! Even he would not make this claim. People say that a man who will honestly and fittingly take care of public matters should not want much but should be beyond the temptation to spend on themselves the funds that pass through their hands. [30] So much for the character of his actions in regard to his brother, but now it is worth hearing about his conduct since he entered politics: you know, he will say that after his family, he loves you the best. I will start with what he did to us. In the charge he brought against my father, gentlemen of the jury, when he prosecuted him for unconstitutional action (*graphē paranomōn*), Theocrines said that the boy who was the subject of the decree was the victim of a plot. My father had proposed that Charidemus, the son of Ischomachus, be awarded free meals in the *prytaneion*.[34] [31] Theocrines contended that if the son returned to his father's home,

---

[29] Archons normally wore a myrtle garland as a badge of their office (Lys. 26.8; cf. *Ath. Pol.* 58.4).

[30] 344/3.

[31] Though the speaker assumes the jurors will find Theocrines' action reprehensible, such a settlement did not violate Athenian homicide law.

[32] For the duties of this magistracy, see *Ath. Pol.* 54.6.

[33] I.e., to substitute for a man who failed the eligibility test (*dokimasia*).

[34] There is no reliable information on this family aside from what the speaker presents. See Davies 1971: 6–7. The provision of meals in this building was not a

he would lose all the property that Aeschylus, his adoptive father, had given him. This was a lie, gentlemen of the jury: this never happened to any adopted person.[35] He also said that Polyeuctus, who was married to the boy's mother, was responsible for all this, because he wanted to have the boy's property for himself. The jurymen were indignant at what had been told them, and though they considered the decree in itself and the gift to be legal, they thought the boy would really be robbed of his property. They fined my father ten talents, thinking he was acting in concert with Polyeuctus, and they believed that Theocrines had helped the boy. [32] This is more or less what happened in the courtroom. But when this *good* man here realized that people were incensed, and that he had persuaded them that he was not entirely impious, he summoned Polyeuctus, indicted him before the Archon for maltreatment of an orphan (*kakōsis orphanōn*), and presented the complaint to Mnesarchides the Assessor.[36] But he accepted two hundred drachmas from Polyeuctus, and for a small sum he sold these shocking allegations, for which he had my father fined ten talents; he gave up the case, retracted the indictment, and abandoned the orphan. [To the clerk] Please call the witnesses to these acts.

[WITNESSES]

[33] If my father had been well off, gentlemen of the jury, and could have produced a thousand drachmas, he would have been completely clear of the indictment for unconstitutional action (*graphē paranomōn*). You see, that is how much this man was asking. [To the clerk] Please call Philippides of the deme Paeania,[37] the man whom Theocrines told about this, and the others who are aware that he spoke of it.

[WITNESSES]

[34] I think you would all believe, gentlemen of the jury, that Theocrines would have withdrawn the indictment of my father if some-

---

form of welfare but a mark of public distinction, best known from Socrates' playful suggestion in Plato's *Apology* (36d) that this be his "punishment."

[35] The speaker's claim is contradicted by Dem. 44.21–23.

[36] A type of magistrate's assistant; cf. Dem. 59.72. This may be the Mnesarchides known from inscriptions to have served as a trierarch.

[37] A rich, politically active man, often honored for his services to the city. Cf. Dem. 21.208.

one had given him the thousand drachmas, even if no one testified to that effect. To show that he has issued many other summonses and entered many other indictments and then took a small payment to give them up and arrange a settlement, I will call for you the very men who made the payments, in order that you not believe him when he says that he was of his own accord guarding against those who make unconstitutional proposals and that the democracy is subverted whenever actions against such proposals are canceled.[38] You know, this is what men who will sell anything customarily say. [35] [To the clerk] Please call Aristomachus the son of Critodemus of the deme Alopece,[39] since he gave him money. Or rather, it was in his house that one and a half minas were paid to this man who does not accept bribes, concerning a decree that Antimedon proposed for the men of Tenedos.[40]

[DEPOSITION]

[To the clerk] Please read also, in order, the similar depositions of the other men, including those made by Hyperides[41] and Demosthenes. You see, this is going too far: this man took the greatest pleasure in getting money by selling indictments to those from whom nobody would think it right to ask for a bribe.

[DEPOSITION]

[36] This man will immediately say that this *endeixis* was brought against him just to keep him from pursuing the indictment (*graphē*) that he has brought against Demosthenes and the one against Thucydides.[42] You see, he is wonderfully clever at lying and saying nothing honest. But we, gentlemen of the jury, have looked into this also, and

---

[38] The practice of prosecuting others for public offenses could be regarded as an act of public service (see Aristoph., *Wealth* 899–919), but it could also be the justification offered by a *sykophant*. A distinguishing mark of the *sykophant* might be his willingness to withdraw a case for a price.

[39] Aristomachus was a man of considerable prominence. Cf. Dem. 59.25.

[40] An island in the Aegean near the northern coast of Asia Minor. Nothing else is known about this decree or the man who proposed it.

[41] Another of the canonical Attic Orators. See *The Oratory of Classical Greece*, Vol. 5.

[42] It was not uncommon to bring a case against someone in order to prevent him from prosecuting some other case. See, for instance, Ant. 6.

we will show you that the city is not at all injured, by Zeus, whether Thucydides' decree is valid or annulled. Still, it is not right to make a defense of this sort before men sworn to judge in accordance with the laws; all the same, you will know from the indictment itself that it is a pretext meant to deal with the *endeixis*. [To the clerk] Please read these indictments.

[INDICTMENTS] [43]

[37] If these decrees, gentlemen of the jury, remain in place or are canceled—to me, at least, it makes no difference—what does the city gain or lose? Nothing at all, I think. People say that the men of Aenus [44] pay no attention to our city and that this is the fault of Theocrines here. You see they were victims of his *sykophantic* conduct at a time when their loyalties were divided between Philip and Athens. When they learned that the decree that Thucydides had proposed concerning their contribution had been indicted as unconstitutional, the decree that Charinus [45] had indicted earlier, and that no conclusion to the business was emerging [38] but that the Assembly was in agreement that the men of Aenus should pay the amount they had agreed to with Chares the general, [46] and they learned that this despicable man Theocrines was planning to resume the same course as Charinus the traitor, they did what they had to do: they chose the least of the evils confronting them. [47] But what must we imagine the men of Aenus were suffering at the hands of the men at Athens drawing up indictments, when they found it preferable to accept a garrison and obedience to a barbarian

[43] Each of these indictments would cite the text of the proposal (*psēphisma*) being challenged for violation of existing law (*nomos*).

[44] A city on the coast of Thrace at the mouth of the Hebrus river that, as a member of the Second Athenian Confederacy founded in 378/7, was obliged to make a certain contribution (*suntaxis*). Nothing else is known about these events.

[45] Din. 1.63 refers to Charinus' banishment from the city for treasonous behavior.

[46] Chares the son of Theochares of the deme Angele served several terms as general, starting in 367/6. He is reported to have stood trial on many occasions. See Aes. 2.72; Dem. 19.232.

[47] I.e., they chose to ally themselves with Philip rather than continue to endure mistreatment by the Athenians.

and to revolt from you? But I suppose that you, and no other Greeks, can tolerate the wickedness of these men here.

[39] So it is pretty clear from what has been said that neither on account of the indictments that have been read out nor for any other reason is it right to acquit Theocrines, for this would violate all the laws about actions of *endeixis*. But, gentlemen of the jury, I think that you have not failed to notice their excuses, their accusations, and their fabricated hatreds.

[40] You have, after all, often seen them in the courts and on the speaker's platform claiming they are mutual enemies but in private working together and sharing the profits, at one moment abusing each other and reviling each other with unspeakable slurs, yet after a little while joining in a party with the very same men [48] and sharing the same sacrifices. Perhaps none of this merits surprise, since they are evil by nature and they see that you accept excuses of this type. So what is to keep them from trying to swindle you by putting these excuses forward? [41] I, however, think that you must consider *this* case exclusively, gentlemen of the jury: if what I say is right and conforms to the laws, help me. Ignore the fact that the prosecutor is not Demosthenes but a very young man,[49] and do not think that the laws should have greater validity if someone presents them to you in skillful arrangement of words than if he uses ordinary language; no, they are the same laws, and you should help inexperienced and young speakers to the degree they would be less apt to trick you. [42] In fact, it is the reverse, and I am the victim of a plot, not Theocrines: and after certain men said they would help me with the litigation but betrayed me because of their political clubs (*hetaireiai*). This will become clear to you in the following way. Let the herald here summon Demosthenes. [The speaker pauses.] He will not come up to the platform. The reason is not that I have been persuaded by certain men to bring this *endeixis* but that the man I just summoned reached a settlement with Theocrines. To show that this is true, I will require the testimony of Cleino-

---

[48] The text is not quite certain, but there seems to be a reference to the party celebrated by a family ten days after the birth of a child.

[49] The word *meirakion* would normally designate a young man, not more than a year or two past eighteen, the age at which he could speak in court.

machus, who brought those men together, and Eubulides,[50] who was with them in Cynosarges to testify.[51] [43] And I will present evidence not less compelling, but more, that this is true, as you will all agree once you have heard it. You see, Theocrines here, prosecuted Demosthenes for an unconstitutional action—this "despicable man," as he soon will say, the one responsible for all his current troubles—but then openly released him from the *graphē* for which he had designated a ten-talent fine. How? Not by doing anything novel but simply what other men like him have done. When the *graphē* was announced, to get a postponement of the trial, somebody swore that Demosthenes was sick—Demosthenes, the man who was going around abusing Aeschines. Theocrines then released his enemy, without swearing a counter-oath[52] or summoning him later on. Aren't these men flagrantly tricking you if you seriously regard them as enemies? [To the clerk] Read the depositions.

[DEPOSITIONS]

[44] Thus the right thing for you to do, gentlemen of the jury, is for your part not to listen to those who will say that they wish to speak on behalf of Theocrines because of their hatred for Demosthenes but instead to direct them, if they are truly Demosthenes' enemies, to indict *him* and not allow him to propose unconstitutional decrees.[53] But these men are clever too and are more credible in your eyes. No, they will not do that. Why? Because they claim to be battling each other, though in fact they are not.

[45] On the subject of their hatred, you could give me a more precise account than I could give you. I would gladly question Theocrines in your presence—*if* he was likely to answer me honestly—I would ask him, given that he says he has adopted the position that he will

---

[50] The former is otherwise known only from Dem. 59.39; the latter has left no other trace.

[51] A place in eastern Attica where there was a shrine of Heracles and a gymnasium. The alleged meeting presumably took place at the latter.

[52] I.e., swearing that Demosthenes was well enough to attend.

[53] The implication may be that the jury simply shout down these speakers (cf. above, 25–26n).

block those proposing unconstitutional action—what in the world he would have done if someone speaking to all the citizens in the Assembly had introduced and passed a decree that permitted disenfranchised men and state debtors to indict and bring *phasis* and *endeixis* actions and, to put it plainly, to do everything the law now forbids them to do? [46] Would he or would he not have brought a *graphē paranomōn* against the proposer? If he says he would not, how is it that we should believe him when he says that he is on guard against those who make illegal motions? And if he *would* indict him, isn't it shocking that he would prevent the decree proposed by another man from taking effect, so that all could not exercise the right, and he would block the business by initiating a suit, in which he wrote down the indictment alongside the specific words of the laws,[54] [47] but right now although he has not persuaded the Assembly or made the business public, he himself brings an indictment—despite the laws forbidding him to do so? In just a moment he will say that he is suffering shocking treatment if he is not allowed to do so, and he will recite the legal penalties to which he will be liable if convicted; but in fact he flouts the laws but demands that you give him a gift so great that nobody has dared even ask for it.

[48] So I think just about all of you know that neither Theocrines nor any one of those speaking on his behalf will have any just claim to put forward concerning the *endeixis*. But I suppose they will try to say that there cannot be an *endeixis* against those whose names are not posted on the Acropolis, and that it is not right to regard people as state debtors if no one has given their names to the official collectors, as if you were ignorant of the law, which states that the debt starts from the day on which the fine is imposed or when the man violates the law or decree, or as if it were not clear to everybody that people fall into debt to the public treasury in many ways and that those who want to obey the laws pay up, and this is clear from the law itself. [To the clerk] Please take this law once again.

[LAW]

---

[54]I.e., in tabular form, the text of the decree juxtaposed with those laws the prosecutor claimed the decree violated.

Do you hear what it requires, you despicable animal?—"from the day on which the fine is imposed on him or when the man violates the law."

[50] Now, I hear that they, and Theocrines too, intend to show you the law that directs that, for those whose names are posted, whatever amount of their debt they pay is to be expunged, and they will ask how they can expunge anything from the account of a man whose name is not posted, as if it were not clear that *this* law was enacted specifically for those whose names *are* posted, whereas those whose names are *not* posted as state debtors are covered by that law that directs that the debt starts from the day on which the fine is imposed or on which the man violates the law or decree. [51] "Why," he will say, "don't you indict me for failure to post the name of a state debtor (*graphē agraphiou*),[55] if I am in debt and my name has not been posted?" Because the law does not stipulate suits for failure to post against those who are state debtors and whose names are *not* posted but rather against those whose names *have* been posted and *have* been expunged, even though they have not paid their debt to the city. [To the clerk] Please take the law and read it.

[LAW]

[52] You hear, gentlemen of the jury, that the law explicitly says that if a state debtor who has not paid his fine to the city has his name expunged, indictments for failure to post can be brought against him with the *thesmothetai* but not against debtors whose names are *not* posted; instead, the law requires an *endeixis* and other penalties against them. [To Theocrines] So why do you instruct me in the ways I should take vengeance on my enemies but do not defend yourself against the charge that I have come to court to bring against you?

[53] Moerocles,[56] gentlemen of the jury, the man who proposed the decree against those who wrong merchants and who persuaded not only you but also your allies to create a guard force to be used against

---

[55] See *Ath. Pol.* 59.3.

[56] Moerocles has the distinction of being among only eight Athenian politicians whom Alexander the Great demanded the Athenians to surrender to him (Plut., *Life of Demosthenes* 23). See also Dem. 19.293 and Arist., *Rhetoric* 1411a.

criminals,[57] will not be ashamed to speak very soon on behalf of Theocrines, contrary to his own decrees. [54] He will have the nerve to argue that you should not punish but acquit a man who is clearly proven to have brought unjustified *phasis* actions against the merchants, as if this was the motive for his legislating that the sea be swept clean, just in order to see to it that those who safely make it over the sea pay out money to these men in the harbor, or as if the merchants would benefit if after making it through a long voyage, they fall into Theocrines' clutches. [55] I suppose it is not you but the generals and those in charge of the warships who are responsible for what happens on sea voyages, but what happens in Piraeus and before the magistrates is your responsibility, since you have authority over all these men. For this reason you must maintain greater surveillance over those who violate the laws here than over those who while abroad do not abide by the decrees: you yourselves should not appear to be nonchalant about what is happening or to connive with the perpetrators. [56] Certainly, Moerocles, we will not fine the Melians ten talents as required by your decree because they gave refuge to pirates[58] and then let this man here go, when he has violated both your decree and the laws by which we administer the city. Will we then prevent the island inhabitants from doing wrong, men whom we must compel to do the right things by manning triremes, and let you despicable characters go, when these men sitting here should, in keeping with the laws, impose punishment on you? [To the jury] Not if you have any sense. [To the clerk] Read what is published on the *stēlē*.[59]

[*STĒLĒ*]

[57] I don't know what more I should say about the laws and the case at hand. I think you have learned enough. But I do wish to ask you for justice for me and my father; then I will step down and not annoy you further. You see, gentlemen of the jury, with the idea that I should

---

[57] The next several sections make clear that this force was specifically intended to deal with pirates.

[58] Melos is an island lying between Athens and Crete. Nothing else is known of this incident.

[59] I.e., the law inscribed on a column.

help my father, and because I thought this course of action was just, I brought this *endeixis,* [58] aware, as I said at the beginning, that those who wanted to insult me would find words to slander my youthfulness and that others would praise me and think I was showing good sense if I chose to take vengeance on my father's enemy. I figured that whatever happened before this audience would happen, regardless, but I needed to do what my father had commanded, especially since it was the right thing. [59] When should I help him? Should I not do so now, when punishment in conformity with the laws is possible, and I am actually sharing my father's misfortune, and he has been left all alone? This is exactly what has now happened. You see, in addition to the other misfortunes, this has happened to us too, gentlemen of the jury: although everybody is goading us on and claiming to share my pain at what has happened, and they say we have been treated terribly, and that Theocrines is liable to an *endeixis,* no one who has said all this is willing to join with us in this suit. They say they do not to want make an open enemy of him. Thus for some men, their desire for justice is weaker than their terror.[60] [60] Although we have suffered many misfortunes over a long period, gentlemen of the jury, because of this Theocrines here, what has happened now is as serious as any of them: because though Theocrines' monstrous and illegal acts were committed against my father and he could expose them to you, he is compelled to keep silent—so the law demands. So it is I, who am not equal to the task, who must speak; other men my age get help from their fathers, but my father now places his hopes in me. [61] Faced with such a trial, we ask you to help us and to demonstrate to everyone that anyone, whether young or old, or of whatever age, who comes before you in accordance with the laws, will get everything he deserves. It is right, gentlemen of the jury, that neither the laws nor you yourselves be put in the power of speakers but that they be put in *your* power and that you distinguish those who speak well and expertly from those who speak what is right.[61] It is, after all, on the basis of justice that you have

---

[60] The translation follows a textual conjecture that replaces the word *parrēsia* (candid speech) with *orrōdia* (terror).

[61] Again, the manuscripts might be in error at this point. The translation follows a conjecture that replaces the transmitted word *saphōs* ("clearly") with *sophōs* ("expertly" or perhaps even "craftily").

sworn to cast your vote. [62] Nobody will persuade you that speakers like this will disappear, nor that the city would in that case be worse off. It's the other way around, from what I hear from the older men. You see, they say that the city fared best when moderate and sensible men were involved in public affairs. Could anyone find that *these* men are good advisers? They say nothing in the Assembly and instead get money by indicting the men who *are* active there. [63] What is astonishing is that while getting their livelihood from *sykophancy*, they claim they are not getting it from the city. They had had nothing to their name before they came before you;[62] now that they are prosperous, they are not even grateful to you; instead, they go around saying that the *demos* is fickle, that it is foul-tempered, that it is ungrateful—as if you were prospering because of them, not they because of the *demos*. But after all, it's natural that they say this, when they see your indifference, for you have given nobody the punishment his wickedness deserves, but instead, you put up with their saying that the security of the democracy depends on men who indict and engage in *sykophancy;* there is no more damnable breed than these men. [64] How could one find these men useful to the city? "These men punish criminals, by Zeus, and reduce their number."[63] Certainly not, gentlemen of the jury. Indeed, they make them more numerous: since those who want to commit some crime know that a portion of their gain must be given to these men, they must necessarily resolve to steal more from others, so they will have something to spend, not just on themselves but also on these men. [65] In the case of criminals who harm anyone they happen to find, it is possible for victims to deflect the attacks of those who intend to do them harm, some by posting a guard at their house, others by staying indoors at night, and yet others by protecting themselves by one means or another. But in the case of *sykophants* like these men here, where can one go to get security from them? You see, the means available to us to take refuge from other crimes are the tools of their profession: laws, courts, witnesses, assemblies. There they flaunt their strengths, regarding those who bribe them as friends, and rich men who mind their own business as their enemies.

---

[62] I.e., before they began bringing legal actions into court.

[63] In classical rhetoric this device, presenting the imagined words of someone opposing the speaker, is known as *hypophora*. For the argument, cf. above, 58.34n.

[66] Keep in mind the evil of these men and remember our ancestors. My grandfather Epichares, the Olympic victor in the boys' foot race, adorned the city with a crown and died with an upstanding reputation among your ancestors. But we, owing to this man whom the gods hate, have been deprived of our citizenship in this state, [67] on behalf of which Aristocrates, the son of Scelius, and the uncle of my grandfather Epichares—my brother here bears his name—accomplished many fine deeds when the city was at war with the Lacedaemonians: he razed Eëtioneia,[64] into which Critias and his band were going to receive the Lacedaemonians, and he tore down the fortification and restored the democracy, braving dangers unlike these confronting us, but ones in which a failure was glorious, and for your benefit he checked the conspirators. [68] For the sake of Aristocrates, it would have been reasonable for you to save us, even if we happened to be men like Theocrines—though in fact we are better than he is and what we say is just. We will not annoy you by repeating this again, since Theocrines has put us into the position that, as I said when I began, we have no hope of sharing in the freedom of speech granted even to aliens.[65] [69] So that we have this consolation, if nothing else, to see this man too forced to keep silent, help us, pity those of our family who have died for their country, force him to give a defense on the subject of the *endeixis* itself, and be the same sort of judges of his words as he was of ours when he prosecuted us. [70] He tricked the jurors and refused to propose a moderate penalty for my father; and though I vehemently begged him and supplicated him at his knees, he set the fine at ten talents, as if my father were a traitor to the city. So we ask you, we beseech you: vote for what is just.

You, whoever you are,[66] help us if you can and speak for us. Step up to the platform.

---

[64] See Thuc. 8.88–92. The speaker is confusing events of 411 with those of 403.

[65] Since he will automatically inherit his father's *atimia*. See above, 58.17n.

[66] This may be the formula, a sort of blank indicated by the speechwriter, into which the speaker would add the name of the man who would speak next. Cf. the ending of Dem. 56.

59. AGAINST NEAERA

〰〰〰

INTRODUCTION

The author of this speech is almost certainly Apollodorus, father-in-law (also brother-in-law) of the man who delivers the first sixteen sections. The style of *Against Neaera* is repetitive and sprawling and shows other signs that the speech is not by Demosthenes himself (see the Introduction, pp. 12–15). Yet *Against Neaera* holds exceptional interest for its picture of aspects of Athenian life seldom touched on with such detail in other texts. We see in particular how *hetairai,* deluxe prostitutes, played a part in the erotic and public lives of many Athenians, some of them very prominent.

Prostitution itself was not a crime in Athens, and men were at no risk of prosecution for employing prostitutes. Moreover, just beneath the surface of the speakers' contempt for prostitutes and their righteous denunciations of Neaera's alleged offenses against the city of Athens and her gods, we can see the possibility that some element of genuine affection and concern might have coexisted with the inherent brutality of paid sex with slave women and with manumitted women at risk of losing their freedom. Lysias was eager to bestow on his favorite the benefits of initiation into the Mysteries (21). Phrastor, when an invalid, felt closer to Neaera and her daughter than to his own relatives, despite the trick the women played on him (55–56). Epainetus, once Neaera's lover, though blackmailed and humiliated, was willing to contribute to a dowry for her daughter (69–70). In addition, in the often-quoted passage distinguishing wives from what we might call "kept" women (122), the speaker assigns the latter group the domains of "pleasure" and "tending," leaving wives only the role of mothering legitimate children and serving as "guardians" of the household.

The legal issue, then, is not prostitution and dissolute living but the integrity of Athenian citizenship. The prosecution has brought a *graphē xenias* against Neaera, a public action charging the fraudulent exercise of rights belonging exclusively to Athenian citizens. Athenian citizenship was highly valued by the Athenians for both its practical and symbolic advantages. Pericles' citizenship law of 451 restricted citizenship to those born to an Athenian father and mother, whereas the earlier practice recognized as citizens men born to an Athenian father and foreign mother. Dwindling manpower during the Peloponnesian War led to lax enforcement of that law. Once the war was over, the Athenians not only reinstated the Periclean law but went on to introduce further restrictions, as can be seen in the law quoted at 16. The procedures for enfranchising a foreigner, known mostly from this speech, were remarkably complex.[1] The prosecution's appeal to a sense of outrage at the alleged offense against citizen rights was certainly a plausible strategy. But it is quite apparent—in fact all but explicit in the opening sections—that the prosecution's real motive is revenge against Stephanus, the man with whom Neaera was living.

In 348, some five to eight years before the trial for which this speech was written, Stephanus had successfully charged Apollodorus with proposing an illegal decree (*graphē paranomōn*), though the jury opted for a fine far smaller than Stephanus had proposed (3–8). Later Stephanus tried, without success, to have him convicted of homicide (9–10). Considering the damage they would have suffered if Stephanus fully succeeded in these court actions, it is hardly surprising that Apollodorus and his family were eager to strike back in the same forum. The prosecution, then, was really aiming at Stephanus, though its legal action was formally lodged against Neaera. If she was convicted, Stephanus would have been fined one thousand drachmas, a large but not crushing sum, and his children's status as Athenians might have been challenged; Neaera would have returned to slavery and lost all her property (16).[2]

---

[1] "The procedure outlined [in *Against Neaera*] is self-consciously defensive with a series of unnecessary hurdles, as if the aim is to restrict eligibility at all costs" (Todd 1993: 176).

[2] Stephanus retreated from a greater risk to his property when threatened by Phrastor with prosecution for marrying off Neaera's daughter to him as if she were a citizen (52).

There is only one other surviving example of a speech written for a trial in which a woman was the defendant: Antiphon 1 *Against the Stepmother.* A few other such trials are mentioned in the course of Demosthenes' speeches (25.57, 57.8). But if our surviving speeches are at all representative of litigation in general, legal action against women was very rare.[3] Athenian men were hardly chivalrous, so we may assume that legal and cultural restrictions on women's power and property rights normally made them not worth prosecuting. Neaera, one of those rare female defendants, was almost certainly in the courtroom to hear the charges against her; at least the speech refers to her as present (esp. at 115). Like other women, even those who enjoyed unchallenged Athenian citizenship, Neaera was not permitted to present her own defense but had to rely on men to speak for her.[4]

By dint of Neaera's profession, the speech received relatively scant attention until classical scholars became interested in the lives of ancient women and could publish their research on sexuality in frank English. English-speaking readers can now consult a rich bibliography, including that in Carey 1992 and the full-scale commentary with translation by Kapparis 1999.

59. AGAINST NEAERA

[1][5] Gentlemen of the jury, many things have spurred me on to bring this action against Neaera and come before you in court. You see, Stephanus has done us—my brother-in-law, myself, my sister, my wife—great harm, and it is because of him that we came into extreme danger. Therefore, I am not taking the initiative in bringing this case, but am seeking retribution. In fact, I am acting in self-defense: he was

---

[3] Note, however, that a woman involved in an inheritance dispute could easily be one of the claimants in a *diadikasia,* a procedure in which, properly speaking, there were no prosecutors and defendants. For an instance in the Demosthenic corpus, see Dem. 43.8, where the speaker mentions serving as his wife's advocate in an earlier *diadikasia.*

[4] Some readers may see Neaera as a sort of Moll Flanders, but Defoe's heroine could at least speak for herself in court.

[5] Theomnestus, the prosecutor, speaks first. Apollodorus, in the role of "co-speaker" (*synēgoros*), takes over at 16 and completes the speech. For discussion, see Rubinstein 2000 (above, p. 11, n. 3), 133–135.

the one who started the quarrel, though he had not had any trouble from our side—not in words, not in action. I want to start by telling you what he has done to us and how we have fallen into the great risk of exile and disenfranchisement. That way you will be more sympathetic to me as I present my defense.

[2] Now then, when the Athenian Assembly[6] voted to make Pasion and his descendants Athenian citizens, in gratitude for the good things he had done for the city,[7] my father agreed with the Assembly's gift of citizenship. He gave his daughter, my sister, in marriage to Pasion's son Apollodorus; and Apollodorus had children by her. Apollodorus was good to my sister and the rest of us and thought of us truly as family, as people who should share all that was his; and I took Apollodorus' daughter, my niece, to be my wife.

[3] Time went by, and Apollodorus was assigned by lot to serve in the Council (*boulē*). He passed the preliminary scrutiny (*dokimasia*) and swore the oath required by law.[8] Then[9] the city found itself in a military emergency, which presented two possibilities. One was that you would prevail and be the greatest city of the Greeks: you would, without question, get your own possessions back in your hands and defeat Philip decisively. The other was that you would be too slow with your help and would forsake your allies; in that case, your army, lacking resources, would be disbanded, which would mean ruining those allies and appearing untrustworthy to the other Greeks; and it would mean also running the risk of losing your remaining possessions: Lemnos, Imbros, Scyros, and the Chersonese. [4] When you were on the verge of marching in full force to Euboea and Olynthus, Apollodorus, as a Council member, introduced a bill in the Council, and it passed,

---

[6]"Assembly" translates the Greek word *dēmos*. Besides this institutional sense, equivalent to *ekklēsia,* the word can also mean "the people" or "the poor people."

[7]Much is known about Pasion's career and the vicissitudes of his family from several speeches of Demosthenes (35, 36, 45) and from Isoc. 17. See p. 112. Pasion's benefactions recognized by the Assembly's decree included the gift of one thousand shields and voluntary service as a trierarch (Dem. 45.85).

[8]Members of the Council of Five Hundred swore that they would act in the best interest of the city and expose any other man selected for this service whom they knew to be "unsuitable" (Lys. 31.1).

[9]In the spring of 348; Apollodorus had entered the Council in the Athenian archon year that started the summer before (349).

an agenda item (*probouleuma*) to be taken to the Assembly, providing for that body to make a choice by its vote whether the leftover funds of the financial administration were to be applied to the military fund or the theoric[10] fund. The laws required that in wartime the funds go to the military, but he thought that the Assembly should have the right to do whatever it wanted when it came to its own resources. He swore he would offer the people of Athens his best counsel, and all of you[11] were witnesses at that critical time. [5] The vote was held, and *nobody* voted against using the funds for the military. In fact, even now, if the matter ever comes up for discussion, everybody agrees that the man who gave the best advice on that occasion was treated unfairly. It's right to be angry at a man who tricks the jurymen with his words— but not at those who got tricked. What happened was that Stephanus, this man here, indicted this decree as illegal;[12] in court he introduced false witnesses to claim that Apollodorus had been in debt to the Public Treasury for twenty-five years[13] and brought up lots of other charges irrelevant to the indictment; and he got the decree declared illegal. [6] If Stephanus thought he had done well to bring this about, we have no complaint. But when the jurors turned to voting on the penalty,[14] we begged him to compromise; he refused and proposed a fine of fifteen talents, meaning to take citizen rights away from Apollodorus and

---

[10]A fund whose name (*theoric* = pertaining to festivals) points to its original function: to help poor Athenians pay for tickets to the theatrical events during the Dionysia and Lenaean festivals. In time, the fund's disbursements extended beyond drama to become a more general subvention for the state festivals and then for other purposes altogether.

[11]Athenian orators often speak as if the jurors in a particular case also participated in or observed certain actions by the Assembly or a lawcourt, even if they were not alive at the time.

[12]See the Introduction to 57.

[13]The Oxford Classical Text, like most other editions of the speech, have transposed this clause ("to claim that . . . twenty-five years") from 9; in the manuscripts it follows "false charge against him." Kapparis (1999) believes that it is not genuine.

[14]This procedure, *timēsis* or *timēma*, was followed if the law did not specify a penalty. Once a jury had convicted a defendant, both he and the prosecutor proposed a penalty, and the jury would in a second vote decide between them. *Timēsis* is best known from Plato's account of Socrates' trial.

his children, and to put my sister and all of us into the deepest poverty, with absolutely nothing to our names. [7] Apollodorus' total property, from which such a big fine would have to be paid, came to not quite three talents; and if he didn't pay off the fine before the ninth *prytany*,[15] the fine would be doubled, and Apollodorus would be listed as owing the treasury thirty talents. Then his belongings would be put on the list of public property, and once they were sold off, he and his children and wife and all of us would end up completely ruined. [8] On top of that, he would not be able to marry off his other daughter. After all, who would marry a girl who had no dowry and whose father was in debt to the treasury and penniless? So Stephanus gave us all such great trouble, though he had not yet been harmed by us. I really do feel grateful to the jurors who decided that case in one point at least, that they did not let him be ruined but instead fined him one talent. That much he could pay off, though it was hard. To Stephanus, though, we have tried—as is only just—to give a dose of the same medicine he was giving to others.

[9] In fact, he not only tried to ruin us but actually tried to run Apollodorus out of his own country. You see, he brought a false charge against him, claiming that once, when he had gone to Aphidna[16] on the trail of a runaway slave of his, he hit a woman, who in the end died of her wounds. Stephanus bribed some slaves and coached them to say they were from Cyrene[17] and then announced that he was bringing a homicide charge against him in the Court of the Palladion.[18] [10] Then

---

[15] A prytany was one tenth of the Athenian year, corresponding to the term of office of each of the Athenian tribes (*phylai*).

[16] A town in Attica northeast of Athens.

[17] On the coast of north Africa (modern Libya).

[18] Though this account of the prosecution is far from clear, it seems likely that the woman who died was a slave owned by Stephanus. First, Apollodorus' assault was presumably intentional, and the trial was held not in the Areopagus, the venue when the victim of intentional assault was a citizen, but in the Palladion, the court that heard cases when the victim was a slave, foreigner, or *metic* (resident alien). Second, the woman is not identified as a relative of Stephanus', hence he would be excluded from prosecuting unless she was a slave and Stephanus was her owner. Theomnestus' claim that Stephanus was disguising the slaves as Cyreneans suggests that this was a ploy to allow them to testify without being subject to torture.

Stephanus, the man before you, presented his case. He swore on his own head, on his family, and on his house that Apollodorus killed that woman with his own hands. But that never happened; and he did not see it happen; and he never heard it from anybody else. It was proved that Stephanus perjured himself and brought a false charge, and it was clear that he had been paid off by Ctesiphon and Apollophanes[19] to drive Apollodorus into exile and take away his citizen rights. He got only a few of the five hundred votes,[20] and people thought he had committed perjury and was a scoundrel.

[11] Gentlemen of the jury, please think over in your minds what makes sense. How could I face myself, my wife, and my sister if Apollodorus was injured by Stephanus' plots against him in either the first or second trials? Imagine my shame and misfortune! [12] Everybody was coming to me in private and urging me to try to get back at him for what he had done to us. They were scolding me, saying I was no man if I didn't get justice for people who were so close to me —my sister, and brother-in-law, and nieces, and my own wife; and I was no man at all if I didn't bring before you in court the woman who was openly defiling the gods, insulting the city, and scorning your laws, and show you that she is guilty. That way I would put *you* in charge, and you could deal with her as you wanted. [13] Just as Stephanus here tried to ruin my people, violating your laws and decrees, so I have come here to show you that he is living with a foreign woman against the law, has brought other men's children before the phratries and deme[21] assemblies, and has married off the daughters of *hetairai* as if they were his own; also that he has committed impiety against the gods and has robbed the people of their power to decide whom *they* want to make Athenian citizens. After all, who will try to get this gift of citizenship from the people, spending money and

---

[19]There are two men named Ctesiphon known from the sources as politicians associated with the sort of action here described, but no candidate has emerged for identification as Apollophanes.

[20]Some manuscripts of the speech have the word "drachmas" after "five hundred." This translation follows those editors who regard the word "drachmas" as a mistaken addition to the original text.

[21]See the note on 57.23.

going to trouble, if it's possible to get citizenship from Stephanus, at a smaller price?—that is, if the same power to grant citizenship falls into his hands.

[14] I have now told you how Stephanus did me wrong before I brought this suit. Next, I will move on to other things you must understand: that Neaera is a foreigner, that she lives with Stephanus as married,[22] and that she has committed many legal offenses against the city. So now I'll ask you, gentlemen of the jury, something that I think proper for someone both young and without experience in public speaking to ask: please let me call Apollodorus up here to help me do the speaking.[23] [15] He is older than I am, more experienced in the law, and has looked into these matters with great care. Stephanus here has done Apollodorus wrong, so you must not be angry with him for taking vengeance for what has happened. And you are obliged, after you have listened to the details in both the prosecution's speech and the defense speech, to cast your vote on the basis of the truth—for the sake of the gods and the laws, justice, and yourselves.

[SPEECH BY APOLLODORUS, THE *SYNĒGOROS*]

[16] Theomnestus has told you, gentlemen of Athens, of the wrongs I have suffered at Stephanus' hands that have led me to rise and accuse Neaera, this woman here. I want to show you clearly that Neaera is a foreigner, and that she is living as married with Stephanus in violation of the law.[24] But first the law that is the basis of Theomnestus' present suit and the reason why this case has come before you in court will be read out.

---

[22]"Lives with" literally translates the Greek word *synoikein*, which in Athens generally connoted legal wedlock. The words "as married" are not explicit in the Greek. See below, 16n and 122, where Apollodorus tries to insist that *synoikein* suggests the intention to present sons produced by the union as eligible for citizenship and daughters as his own.

[23]As the jury did not need to assent to the calling of a *synēgoros*, Theomnestus' request is probably a ploy to win some sympathy for his inexperience and at the same time anticipate and disarm antagonism to Apollodorus on the part of some of the jurors.

[24]The date of this law is uncertain. Kapparis 1999: 202 concludes that it was introduced in the 380s.

[LAW] *If a foreign male by any manner or means lives as married*[25] *with an Athenian woman (aste), let anyone who is entitled to do so and wishes bring an indictment (graphe) before the Thesmothetae of the Athenians.*[26] *If he is convicted, let him be sold into slavery and his property sold. A third part of the proceeds is to go to the successful prosecutor. And if a foreign female cohabits with an Athenian man (astos), the same applies; and the man who cohabited with the foreign woman who has been convicted is to owe [the treasury] one thousand drachmas.*

[17] You have heard the law, gentlemen, which forbids a foreign woman from living with an Athenian man (*astos*), and an Athenian woman (*aste*) from living with a foreign man, and absolutely forbids such couples from having children,[27] by any manner or means. But if someone does so, despite the law, it provides that a public action (*graphe*) be brought against them before the *Thesmothetae,* against both male and female foreigners, and the law orders that they be sold into slavery if convicted. That Neaera here is a foreigner is what I want to lay out for you, from the beginning of the story and in detail.

[18] A woman named Nicarete acquired seven little girls to raise from early childhood.[28] Nicarete was a freed slave of Charisus from Elis; her husband was Hippias, Charisus' cook.[29] She was very shrewd

---

[25] See 14n. Since this law envisions false claims of citizenship on behalf of children born to couples who live together but are not both Athenian citizens, the connotation comes close to "cohabit."

[26] The right of any fully enfranchised Athenian citizen "who wishes" to prosecute is one of the hallmarks of a *graphe;* see the Series Introduction, p. xxvi. The Thesmothetae were six of the nine archons annually elected by lot to administer many of the city's functions; see the Series Introduction, p. xxii. Their judicial responsibilities included the convening of the *dikasteria* ("People's Courts"); see *Ath. Pol.* 59.

[27] This would be understood to mean children who would be falsely presented as the legitimate offspring of two citizen parents and therefore entitled to Athenian citizenship.

[28] These were presumably girls either knowingly handed over to Nicarete by mothers or intermediaries, or exposed and then brought to her for possible adoption.

[29] This speech provides the only contemporary evidence on the woman, her husband, and her former owner.

at sizing up the physical attributes little girls would develop, an experienced expert at raising and educating them. That was the craft she had developed, and from it she made her living. [19] She called these girls her "daughters," so as to get the largest possible fees from men who wanted to be intimate with supposedly free women. She milked the profit of each girl's youthful years, then sold them outright, all seven of them: Anteia, Stratola, Aristocleia, Metaneira, Phila, Isthmias[30]—and Neaera, this woman right here. [20] Just how each man acquired each of the women, and how they won their freedom from the men who bought them from Nicarete, I will tell you in the course of my speech —if you want to hear about it and I have enough time.[31]

But I want to go back to when Neaera belonged to Nicarete and worked with her body, getting paid by those who wanted to have sex with her. [21] Now then, Lysias, the sophist,[32] was a lover of Metaneira. Besides the other money he paid out for her, which he thought all went to Nicarete, her owner, he wanted to pay for Metaneira to be initiated in the mystery cult at Eleusis.[33] The expenses connected with that festival and the rites would be for Metaneira's benefit alone, so she would be grateful to him. He asked Nicarete to come to the ceremony, bringing Metaneira along, so the girl could be initiated, and he promised that he himself would get her initiated. [22] When the women arrived, Lysias did not take them to his own house, since he was embarrassed to do so in front of his wife, Brachyllus'[34] daughter, who was

---

[30] Except for Stratola, who is not otherwise attested, women with these names were notorious courtesans several decades before this speech. Metaneira is reported to have been employed by the orator Isocrates.

[31] As at 14, the speaker acts as if he will respond to the jury's wishes but in fact does not return to the subject.

[32] Almost certainly the celebrated orator. The term "sophist" could be applied to people who received payment (or were thought to do so) for a wide range of intellectual activities (cf. Aes. 1.173, where Socrates is so designated).

[33] Initiation in the Eleusinian Mysteries was not restricted to Athenian citizens: any Greek speaker, male or female, slave or free, was eligible to participate in a ritual that evidently held out some hope for a better lot after death. For a general discussion of mystery religion, see Walter Burkert, *Ancient Mystery Cults* (Cambridge, MA, 1987).

[34] Nothing else is known about Brachyllus. For the consequences of less discreet arrangements, see And. 1.124–125 and 4.14–15.

also his niece, and his elderly mother, who lived there too. Instead, he put up Metaneira and Nicarete with Philostratus of the deme Colonus, a friend of his, still a young man.[35] This woman Neaera came along with them, already working as a prostitute though she was not fully grown.[36] [23] I call Philostratus himself as a witness that I am telling the truth when I say that Neaera belonged to Nicarete, went along with her, and worked as a prostitute for any man willing to pay.

[DEPOSITION] *Philostratus, son of Dionysius, of the deme Colonus, testifies that he knew that Neaera was the property of Nicarete, who also owned Metaneira, and that since their home was in Corinth, they stayed with him when they were in Athens for the Mysteries. Lysias, son of Cephalus, his good friend, put them up with him.*

[24] Well then, men of Athens, after this, Simus the Thessalian[37] came to Athens with Neaera to attend the Great Panathenaea.[38] Nicarete accompanied her, and they stayed with Ctesippus, son of Glauconides, of the deme Cydantidae;[39] Neaera joined the large company of men eating and drinking, just as a *hetaira* does.[40] I will call witnesses to the truth of my statements. [25] Please call up Euphiletus, son of Simon, of the deme Aexone,[41] and Aristomachus, son of Critodemus, of the deme Alopece.[42]

[WITNESSES] *Euphiletus, son of Simon, of the deme Aexone, and Aristomachus, son of Critodemus, of the deme Alopece testify that they know that Simus the Thessalian came to Athens for the Great Panathenaea,*

---

[35] He is known to have been from a rich family and active in politics.

[36] This text is uncertain, but the implication seems to be that she was too young to be engaged in prostitution.

[37] A member of the principal aristocratic family in Thessaly, Simus played an important role in the complex relations of his clan with Philip II of Macedon.

[38] A festival held every four years, by far the most spectacular celebrated at Athens. The Panathenaic Procession is depicted in the Parthenon frieze, much of which is currently displayed in the British Museum.

[39] Not known from other sources.

[40] Respectable women were normally excluded from this sort of social contact with men to whom they were not related.

[41] He is known to have been a member of a rich Athenian family.

[42] A rich man, active in Athenian politics. Cf. Dem. 58.35, Lys. 19.16.

and with him Nicarete and Neaera, the woman now on trial. Also,
that they stayed with Ctesippus, son of Glauconides, and that Neaera
drank with them, in the manner of a hetaira, and that many other
men were present and participated in the drinking in Ctesippus' house.

[26] Afterwards, when she brazenly plied her trade in Corinth and
became a celebrity, Neaera had other lovers, including Xenocleides the
poet[43] and Hipparchus the actor;[44] these men paid to keep her as their
mistress. As far as Xenocleides goes, I cannot provide his testimony
that I am telling the truth, since the laws do not permit him to be a
witness. [27] You see, when at Callistratus' urging you were rescuing
the Spartans, Xenocleides spoke in the Assembly in opposition to giving them assistance.[45] He had bought the two-percent tax on grain
in peacetime[46] and was required to take his payments to the Council building each prytany, and so was exempt under the laws from going out on that military expedition. But Stephanus here indicted him
for not taking part and slandered him in his speech in the lawcourt.
Xenocleides was convicted and disfranchised. [28] Now, don't you
think this is scandalous, that this Stephanus has robbed men of their
right to speak in public, men who are citizens by birth and have had a
legitimate role in the city's affairs, while he thrusts men who are not
part of the city into citizenship—in violation of all the laws? But I will
call Hipparchus himself and force him, in accordance with the law,
to testify or to swear he knows nothing of the business. If he does not
come, I will subpoena him.[47] Please call Hipparchus.

---

[43] He is also mentioned at Dem. 19.331.

[44] An inscription attests that he was six times victorious in competitions as an
actor.

[45] Callistratus (see also 44 and Dem. 57.37) had been prominent in Athenian
politics for nearly a decade at the time of these events. Though once an advocate
of a vigorous anti-Sparta policy, by this time (369) he had come to view Thebes as
the far greater threat.

[46] Under this tax-farming arrangement, a man or group of men making the
highest bid would be granted the exclusive right to collect the duty on all grain
entering or leaving Attica. How well or poorly the tax-farmer would do would depend on the amount of grain subject to the duty as well as his efficiency in making collections.

[47] A man who declined to testify or swear that he knew nothing was liable to a
fine of one thousand drachmas. See Harrison 1968–1971, Vol. 2: 143.

[DEPOSITION] *Hipparchus of the deme Athmonon testifies that in Corinth he and Xenocleides hired Neaera, the woman now on trial, as a prostitute* (hetaira), *one of those who hire themselves out. Neaera would drink with him in Corinth and also with Xenocleides the poet.*

[29] After this, she had two lovers, Timanoridas the Corinthian and Eucrates from Leucas.[48] Since Nicarete was extravagant in her demands—she felt entitled to get all her daily household expenses out of these men—they paid thirty minas[49] to buy Neaera from her, in accordance with the city's laws, and make her, without qualification, their own slave. Then they kept her and used her for as long as they wanted. [30] But when they were about to marry, they told Neaera that since she had been their own mistress, they didn't want to see her working in Corinth or under the thumb of a brothel-keeper.[50] Instead, they would gladly get back less money than they had paid for her and also see her get something good out of it. Accordingly, they told her they would free her from slavery for one thousand drachmas less than the purchase price, five hundred for each man. They told her to find the other twenty minas and pay it to them. When Neaera heard what Eucrates and Timanoridas had to say, she called several of her ex-lovers to Corinth, in particular Phrynion of the deme Paeania, the son of Demon, and brother of Demochares.[51] Phrynion lived a wild life and was a very big spender, as the older men among you will remember. [31] When Phrynion visited her, she told him what Eucrates and Timanoridas had said. She gave him the money she had collected from her other lovers as a contribution toward winning her freedom, together with whatever money she had put aside for herself; and she asked him to add in the rest needed to make up the twenty minas and pay it on her behalf to Eucrates and Timanoridas so she could be free. [32] Phrynion heard this with pleasure. He took the money contributed by her other lovers, added the remainder himself, then gave the twenty minas to Eucrates and Timanoridas for her freedom, on the

---

[48]Nothing is known about these men from other sources.

[49]An impressive sum, given the prices reported for other slaves, e.g., three, five, and six minas for craftsmen mentioned at Dem. 27.9.

[50]Evidently the men regarded the arrangement as incompatible with the more settled life into which they were entering.

[51]From a rich family. He was Demosthenes' cousin.

condition she not work in Corinth. To attest the truth of what I am saying, I call as a witness a man who was there: please call Philagrus of the deme Melite.[52]

[DEPOSITION] *Philagrus of the deme Melite testifies that he was present in Corinth when Phrynion, Demochares' brother, paid twenty minas to Timanoridas of Corinth and Eucrates of Leucas for Neaera, the woman now on trial; and that after he paid the money, he took Neaera with him to Athens.*

[33] Next, Phrynion came here to Athens, with Neaera. He carried on with her in an unruly and reckless way. He would take her along everywhere to eat and drink, and he was always partying with her. He would openly take his pleasure with her[53] whenever and wherever he wanted, showing off to onlookers just how loose he was with her. He visited many men for entertainment with the woman, including Chabrias of the deme Aexone, when he threw a party to celebrate his victory in the four-horse chariot race at the Pythian Games in the archon year of Socratides.[54] He had bought the team of horses from the sons of Mitys of Argos, and when he came back from Delphi, he gave a victory dinner in Colias.[55] There she got drunk, and many men were intimate with her while Phrynion slept—even Chabrias' slaves who were present to serve the refreshments. [34] As witnesses to the truth of what I am saying, I will provide men who were there and saw what happened. Please call up Chionides of the deme Xupete[56] and Euthetion of the deme Cydathenaeum.

---

[52] Aside from this document, all that is known of Philagrus are the names of his father, one or two sons, and his wife.

[53] The Greek can be understood as suggesting sexual intercourse.

[54] Chabrias had by the time of this victory in 374/3 long since distinguished himself as a general, and his winning the chariot competition at these games indicates wealth and prestige. Questionable behavior on Chabrias' part, however, is suggested not only by this passage but also by Dem. 19.287, where his name is associated with various miscreants.

[55] The party took place near, or just possibly in, a famous temple of Aphrodite.

[56] There is some doubt whether the deme name is correctly transmitted in the manuscripts. Nothing else is known about Chionides or Euthetion.

[DEPOSITION] *Chionides of the deme Xupete and Euthetion of the deme Cydathenaeum testify that Chabrias invited them to dinner when he gave a party celebrating his victory in the chariot race, and they were entertained at Colias. They know that Phrynion was present at that dinner and had with him Neaera, the woman now on trial; that they themselves fell asleep, and also Phrynion and Neaera; and that they noticed, during the night, that men got up and went to Neaera, including some of the attendants, slaves of Chabrias.*

[35] Now, since she was badly mistreated by Phrynion, and not loved as she expected she would be, and since he did not do her bidding, Neaera gathered things from his house and as much clothing and jewelry as he had given her, and also two slave girls, Thratta and Coccaline, and escaped to Megara. This was in the year when Asteius was archon, when you were for the second time at war with the Spartans.[57] [36] She spent two years in Megara, the year of Asteius' archonship and the next year, when Alcisthenes was archon. Her work as a prostitute was not bringing in enough money for her to run her household, since she was a big spender, and the Megarians are cheap and fussy; also, there wasn't much foreign traffic because the Megarians had sided with Sparta, and you had control of the sea. Neaera could not return to Corinth, since the terms of her being set free by Eucrates and Timanoridas[58] prohibited her from working there.

[37] But when peace came, during the archonship of Phrasicleides[59] and the Spartans and the Thebans fought the Battle of Leuctra,[60] Stephanus went to Megara and established relations with Neaera as his mistress (*hetaira*) and had sex with her. She told him everything

---

[57] In 373/2. Athenian relations with Sparta went sour in the aftermath of an unprovoked, unauthorized, and unsuccessful attack on Athens engineered by Sphodrias, a Spartan *harmost* (governor). To the horror of the Athenians, a Spartan court acquitted Sphodrias; subsequently, Athens allied herself with Thebes and inaugurated the Second Athenian Confederacy. The first war with Sparta is of course the conflict in the period 431–404.

[58] See above, 32.

[59] 371/0.

[60] In this battle, fought in Boeotian territory, Thebes dealt Sparta a decisive blow from which it never recovered.

that had happened, including how Phrynion had mistreated her, and she gave him what she had taken from Phrynion when she left him. She was eager to have her home here in Athens but was afraid because she had wronged Phrynion: he was angry with her, and she knew his violent and disrespectful manner. She made Stephanus her protector (*prostates*).[61] [38] In Megara, Stephanus inflamed her emotions with his braggadocio, saying that Phrynion would be sorry if he touched her, that he would take her himself as his wife, that he would introduce the children she already had to the *phratries* as his own sons and make them citizens,[62] that nobody would do her wrong. So he brought her from Megara to Athens, along with her three children, Proxenus, Ariston, and a daughter, whom they now call Phano. [39] And Stephanus set Neaera and the children up in a small house near the statue of the Whispering Hermes, between the houses of Dorotheus the Eleusinian and Cleinomachus.[63] That's the house that Spintharus just recently bought from him for seven minas. Seven minas, then, was the extent of Stephanus' wealth, and no more. He brought Neaera to Athens for two reasons, to get himself a good-looking mistress for free and to have her provide for daily expenses by her work as a prostitute and keep the house going. You see, he didn't have any other income, except for what he made as a *sykophant.*[64]

[40] When Phrynion learned that she was at Athens, with Stephanus, he took along some young men, went to Stephanus' house, and tried to take her away. Stephanus took legal action asserting that she was free,[65] and Phrynion made him post bond with the Polemarch. I

---

[61] The term, which literally means "one standing in front," might here carry a technical sense. If so, Neaera was entering Athens as a freed slave required to have an Athenian citizen acting as her official patron (*prostatēs*). The same requirement applied to resident aliens (*metics*). But the term might be used informally to mean merely that Stephanus was looking out for her interests.

[62] See above, 57.23n.

[63] The statue and houses cannot be located, but Stephanus' neighbors are both men of some prominence. Dorotheus was rich enough to have served as a trierarch. For Cleinomachus, see Dem. 58.42.

[64] See 51.16n.

[65] The action is called *aphairesis eis eleutherian,* literally "taking away to freedom" (cf. Dem. 58.19–21). Stephanus would have had to take along men prepared to guarantee her appearance in court (see the deposition that follows).

will bring the man then serving as Polemarch to verify that I am telling the truth. Please call Aeetes of the deme Ceiriadae.[66]

[DEPOSITION] *Aeetes of the deme Ceiriadae testifies that when he was
Polemarch, Neaera, the woman now on trial, was required by Phrynion, brother of Demochares, to post bond; and the guarantors for her
were Stephanus of the deme Eroeadae, Glaucetes of the deme Cephisia,
and Aristocrates of the deme Phalerum.*[67]

[41] With Stephanus as her guarantor, Neaera lived with him and
continued plying her trade no less than before. But now, exploiting
the façade of living with a husband, she demanded higher fees from
men who wanted to engage her. And together with Neaera, Stephanus
would commit legal blackmail[68] on any rich foreigner he caught having sex with her, claiming that the man was a debaucher (*moichos*)[69]
taken in the act. He would lock him in and demand money, lots
of it—as you would expect. [42] Neither Stephanus nor Neaera had
enough resources with which to meet their daily expenses. And their
lifestyle was lavish, since there were the two of them to support and
three young children whom she took along to live with him; also,
three servants, two women and one man. The problem was aggravated
by her having in the past learned to live luxuriously—at other people's
expense. [43] And Stephanus was getting nothing worth mention from
his participation in the city's affairs. He wasn't yet a public speaker,
only a *sykophant*, one of those men who stand around the podium

---

[66]No literary text or inscription mentions Aeetes, which is not surprising for
an Athenian chosen for office by a random process and thus unlikely to have been
part of the small group active in politics or subject to liturgies. Moreover, the
spelling of his name is not certain. The Polemarch, one of the nine Archons, was
involved because he had jurisdiction in matters involving metics.

[67]Glaucetes and Aristocrates are known to be members of rich families.

[68]Lit. "would act as a *sykophant*," i.e., he would bring a legal action, or at least
threaten to do so, in the hope of being bought off by the victim.

[69]*Moicheia* is usually translated "adultery," a word that in modern English refers to extramarital sexual activity of one or more married persons; here Stephanus'
blackmail was based on the pretense that Neaera was his wife. But since *moicheia*
is also used in this speech (64–71) for a situation in which the woman is not married, I prefer to translate it "illicit sex," and the person said to be guilty of "illicit
sex," a "debaucher."

shouting, and is paid to indict people and brings *phasis* actions[70] and puts their names on other people's motions. Then he came under the thumb of Callistratus of the deme Aphidna.[71] I will explain how and why[72] when I show you that this woman Neaera is a foreigner, that she has done you great wrongs, and that she has profaned the gods. [44] Then you will know that on his own, Stephanus deserves a punishment no smaller than Neaera but actually far greater: far greater because he boasts that he is an Athenian, and still he has so much contempt for the laws and for you and for the gods that not even shame for his own crimes restrains him, but he maliciously pursues me and others in the courts. Stephanus has thus brought it about that he himself and this woman have been brought by Theomnestus into court on a very serious charge and caused us to probe into just who she is and expose his wickedness.

[45] Then Phrynion brought suit against Stephanus because he had taken Neaera away from him by asserting her freedom and because Stephanus had received property that she had carried off from his house. But some friends brought the two men together and talked them into letting them arbitrate the dispute. Satyrus of the deme Alopece, Lacedaemonius' brother,[73] served as an arbitrator representing Phrynion; representing Stephanus was Saurias of the deme Lamptrae.[74] They chose Diogeiton of the deme Acharnae[75] as the impartial arbitrator. [46] These men gathered in the temple and heard what happened from both men and from the woman herself. Then they gave their opinion. They granted her her freedom and control over her own affairs, but she was to return everything she had taken from Phrynion, except the clothes, jewelry, and serving women, which had been bought specifically for her. She was to stay with each man on alternate

---

[70] Here the *phasis* is used for the formal denunciation of a man for possession of property belonging to the city (cf. note on Dem. 58.5n).

[71] See above, 27n.

[72] In fact, Apollodorus says no more on the subject (cf. above, 14 and 20n).

[73] Neither man is securely attested in other sources.

[74] Known to be from a rich family.

[75] His service as one of the Treasurers of Athena (attested by an inscription) means that Diogeiton at least officially belonged to the wealthiest property class (the *pentakosioimedimnoi*).

days, but if the men came to some other agreement with each other, that agreement would be valid. The man who had her on any given day was to provide for her needs, and from then on, the men were to be on friendly terms and not bear any grudge. [47] These, then, are the terms of reconciliation in the matter of Neaera decided on by the arbitrators for Phrynion and Stephanus. The clerk will read the deposition to show that I am telling the truth. Please call up Satyrus of the deme Alopece, Saurias of the deme Lamptrae, and Diogeiton of the deme Acharnae.

[DEPOSITION] *Satyrus of the deme Alopece, Saurias of the deme Lamptrae, and Diogeiton of the deme Acharnae testify that, serving as arbitrators, they reconciled Stephanus and Phrynion to each other in the matter of Neaera, the woman now on trial. The terms of the reconciliation are as Apollodorus presents them.*

[TERMS OF THE RECONCILIATION] *Phrynion and Stephanus have settled their quarrel on these terms. Each is to have and enjoy Neaera an equal number of days each month, unless they mutually agree to some other arrangement.*

[48] The reconciliation accomplished, the friends of the two sides left the scene of the arbitration, and something happened that I suppose is common in such matters, especially when a quarrel involves a *hetaira.* They went to dinner at each man's house when he had his turn with Neaera, and she ate and drank with them, just as a *hetaira* does. Please call those who were present as witnesses to the truth of what I am saying: Eubulus of the deme Probalinthus,[76] Diopeithes of the deme Melite,[77] and Cteson of the deme Cerameis.[78]

[WITNESSES] *Eubulus of the deme Probalinthus, Diopeithes of the deme Melite, and Cteson of the deme Cerameis testify that when the reconciliation in the matter of Neaera had been arranged for Phrynion*

---

[76] Eubulus was one of fourth-century Athens' most distinguished politicians. It is startling that he is testifying for Apollodorus, for some five to eight years before he was involved in litigation against him.

[77] Known to have been a rich Athenian.

[78] Cteson has not been securely identified from other documents, but he was probably a member of a wealthy Athenian family.

*and Stephanus, they often ate and drank together, along with Neaera,
the woman now on trial; sometimes they were at Stephanus' place,
sometimes at Phrynion's.*

[49] So far, I have shown in my speech and it has been confirmed
by witnesses that she was from the start a slave, that she was sold twice,
that she used her body working as a *hetaira,* that she escaped from Phrynion and went to Megara, and that when she came here she needed to
post bond as a foreigner with the Polemarch. Now I want to show you
that even Stephanus himself, this man here, gave testimony against her,
saying she was a foreigner. [50] You see, Stephanus gave Neaera's daughter, the one she brought with her to Athens as a little girl, who was
then called Strybele but is now called Phano, in marriage to an Athenian, Phrastor of the deme Aegilla,[79] together with a dowry of thirty
minas—making her out to be his own daughter. But when the girl
went to Phrastor, a conscientious workman, one who had assembled
his wealth by living carefully, she didn't know how to fit in with his
way of doing things; instead, she tried to follow her mother's character, including her wildness. I guess that was how she was brought up.
[51] Anyway, Phrastor saw that she was not a respectable woman and
was refusing to obey him. At the same time, he had learned for certain that she was not Stephanus' daughter, but Neaera's. At first when
he agreed to marry the girl, he had been tricked into regarding her as
Stephanus' daughter, not Neaera's, a daughter whom Stephanus had
with an Athenian woman before he lived with Neaera. Phrastor was
furious at this. Feeling insulted and duped, he threw the girl out of his
house after she had lived with him about a year and was pregnant. He
refused to give back her dowry. [52] Stephanus initiated a private suit
at the Court at the Odeion[80] against him, demanding that he pay to

---

[79] Otherwise not known.

[80] This passage shows that at the time of the trial, there was a specific venue for
specific sorts of litigation. The building where suits for financial support of wives
dismissed by the husbands were heard was originally built as a concert hall
("Odeion" literally means a building for songs). Not long after, the system was altered to make the assignment of magistrates (together with the cases over which
they presided) to the various sites one of several procedural steps decided by lot
the morning of the trial (*Ath. Pol.* 66).

support the girl (*dikē sitou*[81]). Stephanus took this action in accordance with the law that if a man sends his wife away, he is to return the dowry; otherwise, he must pay interest on it at an annual rate of eighteen percent,[82] and the woman's guardian (*kyrios*) can bring suit at the Odeion over the matter of her support. Phrastor initiated a public action (*graphē*[83]) against Stephanus before the Thesmothetae, claiming, in accordance with the following law, that Stephanus had betrothed to him, an Athenian, the daughter of a foreign woman whom he presented as his own but was in fact the daughter of a foreign woman. Please read out the law.

[LAW] *If a man gives a foreign woman in marriage to an Athenian man, claiming that she is his own relative, he is to lose his citizen rights, his property is to be confiscated, and the man who brings a successful prosecution is to receive one-third of the property. The actions* (graphai) *are to be initiated before the Thesmothetae, just like actions claiming usurpation of citizen rights* (graphai xenias).

[53] I have had the law read out under which Phrastor indicted Stephanus before the Thesmothetae. Because he knew that he was in danger of being exposed for marrying off the daughter of a foreign woman and incurring the most extreme penalties, Stephanus came to terms with Phrastor, abandoned the dowry, and dropped his suit for the woman's support. Phrastor in turn dropped his action before the Thesmothetae. I will call Phrastor himself as a witness to the truth of what I'm saying and, as the law provides, compel him to testify. [54] Please call Phrastor of the deme Aegilia.

[DEPOSITION] *Phrastor of the deme Aegilia testifies that when he realized that Stephanus had given him in marriage the daughter of Neaera, as if she were his own daughter, he brought a* graphē *against him before the Thesmothetae in accordance with the law; that he ex-*

---

[81] Lit. "a (private) law case pertaining to grain or in a wider sense to food."

[82] Lit. "at nine obols," i.e., nine obols per mina (600 obols) per month, amounting to 1.5% per month or 18% per year. This is a typical interest rate (it is assumed in the calculations at Dem. 36.38).

[83] Phrastor's move represents an escalation, as a *graphē* was generally more serious than a *dikē*.

pelled the woman from his house and did not continue to live with her; and that when Stephanus started a dikē *for support of the woman in the Court at the Odeion, he and Stephanus came to an agreement with one another that provided that the* graphē *before the Thesmothetae be dropped and also the* dikē *for support initiated against me by Stephanus.*[84]

[55] Now let me present some other testimony, both from Phrastor and his phratry members and clansmen (*gennetai*),[85] that Neaera here is a foreigner. Not long after Phrastor sent Neaera's daughter away, he got sick. His condition was very poor, and he had simply no way to help himself. He had, long before, quarreled with his relatives, and there was anger and hatred on both sides. Besides that, he had no children. With Phrastor in this condition, Neaera and her daughter worked on his emotions, exploiting his need to be cared for. [56] You see, they had gone to him when he was sick and had nobody to nurse him in his illness, and were taking him the right things and watching over him. I'm sure you all realize how useful a woman is when you're sick, being there when you're doing badly. Anyway, Phrastor was talked into taking back and adopting as his own son the little boy whom Neaera's daughter was carrying when she was expelled from his house, pregnant, because he had found out that she was Neaera's daughter, not Stephanus', and he was angry at being tricked. [57] Phrastor put two and two together, as anybody would, figuring that he was in bad shape and there was not much hope he would survive; and so, to keep his relatives from taking his property and so as not to die childless, he adopted the boy as his son and took him into his house.[86]

He would *not* have done this if he had been in good health, as I will show you with clear and compelling evidence. [58] As soon as Phrastor recovered and had pretty well regained his strength, he married an Athenian woman in accordance with the laws—Diphilus' sister, the legitimate daughter of Satyrus of the deme Melite.[87] This should count as proof for you that Phrastor did not recognize the boy willingly. No,

---

[84] The sudden switch from third to first person is one of several peculiarities in this document that have led scholars to question its authenticity.

[85] See 57.23n.

[86] These were common motives for adoption.

[87] Not otherwise known.

he was forced by illness, by his not having other children, by his need to be taken care of by the women, and by his feud with his relatives, whom he wanted to keep from inheriting his property if something happened to him. And what happened next makes the point even better. [59] When Phrastor was sick, he took that boy, the son of Neaera's daughter, to the phratry and the Brytidae—that was Phrastor's clan[88]—the clan members, I suppose, knew that the woman whom Phrastor had first married was Neaera's daughter, and how he sent her away, and that it was because of his illness that he was persuaded to take the boy back. And so, they voted against the boy and would not enroll him in the phratry. [60] When Phrastor brought a suit against them for not enrolling his son, the clan members challenged him to swear, before an arbitrator, over sacrificial offerings that he regarded the son as born to him from an Athenian woman (*astē*), legally married to him. When the clan members made this challenge before the arbitrator, Phrastor refused the oath and did not swear. [61] I will present as witnesses to the truth of my statements members of the clan Brytidae who were in attendance.

[WITNESSES] *Timostratus of the deme Hecale,[89] Xanthippus of the deme Eroeadae, Evalces of the deme Phalerum,[90] Anytus of the deme Laciadae,[91] Euphranor of the deme Aegilia,[92] Nicippus of the deme Cephale[93] testify that they and Phrastor of the deme Aegilia are members of the clan called Brytidae; and that when Phrastor asked that his son be enrolled in the clan, since they knew for themselves that the boy's mother was Neaera's daughter, they prevented his enrolling the boy.*

[62] I will show you, very clearly, that even Neaera's closest friends have testified that she is a foreigner, both Stephanus, who now has her, and Phrastor, who took her daughter in marriage. Stephanus, for

---

[88] See 13 and 55, with notes.

[89] Not otherwise known.

[90] Not otherwise known, unless the manuscripts have misspelled his name and this man is identical with a certain Evalkos of the deme Phalerum whose name is on an inscription.

[91] Not otherwise known.

[92] An inscription records his service as an arbitrator.

[93] Known from inscriptions as a rich man.

his part was unwilling to go to trial in support of his daughter when he was charged by Phrastor before the Thesmothetae with giving him, an Athenian, the daughter of a foreign woman in marriage. Instead, Stephanus relinquished the dowry and would not take it back. [63] Phrastor, for his part, after he married Neaera's daughter, expelled her from his house on learning that she was not Stephanus' daughter and did not return the dowry. Later, when he was persuaded to adopt the boy—owing to his sickness, his childlessness, and his feud with his relatives—he brought him to his *genos,* but the *genos* voted to reject him, and when they challenged him to swear under oath, he refused; instead, he preferred to avoid perjury. Afterward, he married another woman, an Athenian (*astē*), in accordance with the law. These actions were performed in the open, and they give powerful testimony against Neaera and Stephanus that this woman Neaera is a foreigner.

[64] You should also observe Stephanus' shameful, wicked way of turning a profit. That's another way you can know that Neaera here is no Athenian (*astē*). You see, Stephanus plotted against Epainetus, a man from Andros.[94] Epainetus had been Neaera's lover and had spent a lot of money on her. Whenever he came to Athens he stayed with Neaera and Stephanus, since he was her friend. [65] Stephanus here plotted against Epainetus. He invited him to the country, supposedly for a sacrifice, and then seized Epainetus for illicit sex with Neaera's daughter.[95] This frightened Epainetus into settling with him for thirty minas.[96] Stephanus accepted as guarantors Aristomachus, who had served as a Thesmothetes, and Nausiphilus[97] the son of Nausinicus, who had been Archon;[98] then he let Epainetus go on his promise to deliver the money. [66] After Epainetus left and was back in control of his person, he brought an action against Stephanus (*graphē*) for false

---

[94] An island in the Aegean, very near Athens. Epainetus is not known from other documents.

[95] This episode shows that the term *moicheia,* normally used in connection with a breach of a husband's rights (see 41n), could also be applied when the woman is not married.

[96] Cf. the offer to settle at Lys. 1.25.

[97] Neither man is known from any other document.

[98] I.e., eponymous archon (in 378/7).

arrest (*adikōs heirchthenai*[99]). This was under the law that provides that if a man falsely arrests someone on the claim that he is engaged in fornication, he is to be indicted before the *Thesmothetae* for illegal restraint; and if the complainant convicts the man for false arrest, and the verdict is that the complainant is the victim of criminal plotting, the complainant is immune, and the guarantors are released from their guarantee. But if it is decided that the complainant is a debaucher,[100] the law provides for the guarantors to hand him over to the man who arrested him, who can then, in a lawcourt, do to the debaucher whatever he wishes, provided he does not use a weapon.[101]

[67] It was in accord with this law, then, that Epainetus brought a *graphē* against Stephanus. Epainetus admitted having sex with Neaera's daughter but denied that he was a debaucher. He said that she was *not* Stephanus' daughter, but Neaera's. The mother knew her daughter was intimate with him, and he spent much money on the women, supporting the whole household when he was in town. Besides that, he cited a provision of the law that forbids seizing a man as a debaucher if the woman is set up in a brothel or is openly available as a prostitute. Epainetus said that Stephanus' house was a brothel, and prostitution was the business conducted there, and they profited handsomely from that business. [68] Those are the arguments Epainetus made in support of his *graphē*. Now, Stephanus knew that he would be exposed as a pimp and *sykophant*, so he offered to go to arbitration with Epainetus, using those very guarantors as arbitrators. The guarantors would be released from their commitment, and Epainetus would drop his *graphē*. [69] Epainetus was persuaded to accept these terms, and he abandoned the *graphē* he was pursuing against Stephanus. They had a meeting, with the guarantors sitting as arbitrators. Stephanus had no just claim to put forward but said he thought Epainetus should contribute to a dowry for Neaera's daughter. He said she was without means and mentioned the bad luck she had dealing with Phrastor and added that he had lost the dowry and could not provide another one. [70] "You've

---

[99] Lit. "for being unjustly restrained," i.e., for entrapment.

[100] In Greek, "one who commits *moicheia*."

[101] Some sources (admittedly from the comic stage) speak of pushing a radish into the debaucher's anus.

enjoyed the woman," he said, "so it's right that you do something nice for her." And he added other cajoling arguments, the sort of thing a man says when he's in great trouble. After the arbitrators heard both sides, they brought the two men to an agreement. They persuaded Epainetus to contribute one thousand drachmas for the dowry of Neaera's daughter. I will call as witnesses to the truth of what I have said the guarantors, who also served as arbitrators.

[71] [WITNESSES] *Nausiphilus of the deme Cephale and Aristomachus of the deme Cephale testify that they were guarantors for Epainetus of Andros when Stephanus declared that he had seized Epainetus in an act of illicit sex. Subsequently, when Epainetus left Stephanus' house and resumed control of his person, he brought a* graphē *against Stephanus before the Thesmothetae, charging him with false arrest. Later, as arbitrators, they reconciled Epainetus and Stephanus. The terms of reconciliation are the ones presented by Apollodorus.*

[TERMS OF RECONCILIATION] *The arbitrators have reconciled Epainetus and Stephanus on the following terms: They are to bear no grudge in the matter of the arrest, and Epainetus is to give one thousand drachmas to Phano for her dowry, since he enjoyed her company many times. Stephanus is to make Phano available to Epainetus whenever he is in town and wishes to be with her.*

[72] This man Stephanus and this woman Neaera were so outrageous and lacking in decency that they had the brass not just to claim that she was an Athenian (*astē*)—this woman openly acknowledged to be a foreigner and with whom he had dared to seize a man on the pretext of performing illicit sex. No, they went further: they saw that Theogenes of the clan of the Coironidae[102] had been appointed by lot to serve as Basileus.[103] He was well born but poor and inexperi-

---

[102] The manuscripts assign Theogenes, who is otherwise unknown, the deme name Cothocidae, which is inconsistent with 84, where the demotic is Erchia. The translation follows the conjecture "Coironidae," a venerable family associated with the Eleusinian Mysteries.

[103] One of the nine archons, referred to in Greek simply as "king," he mostly discharged religious duties (see *Ath. Pol.* 47.4 and 57 and the Series Introduction, p. xxii). For Greek civic religion in general, see L. B. Zaidman and P. S. Pantel, *Religion in the Ancient Greek City,* trans. by P. Cartledge (Cambridge, 1992).

enced. Stephanus stood by him when he was undergoing his evaluation (*dokimasia*[104]) and helped him meet his expenses when he entered into his office. Then sneaking into Theogenes' affairs, Stephanus bought the office of Assessor (*paredros*[105]) from him; finally he married that woman Phano, Neaera's daughter, to him, making out that she was his own daughter. That's how contemptuous he was of you and your laws.

[73] This woman performed the secret sacrifices on the city's behalf. She saw things that were not proper for her, as a foreigner, to see. A foreigner, she entered where no Athenian—and there are a great many Athenians—other than the wife of the Basileus has ever entered. She administered the oath to the elderly priestesses who tend to the sacred rites. She was given as bride to Dionysus. On the city's behalf she performed the many, secret ancestral rituals honoring the gods. If no one is allowed even to hear about these things, it is certainly a profanity if just any woman whatsoever does them, especially a woman like this, who has committed acts like *that*.

[74] I want to relate these things one-by-one from the beginning in greater detail so that you may give more care to the punishment and so that you realize that you will be voting not only for yourselves and the laws but also for the sake of piety toward the gods, when you take vengeance for acts of impiety and punish the wrong-doers.

Now, gentlemen of Athens, in olden times there was monarchy in the city, passed down through the generations and held by those who had primacy because they were autochthonous.[106] The Basileus performed all the sacrifices, and his wife performed the most solemn and secret, which made sense, since she was the Queen (Basilinna). [75] But when Theseus united the Athenians into a single city[107] and created

---

[104] The procedure for examining a man's qualifications for public office. Aristotle (*Ath. Pol.* 55.2) speaks of the *dokimasia* of the archons, but he does not say what matters were considered.

[105] The Archon, Polemarch, and King each had two *paredroi* to assist them.

[106] Historians and orators often refer to the Athenian boast that, unlike others, their ancestors were not immigrants (e.g., Thuc. 6.2; Lys. 2.17; Isoc. 7.29; Dem. 60.4). Here the distinction is attributed only to the kings.

[107] Like the claim of autochthony, Theseus' *synoikismos*, the political unification of Attica, is a prominent element in the legends of early Athenian history. It is less usual to credit him with founding the democracy.

the democracy, and the city's population grew larger, they continued as before to choose the King by voting, looking for manly excellence (*andragathia*) from a group of pre-selected candidates. And they made a law that he had to marry an Athenian woman (*astē*) who had not had sex with any other man but was a virgin. The object was that the Queen would perform the secret sacrifices in traditional fashion on the city's behalf and that the customary rites would be performed with due reverence for the gods with nothing left out or altered. [76] They had this law inscribed on a stone pillar, and they set it up alongside the altar in the Temple of Dionysus in the Marshes (*Limnae*). The actual pillar is still standing, even now, with its old Attic alphabet, the inscribed letters now faint.[108] With this law the democracy bears witness to its piety toward the god, and for future generations marks a sacred obligation that we should expect a woman to be like this if she is to be married to Dionysus and perform the sacred rites. For this reason they erected the pillar in the most ancient and august temple of Dionysus in the Marshes, to keep the general run of people from knowing what is written on it, for only once a year is the temple opened, on the twelfth day of the month *Anthesterion*.[109]

[77] It is therefore right, gentlemen of Athens, that you give serious attention to these holy and sacred rituals, rituals that your ancestors so nobly and generously tended, and right that you punish those who wantonly dishonor your laws, shamelessly committing impiety against the gods. There are two reasons to do so: to make sure that the violators pay the penalty for their crimes and in order that the others take heed and be afraid to wrong the gods and the city.

[78] I want to call the Sacred Herald who attends the wife of the Basileus when she swears in the elderly priestesses in the ceremony at the baskets by the altar before they touch the sacred objects. This is so you may hear the oath and other things that are said—as much as it is legal to hear—and so you appreciate just how august, sacred, and ancient our observances are.

---

[108] During the archonship of Eucleides (403/2) the city adopted and then consistently used a slightly different alphabet for official documents. The faintness of the letters might refer to actual erosion of the stone's surface or the flaking away of the paint (normally red) applied to the incisions.

[109] Corresponding to late February and early March.

[OATH OF THE ELDERLY PRIESTESSES] [110] *I am pure, chaste, and without taint from things that are impure, including intercourse with men. I celebrate the Festival of the Wine God* (theoinia) [111] *and the Bacchic rite* (iobaccheia) [112] *honoring the god in accordance with the ancestral rule and at the appointed times.*

[79] You have heard the oath and our ancestral practices, to the extent that it is permitted to speak of them. And you have heard that the woman Stephanus gave in marriage, as his own daughter, to Theogenes, when he was serving as Basileus, performed these sacred rituals and swore in the elderly priestesses; also, you have heard that it is not allowed, even for the women themselves who observe the rites, to speak of these things to any other person. And now, let me present testimony to you that is illegal to quote, but that I can still put clearly and truly before you by means of the acts themselves. [80] You see, after these rites had been performed, the nine Archons went up to the Areopagus on the appointed days. The Council of the Areopagus, a worthy body especially in matters of state religion, [113] immediately conducted an inquiry into the identity of Theogenes' wife. They revealed her for who she was and took care for the sacred rites. They punished Theogenes to the extent they were empowered to do. The proceedings were confidential and orderly. They do not, after all, have the right to punish just any Athenian at their whim. [81] There was discussion, and the Council of the Areopagus was indignant and punished Theogenes for marrying such a woman and permitting her to perform the secret rituals for the city. But Theogenes, throwing himself at the Council's

---

[110] Presumably this testimony was given in the standard fashion, i.e., the clerk would read it and the witness (here the herald) would assent to it.

[111] Our only source for this festival (Harpocration, first or second century AD) describes it as involving sacrifices to Dionysus performed by clans in each deme.

[112] The name apparently derives from the cry, "O Bacchus!" (cf. Euripides, *Bacchae* 528).

[113] Besides exercising jurisdiction in homicide cases and a few other criminal matters, the Areopagus is known to have supervised certain sacred lands and sacred olive trees (see Lys. 7) and to have selected certain officials of the cult of the Eumenides. Its precise competence in other religious matters, including the fining of Theogenes, is controversial. For a broad treatment of this court, see Wallace 1989.

mercy and begging, asked them to relent. He said he did not know that she was Neaera's daughter but had been tricked by Stephanus into accepting her as his legitimate daughter, as defined by law. It was because of his inexperience and naïveté that he made Stephanus his assessor,[114] because he thought he would manage that office as a loyal friend, and that was why he became related to him by marriage. [82] "I will show you," he said, "with clear and convincing proof that I am not lying. I will send the woman away, since she is Neaera's daughter, not Stephanus'. If I do that, then you should believe right away what I've told you, that I was tricked. If I do not send her away, then punish me on the spot as an evil man, guilty of impiety to the gods." [83] That was what Theogenes promised when he made his plea. The Council pitied him for his honest ways, and at the same time they thought that he really had been tricked by Stephanus, and so they relented. When Theogenes came down from the Areopagus, he immediately threw the daughter of this woman Neaera out of his house and expelled Stephanus, the man who had fooled him, from his board of assessors. And that is how it happened that the members of the Areopagus ended their trial, and were no longer angry with Theogenes, but instead forgave him because he had been tricked. [84] I now call Theogenes and require him to give testimony that what I say is true. Please call Theogenes of the deme Erchia.[115]

[DEPOSITION] *Theogenes of the deme Erchia testifies that when he was Basileus he married Phano, thinking she was the daughter of Stephanus; but when he found out that he had been tricked, he dismissed the woman and no longer lived with her. He also expelled Stephanus from his board of assessors and no longer allowed him to serve as his assessor.*

[85] Clerk, please take this law on these matters, and read it, so the jury will know that being the type of woman she was and having done the things she had done, Phano should have kept away not only from seeing these sacred things and performing any of the established, ancestral rites for the city, but also from seeing all other things of this sort in Athens. A woman with whom a debaucher (*moichos*) has been found is not permitted to attend any of the city's rites, which the laws allow

---

[114] See above, 72n.
[115] See above, 72n.

even foreign and slave women to attend as observers or suppliants. [86] The law forbids only those women with whom a debaucher has been taken from entering the city's rites. If they enter in contravention of the law, any man who wishes may with impunity do anything to them, short of killing them. The law grants any man the right to administer punishment for these offenses. The law provides that the woman cannot get legal redress for any treatment she suffers except for death, for this reason: that no pollution or impiety sully the sacred rituals. The law frightens women enough to keep them chaste and law-abiding, staying at home behaving properly. The law teaches them that if they commit this sort of crime, they will be expelled from their husband's home and from the city's sacred areas. [87] Once you have heard the law itself read out, you will know that this is so. Clerk, please take the text.

[LAW ON DEBAUCHERY] *When a man catches a debaucher with his wife, it is not permitted for him to continue to live with her. If he does live with her, he is to be disenfranchised. And it is not permitted for the woman with whom a debaucher has been taken to appear at the city's sacred rituals. If she does so, she may be made to suffer anything short of being killed, immunity being granted to the person who punishes her.*

[88] Next, gentlemen of Athens, I want to provide you testimony of the seriousness with which the Athenian *dēmos* regards these religious matters, and how much thoughtful care it has put into these things. You see, the Athenian *dēmos* holds the greatest authority in the city, and it may do whatever it wishes. It considered Athenian citizenship to be so fine and august a gift that it instituted laws for itself that must be followed if it wants to make someone a citizen. These are the laws that now lie in the mud, thanks to Stephanus and those who have married as he has. [89] Still, you will benefit from hearing about them, and you will know how the noblest and most august gift the city can bestow on its benefactors has been defiled. First, there is an established law that prohibits the Assembly (*dēmos*) from making anyone an Athenian citizen who is not worthy of it by virtue of his upright action on the city's behalf.[116] Second, when the city is persuaded to give this

---

[116]"Upright action" normally took the form of lavish expenditure on public works or military equipment.

gift, it does not make the decree valid until, at the next meeting of the Assembly, it is approved by a secret vote of more than six thousand citizens.[117] [90] The law requires the *Prytaneis*[118] to place the ballot urns out for the Assembly before foreigners enter, and the barriers are lifted to make sure that each Assembly member think over entirely by himself whether the man up for citizenship is worthy to receive this gift. Then, the law provides that an indictment for an illegal proposal (*graphē paranomōn*[119]) can be instituted by any Athenian who wishes. He is allowed to go to court to expose a man as not worthy of the gift of citizenship and holding it in violation of the laws. [91] Already in some cases after the Assembly, hoodwinked by the speeches of the petitioners, granted citizenship, a *graphē paranomōn* was instituted: the man who had received the gift was exposed as unworthy, and the court stripped him of citizenship. Now, it would be a major project to go through the many cases from the past, but you all remember that the court canceled the citizenship given to Peitholas of Thessaly[120] and Apollonides of Olynthus.[121] [92] These cases are not too ancient for

[117] The prosecution might be suspected of exaggerating the distinction involved in naturalization (see above, 2), but the gift was in fact rarely bestowed, and the process was in fact difficult to transact. "The double procedure was introduced in about 370, and between 368 and 322 we have knowledge of fifty grants of citizenship, to sixty-four foreigners; since the sources are fragmentary as usual, it may be conjectured that several hundred people obtained citizenship by naturalization in those forty-seven years, but that is no great number, and most of them were foreign princes and statesmen who had no intention of settling in Athens, so that their citizenship was in practice honorary" (Hansen 1999: 94).

[118] Fifty members of that tribe currently serving as a sort of executive committee of the Council of 500.

[119] See the Introduction to 58.

[120] Son of Jason, the tyrant of Pherae who brought all of Thessaly under his control. Peitholas joined Athens in supporting Phocis in the Second Sacred War (a struggle for control of Delphi) that began in 355. This alliance was, presumably, behind the grant of citizenship. Evidently, there followed a breach between him and the city, or possibly an allegation of bribery (see Arist., *Rhetoric* 1410a) that precipitated the cancellation.

[121] Olynthus, the main city of Chalcidice, a peninsula in northeast Greece just below Macedonia, was first allied with Philip II, then with Athens (see Dem. 1–3). Apollonides led the faction opposed to Philip and was exiled from Olynthus. There

you to remember them. And although the laws on citizenship regulating how one becomes an Athenian are so excellently and effectively composed, there is another law of the greatest authority that has been enacted in addition to all the others. Such was the care the *dēmos* devoted on its own behalf and on behalf of the gods, to ensure that the sacrifices on the city's behalf are made in piety. The law explicitly forbids those made citizens by an act of the Athenian Assembly from holding any of the nine archonships or participating in any priesthood. The *dēmos* does, however, grant a share in all these privileges to the second generation, adding the qualification, "if they are born to a woman who is an Athenian (*astē*) and legally married." [93] And I will show that this is true by strong, clear evidence. I want to go back to the beginning in telling you about this law, how it was established and with what sort of people, what upstanding and reliable friends of the *dēmos* it had in mind. From all this you will learn that the *dēmos'* gift, one reserved for the city's benefactors, has been besmirched, and what great benefits are being taken out of your hands by this man Stephanus and those who have married and had children in the same way.

[94] You see, gentlemen of Athens, the Plataeans were the only Greeks who came to your aid at Marathon when Datis, general of King Darius, left Eretria after bringing Euboea under his control.[122] He entered Attica with a large force and was laying it waste. To this day a memorial, a painting in the Stoa Poikilē,[123] memorializes the Plataeans' manly virtue. They are the men in the Boeotian helmets, each one coming to help as fast as he can. [95] And again, when Xerxes marched against Greece and the rest of the Thebans took the Persian side, the Plataeans had the moral strength to remain your friends.[124]

---

is no specific information on either the grant of citizenship to Apollonides or its later cancellation.

[122] Events of 490. Marathon is in Attica; Eretria is in Euboea, the large island just off the east coast of Attica.

[123] The "Painted Porch" on the north side of the Agora in Athens, famous for its fifth-century murals by prominent artists of the time.

[124] Events of 480–479. These naval battles were fought in 480, the first off the northern end of Euboea, the second in the narrow strait between the island of Salamis and the coast of Attica. The Battle of Plataea, a Boeotian town near the border with Attica, took place in 479.

Alone among the Boeotians, they fought on the Greek side. Half of them, standing side-by-side with Leonidas[125] and the Spartans, fell in the Battle of Thermopylae. The other half embarked on your triremes, since they did not have their own ships, and fought with you at the battles of Artemisium and Salamis. [96] And at the final battle at Plataea against Mardonius, the Persian King's general, they fought alongside you and the other Greeks in the struggle for Greek liberation and won freedom for the other Greeks. Then Pausanias, the Spartan king, tried to insult you and was not content that the Greeks thought the Spartans alone worthy to be their leader.[126] Although Athens was truly freedom's champion for the Greeks, it did not compete with Sparta from fear that the allies would be jealous. [97] In these circumstances Pausanias, a king of Sparta, puffed up with pride, put the following inscription on the tripod in Delphi erected by the Greeks who fought together at Plataea and won the victory at sea in the Battle of Salamis. The tripod, a memorial of valor from the spoils of war taken from the barbarians, was dedicated to Apollo:

> Commander of the Greeks, when he destroyed the army of the Persians,
>   Pausanias dedicated this monument to Phoebus Apollo.

The implication was that the deed and the dedication belonged to him, not to the allies working in common.

[98] The Greeks were angry, and at the Amphictyonic Council[127] the Plataeans, on behalf of the allies, instituted a suit against the Spartans for one thousand talents and forced them to chisel out the letters and inscribe instead the names of the cities that shared in the deed. This was the main reason the Spartans and their royal family began to hate the Plataeans. At the time, they had no way to attack the Plataeans,

---

[125]One of the two Spartan kings at the time. Spartan kings were, above all, hereditary military leaders.

[126]Although Apollodorus calls him "King," Pausanias was in fact serving as regent for his young cousin, King Pleistarchus. Apollodorus' account, although it clearly derives in the main from passages in the first three books of Thucydides' history, deviates from it at a number of points.

[127]A council that administered the affairs of Delphi.

but fifty years later,[128] in time of peace, Archidamus son of Zeuxida-
mos, a king of the Spartans, tried to capture their city. [**99**] He worked
from Thebes with the assistance of Eurymachus, the son of Leontiades
the Boeotiarch.[129] Naucleides, together with a few others, was bribed
to open the gates of the city during the night. When the Plataeans realized that the Thebans had entered during the night and that their city
had suddenly been captured in peacetime, they organized and came
to their city's defense. At daybreak they saw that the Theban contingent was not large—only the vanguard had entered, as heavy rain
during the night had kept the full force from entering. The Asopus
river was running high and was not easy to cross, especially at night.
[**100**] Now, when the Plataeans saw the Thebans in the city, but realized they did not have their whole army, they attacked and defeated
them in battle. They were able to crush them before the other Thebans could come to their assistance. Then they immediately sent a
messenger to you to report what had happened, announce their victory in the battle, and ask you to help them if the Thebans ravaged
their land. When the Athenians heard this, they quickly sent help to
Plataea. When the Thebans saw the Athenians helping the Plataeans,
they returned home.

[**101**] Since the Theban attempt failed and the Plataeans put to death
the prisoners they took in the battle, the Spartans were angry and right
away, without offering any excuse, they launched an attack on Plataea.
They ordered all the Peloponnesians, with the exception of the Argives,
to send two-thirds of their forces from each city to take part in the expedition; to the Boeotians, including the Locrians, Phocians, Malians,
Oetaeans, and Aenians, they sent the order to join the campaign with
their full forces. [**102**] Once the Spartans had laid siege to the Plataean
wall with this large contingent, they sent messages to the Plataeans,
saying that if they were willing to hand over their city, they could re-
tain the land and enjoy the use of their property, but they would have
to abandon their alliance with Athens. The Plataeans refused and answered that they would do nothing without the Athenians. So the
Spartans encircled the city with a double wall and continued the siege

---

[128] In 431, just before the outbreak of the Peloponnesian War.
[129] A leader of the Boeotian League.

for two years,[130] making many attempts to take the city by various means. [103] When the Plataeans were exhausted, and had no resources left and despaired of rescue, they divided themselves up by lot. One group stayed in the besieged city, but the others waited for a night with rain and strong wind, then escaped from the city, then scaled the enemy's siege walls without being detected, killed the men on watch, and against all expectations made their way safely here—though in a terrible state. Plataea was taken by force, and of those who had remained, all the adult men were slaughtered, and the women and children enslaved. But those who did not stay in the city when they realized the Spartans were attacking escaped to Athens.

[104] Now consider again how you gave a share in Athenian citizenship to men who so clearly demonstrated their goodwill toward our *dēmos,* giving up all that was theirs, even wives and children. The law will be clear to all from your decrees, and you will know that I am telling the truth. Clerk, please take this decree and read it to the jury.

[DECREE CONCERNING THE PLATAEANS] *Hippocrates made the motion.*

The Plataeans are to be Athenian citizens from this day forward, with the rights enjoyed by the other Athenians, and they are to have a share of all that the Athenians share, sacred and secular, except for a priesthood or rite belonging to a clan and service as one of the nine Archons,[131] *though their descendants may do so. The Plataeans are to be distributed among the demes and tribes.*[132] *Once the distribution takes place, it will not be permitted for any other Plataean to become an Athenian citizen, unless he obtains that right from the Athenian* dēmos.

[105] You see, gentlemen, how fine and just a decree the speaker proposed for the Athenian *dēmos.* He required, first, that the Plataeans take the gift only after undergoing the scrutiny (*dokimasia*), man by man, in court, to see whether each one was a Plataean and a friend of the city. This provision guarded against many getting citizenship by false claim. Second, the names of those who passed the scrutiny were

---

[130] This translates an emendation of the manuscripts, which read "ten years," but some scholars believe that "ten" is correct.

[131] Cf. above, 16n.

[132] Cf. above, 13 with n.

to be inscribed on a stone pillar to be erected on the Acropolis next to the temple of Athena, so that the gift of citizenship would be preserved for the Plataeans' descendants, and it would be possible for any individual to prove his relationship. [106] And the decree does not allow anyone to become an Athenian citizen later who did not become one at this time after scrutiny by the court. The purpose was to prevent a multitude from claiming to be Plataean and thereby concocting citizenship for themselves. Further, in the decree he prescribed the law for the Plataeans, in the interests of both the city and its gods, that effective immediately no Plataean could obtain any of the nine archonships nor any priesthood, though their descendants may, if born to a legally married Athenian woman (*astē*).

[107] Isn't it shocking? On the one hand, when it comes to our neighbors, men acknowledged to be the best of all the Greeks in their dealings with our city, you have legislated with such precise care the conditions under which each individual may enjoy the gift of citizenship; while on the other, you will allow this woman, a whore known to all Greece, to treat our city with disgrace and contempt and get away with profaning the gods, this woman who is not Athenian by her birth and not a citizen by act of the *dēmos*. [108] Is there a place she has *not* sold her body? Is there a place she has *not* gone to earn her daily living? She's been all over the Peloponnese, in Thessaly, and in Magnesia with Simus from Larissa [133] and Eurydamas the son of Medeius; [134] in Chios and in most of Ionia she followed Sotades from Crete around,[135] rented out by Nicarete, who still owned her. What do you suppose a woman will do when under the thumb of different men, traipsing after any man who pays her? Isn't she going to serve up every sort of pleasure to the men who use her? And *then,* will you vote citizenship for a woman of this character, notorious to all for making her living from three holes,[136] street-walking the world?

---

[133] See above, 24.

[134] A member of the same aristocratic family as Simus, he came to a lurid end alluded to by the poets Callimachus and Ovid. Eurydamas killed Simus' brother; Simus then killed him and dragged his corpse around his brother's tomb.

[135] Another prominent man, Sotades was a victor at the Olympic Games of 384.

[136] Hermogenes, a second-century AD writer on rhetoric, reports that the words "making her living from three (drilled) holes" appeared in some texts of this

[109] If someone asks you, just what fine deed will you say you have accomplished? What shame and impiety will not rightfully be blamed on you? Before she was indicted and came to trial and everybody learned her true identity and profane acts, the crimes were her doing, and the city was merely negligent. Some of you did not know. Others, when they looked into it, were furious and said so, but there was nothing they could do to her as long as no one brought her to court and gave you the chance to vote on her. But now that you all have the information and the power and authority to punish her, the impiety is *yours,* if you fail to punish her. [110] If you acquit this woman, what will each of you say when you return home to your wife or daughter or mother when they ask you, "Where were you?" You answer, "We were judging a case." The next question will be, "Who was on trial?" Of course you'll answer, "Neaera. The charge was that she is a foreigner who lived with an Athenian as married to him, in violation of the law, and that she gave her daughter, a corrupted woman,[137] to Theogenes when he became Basileus; and that she performed the secret, holy sacrifices for the city and was made the wife to Dionysus." And you will go through the rest of the accusations against her, recalling how memorably and carefully each of the charges was presented. [111] When they hear this, they will ask, "Well, what did you do?" And you will say, "We acquitted her." At once, the most upright of the women will be angry with you for having thought it proper that this woman share the city and its religion on an equal basis with them. As for the women with less sense, you will plainly be directing them to do whatever they want, since you and the laws have granted them immunity. You will seem to be reckless, lazy, and in sympathy with Neaera's way of life. [112] The result will be that it would be better for this trial not to have taken place at all than for you to acquit her, because in that case there will be complete license for whores to live with whomever they wish and to claim that their children were fathered by just anybody. As far

---

speech. They are not to be found in any surviving manuscript, and most scholars believe that the expression is too crude for Attic oratory. But since the entire passage passes the normal limits of decorum, Apollodorus probably did venture this gibe.

[137] The Greek suggests that she was irreversibly ruined by *moicheia* (see above, 41n).

as you are concerned, the laws will lose their force, and the lifestyle of *hetairai* will have the authority to bring about whatever those women want. Give a thought to the interest of our female citizens so that the daughters of poor men will not go unmarried. [113] As it is now, even if a girl is without resources, the law contributes a sufficient dowry if her looks are halfway presentable.[138] If you trample this law in the mud and invalidate it by acquitting Neaera, the business of prostitution will be the lot of the daughters of Athenian citizens who cannot be married off owing to poverty; while the *hetairai* will achieve the dignity of free women if they can with impunity have whatever children they want and share in the city's rituals, religion, and honors.

[114] So each one of you should think of himself as casting his vote in the interests of his wife, or daughter, or mother, or of the city and its laws and its religion. Your purpose is to keep the women in your care from being brought down to the same level of honor as this whore. You must keep women who are brought up in strict chastity and care by their family and given in marriage according to the laws from publicly attaining the same honor as a woman who has spent each day in obscene practices, over and over complying with each customer's desires.

[115] Do not suppose it is I, Apollodorus, who is speaking, nor the citizens who will speak to defend and support her, but imagine that the laws are actually in litigation with Neaera here over the things she has done. When you are hearing the prosecution, listen to the laws themselves, those laws that govern the city and that you have sworn to follow in your judgments. What do those laws require, and how have these people violated them? When you hear the defense, keep in mind the laws' accusations and the speakers' clear proofs. Observe her appearance and consider only this: being Neaera, did she do these things?[139]

---

[138] It is not known whether Apollodorus is referring accurately to any real law. The qualifying final phrase perhaps hints at physical characteristics the society deemed outright deformity.

[139] The meaning of this instruction to the jury is obscure: perhaps Neaera, though a woman well into middle age, was still flaunting her beauty in a way the jurors might find shocking. Or perhaps, just because she strove for a look of decorous respectability, Apollodorus was inducing the jury to look past this disguise

[116] It is also worth considering this, gentlemen of Athens. You punished Archias, who had been the hierophant,[140] when he was shown in court to have committed an impiety by sacrificing in violation of our ancestral practices. There were many charges against him, but the main one was that at the Haloa[141] on the altar in the Eleusinian court he sacrificed an animal brought to him by the *hetaira* Sinope,[142] even though it was not legal to sacrifice animals that day, and the sacrifice was not for him to perform, but for the priestess. [117] Would this not be shocking? You punish a man of the Eumolpidae clan,[143] with ancestors of the highest quality, a citizen of Athens, because he appeared to have violated some element of the laws. The pleas of his relatives and his friends did not help, nor did the liturgies[144] that he or his ancestors had performed for the city, nor his ancestry, nor his position as hierophant. No, you punished him because you decided he had done something wrong. Will you then turn around and *not* punish this woman Neaera, guilty of impiety towards the same god and towards the laws—the woman herself and her daughter?

[118] I, for my part, am wondering what in the world they will say to you in their defense speech. Will they claim Neaera is an Athenian woman (*astē*) and that she lives with Stephanus in conformity with the laws? There has, however, been testimony that she is a *hetaira* and was Nicarete's slave. Will they claim that she is not his wife but is living

---

by remembering the lurid past associated with her name. Merely that her name is mentioned at all, perhaps aggravated by her presence in court (see the Introduction to this speech), may in the etiquette of the Athenian courts have marked her as a prostitute.

[140] The priest who served the special function of exhibiting sacred objects during the rituals of the Eleusinian Mysteries. Archias is known to have taken sides in Theban civil strife, and this action was probably the motive for his political enemies to have instituted his prosecution for a religious offense.

[141] A fertility festival that took place in early winter. Men were excluded from at least part of the festival.

[142] She is mentioned at Dem. 22.56.

[143] One of the two great clans that supplied the main priests for the mystery cult at Eleusis.

[144] Payments made by the richest men to support the city's military, religious, and cultural activities. See the Series Introduction, p. xxiii.

with him as a concubine (*pallakē*)? But Stephanus presented the boys
to the phratry as sons of Neaera and gave her daughter in marriage to
an Athenian, clearly demonstrating that he did keep her as his wife.
[119] I do not think that either Stephanus himself or anyone speaking
for him will show that the charges and testimony are not true and that
Neaera is an Athenian (*astē*). I hear that he will present a defense going something like this: he did not keep her as a wife but as a *hetaira*,
and the children were not hers but were his by another woman, an Athenian (*astē*), a relative of his, whom he will say he had married earlier.

[120] In response to the shamelessness of his speech, and the trick-
ery of his defense, and of the witnesses he had coached, I issued a specific and just challenge, which would have made it possible for you
to know the whole truth: he should hand over for torture[145] Thratta
and Coccaline, the slave women who remained in Neaera's service
when she came from Megara to Stephanus' house, and also the women
she acquired later, when she was with Stephanus, Xennis and Drosis.
[121] They have accurate information about Proxenus, who has died,
and Ariston, who is still alive, and Antidorides the runner, and Phano
—I mean the woman called Strybele, the one who lived with Theogenes when he was Basileus—all these are Neaera's children. And if the
interrogation under torture showed that Stephanus married an Athenian woman, and the boys were born to another Athenian woman
(*astē*), not to Neaera, I was willing to abandon the trial and not pursue this indictment. [122] "Living with a woman" means, after all, that
a man has children with her and introduces his sons to the phratry and
deme, and he gives his daughters away to be married, presenting them
as his own. We have *hetairai* for the sake of pleasure, concubines (*pallakai*) for meeting our bodily needs day-by-day,[146] but wives for having legitimate children and to be trustworthy guardians of our household. So *if* he had married an Athenian woman (*astē*) before, and these
sons were born to her, not to Neaera, he could have presented proof

---

[145] For evidence taken under torture, see Dem. 52.22n.

[146] This often-quoted statement must be taken in context: Apollodorus' intention is to distinguish sharply between wives and other women, and he therefore
does not bother to distinguish clearly between the services provided by *hetairai* and
pallakai.

coming from the most accurate testimony—by handing over these slave women for torture. [123] To prove that I issued a challenge, the clerk will read out the testimony and the challenge. Please read the testimony and then the challenge.

> [DEPOSITION] [147] *Hippocrates the son of Hippocrates, of the deme Probalinthus,*[148] *Demosthenes son of Demosthenes, of the deme Paeania,*[149] *Diophanes son of Diophanes, of the deme Alopece,*[150] *Deinomenes son of Archelaus, of the deme Cydathenaeum,*[151] *Deinias son of Phormos, of the deme Cydantidae,*[152] *and Lysimachus son of Lysippus, of the deme Aigilia*[153] *testify that they were present in the Agora when Apollodorus challenged Stephanus and demanded that he hand over his slave women for interrogation under torture concerning the charges Apollodorus has brought against Stephanus concerning Neaera. Stephanus refused to hand over the slave women. This is the challenge that Apollodorus made:*

[124] Read the very challenge, the one I presented to this man Stephanus.

---

[147] Probably a trustworthy document, since it contains names of men not mentioned in the text but whose existence is recorded on inscriptions. The authenticity of documents found in the manuscripts is a matter of long-running controversy. Scholars have sought to identify documents that can be confirmed as genuine by external testimonia, often epigraphic, and distinguish that type from those documents that might have simply been composed from internal references long after the speech was written.

[148] Not otherwise known.

[149] The father's name and deme identification make it certain that this is the very Demosthenes to whom the manuscripts attribute the entire speech (see the Introduction). As with Eubulus (see above, 48 with note), we cannot confidently trace the shifting political alliances that brought it about that the orator who composed (and possibly delivered) a speech in defense of Phormio (36), with whom Apollodorus has been quarreling (see p. 13) appears to support Apollodorus.

[150] A stone of the third century includes a man of this name in a list of ephebes; presumably he was a grandson of the man mentioned here.

[151] The manuscripts give "Diomenes," but most editors read Deinomenes in light of epigraphical evidence (which also demonstrates that the man was rich).

[152] Again, epigraphical evidence indicates a spelling different from what is found in the manuscripts, i.e., Phormides.

[153] Not otherwise known.

[CHALLENGE] [154] *Apollodorus challenged Stephanus concerning the indictment he had brought against Neaera,[155] charging that she is a foreign woman living with an Athenian (astos). Apollodorus is prepared to take Neaera's slave women for interrogation under torture, both those she brought with her from Megara, Thratta and Coccaline, and those she acquired later when living with Stephanus, Xennis and Drosis. These women have accurate knowledge concerning Neaera's children, that they are not Stephanus'.[156] They are Proxenus, now deceased, Ariston, who is still living, Antidorides the runner, and Phano. And if the slave women agree that these are Neaera's children, Neaera is to be sold in accordance with the laws, and her children are to be classified as foreign. If, however, they agreed that they are not Neaera's children but from another woman, an Athenian (astē), I was willing to abandon my case against Neaera; and if the women were injured in the torture, I was willing to pay compensation for the injuries.*

[125] This, gentlemen of the jury, was my challenge to Stephanus, which he refused to accept. Doesn't it seem to you that Stephanus himself has already delivered the verdict, finding Neaera guilty of the charges I have brought against her? And that I have told you the truth and have presented truthful testimony? And that everything he tells you will be a lie? And that he will convict himself of saying not one

---

[154] The text presents several textual problems and puzzles (for more detailed discussions, see Carey 1992 and Kapparis 1999), but as with the deposition just before, details that cannot be derived from the text strongly suggest an authentic document.

[155] A problematic statement, since Theomnestus makes out that he is the prosecutor and Apollodorus only a *synēgoros* (see 1 and 14). Perhaps Apollodorus is relating an action he initiated and then abandoned; more likely he regards himself as the *de facto* prosecutor. In the next two sections Apollodorus again speaks of himself as the principal. There is also a discrepancy between the third person used at the start of the challenge and the first person (except in one manuscript) near the close.

[156] This translation follows the Oxford Classical Text, which follows the manuscripts in the order "Neaera's"/"Stephanus'" and adds "not." Other editors, thinking that the children's maternity is the real issue, switch the position of "Neaera's" and "Stephanus'." Others accept the manuscript reading whereby Neaera's children are also Stephanus': this is a stronger claim than is made earlier in the speech.

honest word?—all this by refusing to hand over for interrogation under torture the slave women I requested?

[126] Gentlemen of the jury, it was to avenge the gods against whom these people have committed impiety and to avenge myself that I have brought them to trial and subjected them to your vote. With the understanding that the gods, whom they have offended with their crimes, will observe how each of you will cast his ballot, you must vote for what is right and bring vengeance—in the first place for the gods and then for yourselves. If you do this, all will think that you have well and fairly tried this case that I have brought against Neaera, that she is a foreign woman who lives as though married to an Athenian (*astos*).

INDEX